D0550348

To the Other Shore:

Cross-currents in Irish and Scottish Studies

Edited by Neal Alexander, Shane Murphy
and Anne Oakman

Cló Ollscoil na Banríona
Belfast 2004

First published in 2004
Cló Ollscoil na Banríona
Queen's University Belfast
Belfast, BT7 1NN

Belfast Studies in Language, Culture and Politics
www.bslcp.com

© Cló Ollscoil na Banríona and Contributors

The publication of this book has been supported by the AHRB Research Centre
for Irish and Scottish Studies

British Library Cataloguing-in-Publication Data
A catalogue record for this book is available from the British Library.

ISBN 0 85389 863 4

Cover illustration, 'Teacup', by Dorothy Cross, is reproduced with kind
permission of the artist and Frith Street Gallery, London

Cover design by Colin Young
Typeset by John Kirk in Times New Roman
Printing by W. & G. Baird, Antrim

The papers in this volume were first presented at two conferences entitled
Cross-currents in Irish and Scottish Studies
each focusing on single-discipline, comparative and interdisciplinary research in
the areas of literature, film studies, history and Celtic studies, and held at the
University of Aberdeen from 5-7 April 2002, and at Queen's University Belfast
from 25-27 April 2003, within the AHRB Research Centre for Irish and Scottish
Studies

Editorial Disclaimer
The views expressed in each paper are those of the author. Publication in this
volume does not signify either editorial agreement or disagreement or editorial
responsibility for these views.

Publisher Disclaimer
The publisher has used its best endeavours to ensure that the URLs for external
websites referred to in this book are correct at the time of going to press. However,
the publisher has no responsibility for the websites and can make no guarantee that
a site will remain live or that the content is or will remain appropriate.

CONTENTS

Notes on Contributors

CONTRIBUTORS

Cassilda Alcobia is a PhD student at the Research Institute of Irish and Scottish Studies, University of Aberdeen. Her work explores the various possible discourses developing in the face of violence in Northern Ireland and focuses, on the one hand, on institutional representations of the conflict (namely the attempt to legitimize or to occlude state violence and to lessen the complex ramifications of the conflict) and, on the other hand, on a broad range of cultural and artistic representations of violence (in poetry, novel, drama, film, the visual arts, posters and murals).

Neal Alexander is completing a PhD on Irish writing at Queen's University Belfast.

Mary Burke is the current NEH Keough Fellow at the University of Notre Dame, Indiana. She is writing a book on the subject of the "tinker" figure in Irish writing, and will join the English Department at the University of Connecticut in the autumn. She has published in *The Australian Journal of Irish Studies* (2002), *Travellers and their Language* (2002), *New Voices in Irish Criticism 3* (2002), and *The Irish Revival Reappraised* (2004).

Denis Condon undertook his MA research on East German feature films at the School of Applied Languages and Intercultural Studies, Dublin City University. He is currently completing a PhD with the Centre for Media Studies at the National University of Ireland, Maynooth, on the cinema in Ireland before 1923.

Niav Gallagher is finishing a PhD in Medieval History at Trinity College Dublin. Her thesis examines the involvement of the Mendicant Orders in the North of Ireland, Scotland and Wales.

John Gibney is a PhD student in the Department of Modern History, Trinity College Dublin where he is completing a thesis on 'Ireland and the Popish Plot, 1678-81'. He is a contributor to the Royal Irish Academy's *Dictionary of Irish Biography* (Cambridge University Press, forthcoming).

Scott Hames is completing a PhD on James Kelman at the University of Aberdeen. His work examines contemporary fiction from the standpoint of (belatedly) 'modernist' narrative politics.

Richard Harris is a PhD student in the English Department of Sheffield University. His thesis examines the narrative strategies employed in the fiction of Irvine Welsh and James Kelman.

Jim Kelly is in the final year of a PhD on Charles Robert Maturin and Irish fiction in the Romantic period. He currently teaches Scottish and Irish literature in the Department of English literature and Office of Lifelong Learning at the University of Edinburgh.

Ruth Lysaght has researched and worked in Irish language film, speaking on this subject at several European conferences and mini film festivals. Her work to date has focused on TG4 and Celtic language broadcasters. She is currently teaching languages in Dublin, and plans to continue her research into minority language film and television initiatives in other countries, including issues of cultural identity and location. She has written for stage, screen and radio in Irish and English.

Kirsty A. Macdonald is a PhD student in the Department of Scottish Literature at the University of Glasgow. Her thesis is on "Madness and the Supernatural in Scottish Literature."

Claire McEwen is a PhD student at the Research Institute of Irish and Scottish Studies (RIISS) at the University of Aberdeen. Her thesis examines contemporary women's poetry from Scotland, Ireland and Northern Ireland, and she has published an essay on Carol Ann Duffy in *ecloga* (2003) and is a contributor to the forthcomming *Irish Women Writers: An A-to-Z* (Greenwood Press, 2005).

Patricia Silva McNeill has a MLitt in Anglo-Irish Literature from University College Dublin (2002), and is currently a PhD student in the Department of Portuguese and Brazilian Studies at King's College London. Her thesis is entitled "Affinity and Influence: a comparative study of the poetry of Fernando Pessoa and W.B. Yeats". She has published in *PaGes* (2000) and *New Voices in Irish Criticism 3* (2002).

Katherine Meffen is a PhD student at the Research Institute of Irish and Scottish Studies (RIISS) at the University of Aberdeen. Her thesis examines how working experience is represented in contemporary Irish and Scottish novels, focusing particularly on works by Roddy Doyle, James Kelman, James Plunkett, Dermot Bolger, and William McIlvanney.

James Moran has recently completed a PhD thesis on "The Drama of Easter 1916" at Downing College, Cambridge. He has published in *New Theatre Journal, Having Our Own Field Day* (forthcoming), and his short story, "Vise Placute", appeared in *Inprint* in 2003.

Shane Murphy is a lecturer in English at the University of Aberdeen.

Anne Oakman completed her PhD on Irish writing at Queen's University Belfast in 2004.

Kersti Tarien Powell completed a DPhil. in English at Oxford University and has published a number of articles on contemporary Irish writers. Her book, *Irish Fiction: An Introduction*, is due to be published by Continuum Press in 2004.

Daniel Smith is currently completing a thesis on the representation of the violence of the Northern Irish Troubles at the Research Institute of Irish and Scottish Studies, University of Aberdeen.

Nadia Clare Smith received a PhD in History from Boston College for a dissertation on Irish women historians. She was awarded a Government of Ireland Post-Doctoral Fellowship in 2003.

Enrico Terrinoni is a Government of Ireland Scholar (IRCHSS) and PhD student at University College Dublin. His thesis is entitled, "Joyce and the Occult: Hidden Patterns into the Narrative of Ulysses". He has published in *Pages, Joyce Studies in Italy, James Joyce Broadsheet* and has translated works by Brendan Behan, Muriel Spark, and Gerard Mannix Flynn into Italian.

To the Other Shore: Introduction

Neal Alexander, Shane Murphy and Anne Oakman

> That stretch of water, it's always
> There for you to cross over
> To the other shore … (Tom Paulin, "States")

Once marginalized due to a traditional Anglo-centric emphasis, scholarly interest in Irish-Scottish studies has gained momentum in recent years, due in no small part to the new political realities stemming from the Good Friday Agreement and Scottish devolution. What the Taoiseach Bertie Ahern has called "a new era in relations" between Scotland and Ireland has resulted in several key institutional developments: the establishment of an Irish-Scottish Academic Initiative, an innovative consortium of five universities (Aberdeen, Trinity College Dublin, Strathclyde, The Queen's University Belfast, Edinburgh); the inauguration of The Research Institute of Irish and Scottish Studies by the Irish President Mary McAleese in 1999; and the formation of the UK Arts and Humanities Research Board (AHRB) Centre for Irish and Scottish Studies in 2001. Each, in its own way, has provided a forum for scholars to provide an informed understanding of the cultural and historical forces that have shaped relations between Scotland, Northern Ireland and the Republic of Ireland. The comparative and inter-disciplinary research fostered by such initiatives have allowed for a more thorough recognition of what W. R. Rodgers terms "through-otherness", a compound word meaning "things mixed up among themselves": Scotland is no longer viewed as "other" from an Irish perspective, and vice versa.

As part of its programme of postgraduate training, the AHRB Centre instituted a series of conferences entitled *Cross-currents*, each focusing on single-discipline, comparative and interdisciplinary research in the areas of literature, film studies, history and Celtic studies. To date, two such conferences have taken place: the first at the University of Aberdeen, (where the AHRB Centre has its base), and the second at Queen's University Belfast. The aims of these conferences are manifold: to develop intellectual synergies between young academics from diverse institutions; to facilitate the establishment of scholarly networks; to provide a supportive, stimulating and challenging environment in which young scholars can debate with more established members of the research community; to broaden the contextual awareness of academics working within the single disciplines of Irish and Scottish Studies. Indeed, bringing postgraduates and the diversity of their research together promotes a collaborative dialogue that creates its own originality through its ongoing dialectic with the work of its colleagues, peers and predecessors. The intellectual generosity and shared debate exhibited throughout these conferences proved that emergent scholarship within and across these shores was not only full of new ideas, but that those ideas were ripe to be talking to each other and fashioning innovative links both within and without the specificities of the conference's Irish-Scottish tenor.

Yet these conferences and publications are also intended to encourage postgraduate students to make their voices heard in the academic arena and further catalyse student initiative to create and implement their own postgraduate events. Within the arena of postgraduate research there appears to be a critical emphasis on the necessity and ability of young scholars to 'aerate' with new 'lines of enquiry' what could otherwise become a 'stifling institution' of literary and cultural studies. Alongside this, however, there is perhaps also a need to firmly acknowledge and encourage the equally refreshing exposure of certain academic creeds of professionalism which have a practical and pervasive impact on those doctoral students intending to build a career within higher education. The knowledge and experience gained through both the organisation of and participation in postgraduate conferences becomes a vital asset in facing the difficulties which beset young critics attempting to forge an academic career in an often isolating academic environment.

The collaborative and interdisciplinary ethos that has sustained both the organisation of the first two *Cross-currents* conferences and the editorial and structural facets of this publication arguably go some way towards deconstructing certain institutional and cultural ideologies of individualism within the humanities. The politicised value-system that bestows scholarly merit and recognition to perceptibly autonomous scholars looms all too large for those postgraduates slowly nearing postdoctoral status. The pressure to (singly) publish that vital monograph, gain academic recognition, produce almost aggressively 'original' research proposals for postdoctoral fellowships, score points in a department's RAE, and be eligible for tenure and promotion stills feeds off a rhetoric of romanticised egotism which effaces the more collaborative norms of practice governing the realities of research, teaching and conference culture. At the pinnacle (and within the stormy currents) of these anxieties postgraduate students and their conferences have the potential to challenge the currently normalised attitudes that reign over these issues and make a significant impact on the governance and attitudes of the future institutions we are, after all, becoming an increasingly important part of.

Any collection of essays that aspires to delineate some of the critical and contextual crosscurrents between distinct academic disciplines must, of necessity, pay careful attention to the textual politics of its own formal presentation. The essays collected in this volume are arranged alphabetically by author in an effort to accommodate the full range of unlikely affinities and productive juxtapositions such a diversity of critical perspectives offers, an expansive remit of overlap and dissension that might be obscured by an over-zealous editorial impulse towards thematic structuration and discrete sub-sections. We hope to foster a similarly fertile miscellaneity to that highlighted by Aaron Kelly and Alan Gillis's edited collection, *Critical Ireland: New Essays on Literature and Culture* (2001), and also to shuffle our Irish and Scottish decks together more fully where comparative analyses do not emerge of their own accord. Ideally, what will arise from this implementation of the alphabet's arbitrary logic is a play of friction and confluence that is stratified by the constellation of competing factors and alternative groupings, allowing each reader to follow their own connective threads or to leap the sometimes precipitous topical gaps that open up between adjacent essays. Nonetheless, it may be apposite here to sketch some of the more obvious linkages and intersections that immediately suggest themselves between essays, as a preliminary set of interpretative co-ordinates that may be expanded upon, adapted, or discarded as the reader sees fit.

Three of the essays collected here focus upon the work of twentieth century Irish poets, paying particular attention to the way in which aesthetic and political imperatives collide in the formation of a distinctive poetic voice. **Patricia Silva McNeill's** comparative reading of W.B. Yeats and Fernando Pessoa is both a re-evaluation of two important modernist writers and also an exemplary demonstration of the way in which Irish (and Scottish) Studies may benefit from a more consciously European perspective. Her illustration of the parallels between Yeats's "theory of the Mask" and Pessoa's "heteronymy" unravels the complexities of self-presentation in each poet's work, illuminating the means by which a number of poetic *personae* are developed and manipulated for dramatic and expressive purposes. Self-presentation is also an important thematic frame in **Claire McEwen's** essay on Eavan Boland, whose poetry is often concerned to address the wholesale objectification of women within Irish literature. At the same time as she is critical of Boland's tendency to fall back upon the very assumptions she wishes to challenge and critique, McEwen also discovers in her emblematic use of objects a more radical poetic strategy through which the masculine tradition of woman as object may be subverted, as objects and emblems become representative *of* woman instead. **Cassilda Alcobia's** essay on Derek Mahon tackles a different representational dilemma, discussing the simultaneously moral and aesthetic demands placed upon the Northern poet by the pressures and intensities of historical circumstance. She argues that obliquity figures as a textual strategy in Mahon's work, providing him with a means of approaching the emotional lacerations attendant upon the experience of violence and political murder without succumbing to the powerful public pressures that would turn the poet into a mouthpiece for community or creed.

Another trio of papers turn their attention to the history and development of Irish film. **Ruth Lysaght's** survey and assessment of the growth of Irish language film-making emphasises the important role played by TG4, particularly its *Oscailt* scheme, which has been instrumental both in promoting a new image of Irish as a modern language and in creating a much wider audience for Irish language cinema. Lysaght ascribes this success to a decisive contemporaneity of vision that eschews the clichéd Gaelicisms of previous productions, although she also notes that many films are now made from the perspective of the 'outsider' and registers the absurdity of a situation whereby some directors are now forced to coach their actors in the delivery of lines whose meaning escapes them. **Denis Condon** examines the generic and representational underpinnings of the surviving "O'Kalem" rebel-and-redcoat films made by the US-based Kalem Company, outlining their relationship with the theatrical genre of Irish political melodrama. Both espouse a popular militant nationalism that draws impetus and material from the rebellions of 1798 and 1803, and Condon argues persuasively that the conventions and techniques epitomised in the plays of Dion Boucicault affected the production and reception of the O'Kalem films in the early twentieth century. **Daniel Smith** fast forwards to the beginning of this century in order to critique the representational agenda informing Paul Greengrass's *Bloody Sunday* (2001), particularly its self-conscious production of 'authenticity'. Utilising Jacques Derrida's concept of the 'supplement', Smith focuses upon the director's commentary appended to the DVD release of the film, finding in its documentary overlay a point of rupture or dissonance from which he proceeds to deconstruct the film's anxious self-projection as unmediated reportage, uncovering its artificial creation of what Greengrass deems "a credible account".

This interest in film is continued and also elaborated through its imbrication with literary-critical analysis in a number of other essays. **James Moran** intimates the complex and unusual experience of "Being Sir Rogered" by first relating the circumstances of an aborted attempt to make a Hollywood film of Roger Casement's life, a drama that features Eamon de Valera and George Bernard Shaw as principal actors. Through careful archival research he goes on to elucidate the personal and literary-historical relationships between Shaw and Casement, and discovers the latter waiting in the wings of Shaw's *Saint Joan* (1923). **Kersti Tarien Powell's** essay on Elizabeth Bowen's *The Last September* (1929) provides parallel readings of both the novel itself and its 2000 screen adaptation by John Banville and Deborah Warner. Playing close attention to the ambivalences attached to Bowen's conceptions of 'place' and 'belonging', Powell provides a succinct overview of the novel's historical and geographical contexts before going on to argue that the film version elides or simplifies many of the political and psychological nuances of Bowen's text through a constitutive indecision between its art-house pretensions and courting of commercial success. Another comparative reading is undertaken by **Kirsty A. Macdonald**, who addresses questions about the thematic and political importance of preternatural characters and motifs in Troy Kennedy Martin's television serial, *Edge of Darkness* (1985) and A.L. Kennedy's novel, *So I Am Glad* (1995). Drawing upon psychoanalytic theory and critical perspectives on the literary fantastic, MacDonald argues that in both cases these supernatural figures not only symbolise the continued irresolution of personal loss and individual pain, but also gesture allegorically towards a larger public malaise.

Scottish fiction is the subject of two further essays here, although they also deliberately seek to expand the frameworks for critical discussion beyond the narrow remit imposed by the 'national problematic'. Taking his theoretical orientation from Antonio Gramsci and Michel Foucault, **Scott Hames** interrogates the relationships and complicities between educational discipline and narrative authority in novels by Muriel Spark, George Friel and James Kelman. His essay undertakes a formalist inquiry into the nexus of politics, education, and narrative as it is manifest in each and shows how these three writers raise radical, self-critical questions about the authority of knowledge and its dissemination. **Richard Harris's** essay on James Kelman begins with a consideration of the furore that erupted when his novel, *How Late it Was How Late*, was awarded the Booker Prize in 1994. Uncovering the prejudices which gave rise to such a response from within the liberal literary establishment, he goes on to read Kelman's novel in light of the cultural politics of subaltern representation and offers a provocative materialist critique of some popular themes in postcolonial theory. **Katherine Meffen** draws a suggestive parallel between Kelman's writing and that of the Irish novelist Roddy Doyle, arguing that their attitudes towards language and employment of 'regional' Englishes imply congruent narrative strategies. However, Kelman's recurrent internal monologues are typically replaced by an emphasis on dialogue and external focalisation in Doyle's work, and Meffen's linguistic analysis of *The Snapper* (1990) pays particular attention both to his use of 'nonstandard' English and his deployment of narratorial interventions.

Jim Kelly builds upon recent work by John Kenny and Aaron Kelly to argue that much criticism of Irish fiction has been characterised by a divisive tendency towards formalist straitjacketing, proposing the steady, realist novel as the normative category of prose fiction and therefore the only suitable model for a 'national narrative'. He calls for a methodological approach that would place Irish fiction within a larger network of literary and cultural production, and goes on to offer an examination of the politics of form in Charles Robert Maturin's *The Wild Irish Boy* (1808). **Enrico Terrinoni** argues for a reconsideration of James Joyce's supposedly peripheral or ephemeral interest in spiritualism and the occult. Concentrating on his responses to the writings of Jacob Boehme, Emanuel Swedenborg, and particularly the early Yeats, Terrinoni suggests that Joyce's interest in mysticism was much deeper and sustained than is usually acknowledged, and may help to elucidate some of the clandestine meanings and obscurities in his later works.

Shifting the focus from literature to history, **Nadia Clare Smith's** essay examines the careers and writings of two 'non-professional' historians, Helena Concannon and Agnes Mure Mackenzie, who worked in Ireland and Scotland respectively during the 1920s and 1930s. Despite differences of approach and political affiliation, both women complicate accepted paradigms concerning Western women historians and their work can shed light on questions of historical practice in both Irish and Scottish contexts. **John Gibney's** account of events surrounding the alleged Popish Plot of 1678 addresses the importance of a broader context that is typically overlooked by English and Irish historians alike. Deriving his approach from 'British' history perspectives, Gibney argues that the plot had an internal dynamic within the island of Ireland, causing concern amongst the Irish Protestant community, but also reached beyond it, generating English fears over an 'Irish Plot', and he is keen to stress the complex political and historical interactions between both islands during this period. Reaching several centuries further back in time, **Niav Gallagher's** essay looks at the experience of the Franciscan friars who first arrived in England in 1224, subsequently spreading into Ireland, Scotland and Wales. She follows their progress and reception in Ireland and Scotland, where they gradually advanced from mendicancy and a peripheral status on the fringes of society to a position of considerable political influence and power. Finally, **Mary Burke** traces the ethnographical construction of the "Gypsy" or "Tinkler" by Scottish scholars and writers, and examines the forms in which this figure appears in works of Scottish literature by Sir Walter Scott and Robert Burns. For conservative writers such as Scott, she argues, these colourful, exotic figures functioned as a repository of all that contemporary civilisation had necessarily abandoned, effectively existing in an earlier cultural time and always seemingly on the point of vanishing from the public view altogether.

The narrative that is briefly sketched out above is, of course, only one of many possible routes through this book, each of which will highlight particular overlaps or disagreements. If the notion of 'cross-currents' implies confluence and interaction then it may also signify points of tension or antagonism where trains of thought pull in contrary directions. Even a cursory glance at the contents page of this volume indicates some of its particular idiosyncrasies or fault lines, three of which may be worth mentioning here: a noticeable imbalance towards Irish

Studies subjects; a preponderance of literary-critical analyses in comparison to other perspectives and approaches; a relative scarcity of comparative readings tackling both Irish and Scottish material. These are issues that should be addressed in subsequent conferences and publications, but as they stand these essays both offer a window onto the diversity of current research interests and promise to catalyse further developments in Irish *and* Scottish Studies. Consequently, it is our hope that this collection may contribute to an ongoing project that would make the distance between these separate disciplines and cultures brilliant, and therefore mutually illuminating.

It takes many people to put on conferences and publish their proceedings, and we would like to thank some of our collaborators here. We gratefully acknowledge the financial assistance provided by the AHRB and RIISS at the University of Aberdeen. Invaluable advice, encouragement and practical assistance of various sorts was generously given by Tom Devine, Eamonn Hughes, John Kirk, Edna Longley, Elaine Stockman, and George Watson. Leontia Flynn and Conor Wyer aided and abetted the running of the Belfast conference and the following were good enough to participate in a panel discussion on history and literature as part of the 2003 programme: Andrea Binelli, Patrick Crotty, Enda Delaney, Scott Hames, Christopher Harvie, and Sinéad Sturgeon. Further thanks are due to Kate Clanchy and Sinéad Morrissey who read from their work at the Belfast conference.

"Working on the Circumference": Obliquity in the Poetry of Derek Mahon

Cassilda Alcobia

One of the demands that the Northern Irish context has placed on literary texts for the past thirty-five years, a demand both moral and aesthetic, is that which concerns the representation of violence. That the strategies employed by writers in this representation often involve an avoidance of direct reference to the conflict is both telling of its complexity and, given its extreme nature, of the difficulty of engaging in any response capable of sidestepping the powerful logic established by the phenomenon of violence.

As a textual strategy, obliquity presents the advantage of allowing poets to address difficult issues in a playful manner, to obtain the necessary critical distance with which to explore the multiple possibilities of perception of what are extreme phenomena, as well as to uncover the encoded narratives within dominant discourses surrounding violence. The ambiguity of subject-matter, the allusions to other texts and sources of authority, the layering of surface and inner meanings produced by irony, the ambiguity of authorial voice, combined with a strong alertness to the *re*-presentational nature of their creative process provide poets with a frame of authorial control which counteracts powerful public pressures, not least those towards serving as mouthpiece to a community or a creed.

Witnesses to the way in which language manipulates perceptions, and having themselves to resort to language in order to create alternatives to these perceptions, Northern Irish poets display a scrupulous self-reflexivity in their work, repeatedly focusing on language's failure to live up to the reality it aims to describe. This is a concern voiced by Derek Mahon as early as his first published collection, *Night-Crossing* (1968).

> This is a circling of itself and you –
> A form of words, compact and compromise,
>   Prepared in the false dawn of the half-true
> Beyond which the shapes of truth materialize.
>   This is a blind with sunlight filtering through.
> This is a stirring in the silent hours,
>   As lovers do with thoughts they cannot frame
> Or leave, but bring to darkness like night flowers,
>   Words never choosing but the words choose them –
> Birds crowing, wind whistling off pale stars.

"Preface to a Love Poem" (1968: 13) is doubly a metatext: a poem about a preface about a poem. The anaphoric insistence on the assertive "This is" paradoxically brings to light the anxiety building out of the elusive endeavour of definition, of "circling" reality. The "shapes of truth materialize" in an indeterminate beyond, as we are left with the text, which is "at one remove – a substitute/For final answers".

Since the centre is ultimately unattainable, for Mahon the representational effort can be subsumed to a "working on the circumference", and the permanent division between art and reality is embodied in the artist's own position, the place he must learn to know for himself:

Why am I always staring out
of windows, preferably from a height?
I think the redemptive enterprise
of water – hold it to the light! –
yet distance is the vital bond
between the window and the wind,
while equilibrium demands
a cold eye and deliberate hands. ("The Sea in Winter", 1990: 113)

Mahon's poetic personae are often isolated, staring out of windows – these being an apt metaphor both for the limited knowledge framed within any single perspective, and the inescapable division between reality and its representation. Yet in Mahon's poetry there is always a sense in which art keeps encroaching on the "real" world. If, as Kathleen Mullaney notes, "birds and wind appear throughout Mahon's work to suggest [a] very piercing sort of expression that nonetheless in no way partakes of human language" (1995: 50), the cyclical nature of the assonance in "the window and the wind" is more indicative of a relationship of exchange than of estrangement.

"Yet distance is the vital bond". In this paper I propose to examine some of the textual strategies with which Derek Mahon achieves this distance. To do so I have divided my approach into four categories: temporal and geographical displacement, "germinal ironies", metonymy, and ekphrasis.

In his article "Place and Displacement: Reflections on Some Recent Poetry from Northern Ireland", Seamus Heaney describes the "Troubles generation" of Irish writers as condemned to lead a bilocated existence:

They belong to a place that is patently riven between notions of belonging to other places. Each person in Ulster lives first in the Ulster of the actual present, and then in one or other Ulster of the mind. The Nationalist will wince at the Union Jack and *God Save the Queen* as tokens of his place in the world .... Yet ... [he] conducts his daily social life among Unionist neighbours for whom these emblems have pious and passionate force. (1992: 127)

Whereas in Heaney's text the 'Ulster of the mind' is a space of ideological construction of 'national' identities which are passed down the generations in two separate communities, Mahon fashions for himself an "Ulster of the mind" of imaginative literary tradition that is not necessarily Irish or British.

In "Death and the Sun", a poem in which Mahon acknowledges his indebtedness to existentialist writer Albert Camus, the Northern Irish landscape becomes interspersed with Algerian "climatic privileges":

When the car spun from the road and your neck broke
I was hearing rain on the school bicycle shed
Or tracing the squeaky enumerations of chalk;
And later, while you lay in the *mairie*,

> I pedalled home from Bab-el-Oued
> To my mother silently making tea,
> Bent my homework in the firelight
> Or watched an old film on television –
> Gunfights under a blinding desert sun,
> Bogartian urgencies in the Ulster night. (1985: 35)

Northern Irish school sheds find themselves occupying the same space as exotic Bab-el-Oued as naturally as "*mairie*" is made to rhyme with "tea". Furthermore, the landscape is able to accommodate cinematic references to other regions of "blinding desert suns", while the notion of "Bogartian urgencies", as juxtaposed to the "Ulster night", brings darker overtones to this Ulster of the imagination, particularly since both cinematic references belong to genres – the *western* and the *gangster film* – deeply dependent on the semiotic code of violence for the development of their particular narratives. What can hardly be attributed to the imagination is the parallelism between the historical circumstances of Northern Ireland and of Algeria's war of independence in the early 1960s:

> We too knew the familiar foe, the blaze
> Of headlights on a coast road, the cicadas
> Chattering like watches in our sodden hedges;
> Yet never imagined the plague to come ...

Nevertheless, as a textual strategy, temporal and geographical displacement attains its full effect in Mahon's work when the 'home'-land is left unmentioned, as is the case in the poem "The Snow Party":

> Basho, coming
> To the city of Nagoya,
> Is asked to a snow party.
>
> There is a tinkling of china
> And tea into china;
> There are introductions.
>
> Then everyone
> Crowds to the window
> To watch the falling snow.
>
> Snow is falling on Nagoya
> And farther south
> On the tiles of Kyoto;
>
> Eastward, beyond Irago,
> It is falling
> Like leaves on the cold sea.
>
> Elsewhere they are burning

> Witches and heretics
> In the boiling squares (1975: 8)

Here Mahon juxtaposes the polite society of seventeenth-century Japan with the contemporaneous European scene, a brutal world of religious persecution. The repeated references to the snow which covers Basho's country, as well as the stance of immobility adopted by the guests of the snow party – reflected in the stilted cadence of the first five stanzas – are reminiscent of Joyce's mantle of snow over Ireland at the end of 'The Dead'.[1] Thus, while bringing into play different spaces and times, Mahon is nonetheless offering a commentary on present-day Ireland: in the 1970's, as in the seventeenth century, social chaos and violence seem to coexist with purely contemplative, passive existences, and Mahon criticises this stance most keenly when it reveals itself in a certain aesthetic apathy on the part of the poet, a criticism further developed in "Rage for Order":

> Somewhere beyond
> The scorched gable end
> And the burnt-out
> Buses there is a poet indulging his
> Wretched rage for order—
>
> Or not as the case
> May be, for his
> Is a dying art,
> An eddy of semantic scruple
> In an unstructurable sea. (1972: 22)

However, the lines "Or not as the case/May be", which open the second stanza, announce that this is to be a poem of reversals. In effect, the repeated claim that poetry "Is a dying art" is belied by the flawlessness of the formulation "An eddy of semantic scruple/In an unstructurable sea": such a description of the violent unpredictability of the world and of how poetry counteracts this by affirming itself as a unit of meaning, even if a small or tentative one ("eddy", "scruple") could hardly have been achieved as effectively by any other literary form. Nonetheless, the reversals continue in this poem, for if it is Mahon's intention to put forward the urgency of the world outside ("the fitful glare/Of his high window is as/Nothing to our scattered glass") as opposed to the self-centred ("His talk of justice and his mother"), dithering poet ("as the case/May be", "if you prefer"), this urgency is surely undermined by the triteness in the description of the poet's indifference "in the face of love, death and the wages of the poor". Mahon's purpose is very likely to forewarn against the opposing dangers of apathy and sentimentalisation in the response to extreme realities, but what stands out in this poem is the instability of the poetic voice itself. Not only are we never sure as to its degree of earnestness but also as to its place within the poem. While siding initially with those who experience violence firsthand (*"our* shattered glass"), this voice then gains an

---

[1] Hugh Haughton points to the Joycean reference in his essay "Place and Displacement in Derek Mahon" (1992: 107).

individual identity, emphasized in the profusion of personal pronouns, another reversal which further complicates interpretation:

> Now watch *me*
> As *I* make history,
> Watch as *I* tear down
> To build up
> With a desperate love,
> Knowing it cannot be
> Long now till *I* have need of his
> Germinal ironies. (emphasis added)

Furthermore, the opposed value of literal and non-literal readings of the above statement indicates that the poet's "Germinal ironies" may already be in use. Read literally, the announcement "watch me/As I make history" is a declaration of radical intent. A non-literal reading, however, might point to the performative, self-promoting aspect of this same statement – the demand that we watch is, after all, pronounced twice. The promise to "make history", in this sense, might be no more than the adherence to a well-sounding formula, announcing an empty act, its meaning dependent, for its validation, on an audience.

In either case, the slipperiness of the poetic voice is a statement of its refusal to be pinned down to any particular ideological stance. This elusiveness of posture is also reinforced by Mahon's constant revisions. As it appears in *Lives* (1972), the last line of the poem reads 'Germinal ironies'. In the version included in the collection *Poems 1962-1978* (1979), it is "Desperate ironies", and finally, in the more recent *Collected Poems* (1999), "Terminal ironies". While these changes are perhaps indicative of a diminishing belief in irony – "germinal" contains associations of birth and creation/creativity which are denied to the extreme in "terminal" – Mahon's adoption of the ironic mode has nonetheless served as yet another way of attaining the necessary distance with which to relate to his native Northern Ireland. As he explains in an interview:

> Somehow, Ulster Protestants are expected to be ironical. This is a way
> of explaining the liberal Ulster Protestant and apologizing for him, be
> it Louis MacNeice or Terry Brown or myself or whoever. By being
> ironical we somehow escape culpability. (Murphy, 1999: 196)

Culpability, but not guilt. It is when his ironies are at their most "terminal" that Mahon expresses the most acute anxiety at being apart from a community with which he cannot identify himself. In "Afterlives" the poetic voice begins in the recognizable isolated room:

> I wake in a dark flat
> To the soft roar of the world.
> Pigeons neck on the white
> Roofs as I draw the curtains
> And look out over London
> Rain-fresh in the morning light. (1975: 1)

This distance, however, is twofold, since not only do the curtains serve the function of barrier from the world, but the speaker is also physically removed from the "burnt-out buses" of Belfast, and in London, where the noises outside are no more than "a soft roar", the oxymoron indicating that they might deserve a response but could as easily be ignored.

"Rain-fresh" London, however, seems to provide the safety of rational answers and dialogue, representing, we may infer, all that Belfast is not:

> This is our element, the bright
> Reason on which we rely
> For the long-term solutions.
> The orators yap, and guns
> Go off in a back street;
> But the faith does not die
>
> That in our time these things
> Will amaze the literate children

Enlightened reason is soon taken apart as yapping, oratory; the inflated language of "bright/reason" and "long-term solutions". In particular, the enjambment of the second and third stanzas preserves one further cliché, "the faith does not die". People, however, do. This is nonetheless left unsaid, the unadorned reality which will not fit within the idiom of cliché.

The word "home" is present at the beginning and end of the second part of the poem. If London offers the bright light of reason, Belfast should offer the comfort of recognizable childhood memories, traceable spatial equivalents to the formation of individual identity.

> And I step ashore in a fine rain
> To a city so changed
> By five years of war
> I scarcely recognize
> The places I grew up in,
> The faces that try to explain.
>
> But the hills are still the same
> Grey-blue above Belfast.
> Perhaps if I'd stayed behind
> And lived it bomb by bomb
> I might have grown up at last
> And learnt what is meant by home.

The immutability of the "imaginary homeland", however, finds no equivalent in the Belfast of the Troubles, where only the fragile light of a "naked bulb" greets the poetic voice, the constant hills serve as a reminder of just how inconstant life around them is and "home" is made to rhyme with the bombs that deface it beyond recognition. That the speaker may not have grown up is verifiable in the puerile extended cliché of the last two verses: "I might have grown up at last/And learnt what is meant by home." The irony, of course, is that the speaker seems reasonably taken with the notion of having stayed behind in an immutable "home" that does not really exist to carry out the doubtful achievement of living "bomb by bomb".

In the Belfast of "Afterlives" violence is identifiable through the changes generated in its aftermath. In Mahon's poetry the violent act is never represented as it occurs, but rather, metonymically, derelict landscapes and abandoned sheds standing in for past moments of destruction. This strategy is effectively carried out in "Ecclesiastes", where the urban landscape, forlorn and stripped bare, seems to stand as a monument to the Protestant faith and its "dank churches, empty streets/the shipyard silence, the tied-up swings" (1972: 3), an ironic legacy of the Calvinist ethos of austerity. The distilled faith of puritan ideals is thus metonymically demonstrated to be essentially destructive.

The last textual strategy examined in this paper is ekphrasis, a term used to denote writing in response to visual art. Since it involves an exchange between two kinds of artistic texts (verbal and visual), this technique necessarily foregrounds issues of representation and artistic originality, and allows for the layering and multiplication of meaning which characterizes intertextuality. Nonetheless, poems about paintings that seek to produce something more than art criticism – to be more than a derivative of the visual work which has inspired them – must set up their own discursive universe, and I shall examine how Mahon achieves this in the poem "Girls on the Bridge".

The first stanza of the poem seems to be purely descriptive, a sensation enhanced by the almost total absence of verbs and its stilted pace:

> Audible trout,
> Notional midges. Beds,
> Lamplight and crisp linen, wait
> In the house there for the sedate
> Limbs and averted heads
>   Of the girls out
>
> Late on the bridge. (1982: 32-3)

However, what the poem describes is, for the most part, nowhere to be seen in Munch's painting, and the use of the term "notional" is not innocent in this context.[2] In fact, as Terence Brown points out, "the evocations of a domestic interior which Mahon discerns in it are more suggestive of the images of a Dutch Golden Age canvas than of the expressionist *angst* of Munch's universe" (1994: 46). Mahon does not so much *describe* the painting as *inscribe* it with images of a languorous, untroubled, but also passive existence of "sedate limbs" and "averted heads", a characterization further developed in the semantic range of the third stanza:

> But *stops* to find
> The girls *content* to *gaze*

---

[2] In fact, this word was introduced in Mahon's revision of the poem from an earlier version included in the interim collection *Courtyards in Delft* (1981).

> At the unplumbed, *reflective* lake,
> Their plangent conversational quack
>   Expressive of *calm* days
>   And *peace of mind*. (emphasis added)

The world imagined by Mahon in this stanza fits perfectly the description of a "cold dream/Of a place out of time". Here, even the road stops. Yet the casual introduction of the adjective "plangent" which describes "a full, deep, or rich sound", but which ultimately derives from the Latin word *plangere*, meaning "to beat", "to strike noisily", especially "to strike the breast or the head as a sign of grief" disrupts this world even as it is being built – it would thus seem that Mahon's rewriting of the painting is not as distanced from Munch's disquiet as Terence Brown suggests. The last three stanzas of the poem carry out the threat to transform a world of dreamy chattiness into nightmare and scream, its final word constituting a reference to Munch's *The Scream* (1893), a painting whose spirit can be said to haunt Mahon's poem. Just as in *The Scream*, there is a very deliberate attempt, in "Girls on the Bridge", to represent sound: the poem is charged with auditive evocations, beginning with its opening word, "audible", followed by "plangent conversational quack", "laughter", "calls" and ending with "screams".

"Girls on the Bridge" thus follows a trajectory which moves away from the painting only to return to it, thereby achieving a delicate balance between an immersion in Munch's aesthetic concerns, namely his turn-of-century existential anguish, and Mahon's own apocalyptic vision:

> Grave daughters
> Of time, you lightly toss
> Your hair as the long shadows grow
> And night begins to fall. Although
>   Your laughter calls across
>   The dark waters,
>
> A ghastly sun
> Watches in pale dismay.

Just as in "The Snow Party" there is an "elsewhere" of violence and disquiet alongside the placid landscape of snow and of polite society, the "averted heads" of the girls on the bridge may indicate the refusal to face a world of violence to come. By choosing to reflect on matters of violence and its representation in such an oblique manner, Mahon is "keeping time", in Heaney's double sense of poetic musicality and of acknowledging a particular contemporary phenomenon (1996: 247-62), thus moving beyond the simplifying and deterministic discourses that rationalize and justify violence, that label, accuse and choose sides, as well as refusing a thirty-five year-old "journalistic" tradition which has produced little more than congealed, "self-evident" truths and the language of stereotypes.

References

Brown, Terence. 1994. "Derek Mahon: The Poet and Painting". *Irish University Review*. 24.1: 38-50

Haughton, Hugh. 1992. "Place and Displacement in Derek Mahon". *The Chosen Ground:Essays on the Contemporary Poetry of Northern Ireland*. Ed. Neil Corcoran. Dufour: Seren. 87-120

Heaney, Seamus. 1992. "Place and Displacement: Reflections on Some Recent Poetry from Northern Ireland". *Contemporary Irish Poetry: Critical Essays*. Ed. Elmer Andrews. London: Macmillan. 124-44

Heaney, Seamus. 1996. "Keeping Time: Irish Poetry and Contemporary Society". *International Aspects of Irish Literature*. Eds. Toshi Furomoto et al. Gerrards Cross: Colin Smythe. 247-62

Mahon, Derek. 1968. *Night-Crossing*. London: Oxford University Press

Mahon, Derek. 1972. *Lives*. London: Oxford University Press

Mahon, Derek. 1975. *The Snow Party*. London: Oxford University Press

Mahon, Derek. 1981. *Courtyards in Delft*. Dublin: Gallery Press

Mahon, Derek. 1982. *The Hunt by Night*. Oxford: Oxford University Press

Mahon, Derek. 1985. *Antarctica*. Dublin: Gallery Press

Mahon, Derek. 1990. *Selected Poems*. London: Penguin

Mahon, Derek. 1999. *Collected Poems*. Meath: Gallery Press

Mullaney, Katherine. 1995. "Derek Mahon's Poetry". *Politics and the Rhetoric of Poetry: Perspectives on Modern Anglo-Irish Poetry*. Eds. Tjebbe A. Westendorp and Jane Mallison. Amsterdam: Atlanta. 47-55

Murphy, James J. et al. 1999. "Derek Mahon". *Writing Irish*. Eds. James P. Myers, Jr. New York: Syracuse University Press. 185-99

Dwellers in archaic cultural time: "Gypsies", "Tinkers" and "Gaels" in early nineteenth-century Scottish writing

Mary Burke

> Everywhere the Gypsies appear in nineteenth-century narrative, they
> begin to hold up ordinary life, inducing local amnesias or retrievals
> of cultural memory, and causing blackouts or flashbacks in textual,
> historical, and genre memory as well.[1]

Although it was only published in 1865, Walter Simson's ponderous 575-page *A History of the Gipsies* was collated decades earlier during the lifetime of his acquaintance and correspondent, Sir Walter Scott (1771-1832). Scott and Simson communicated frequently, and conversed at Abbotsford on the subject of the Gypsies; the great novelist considered Simson's work to be extremely important, and urged the task of writing a history of the Gypsies upon him,[2] a fact that Simson is keen to stress in his introduction. In this investigation, *History of the Gipsies* is considered as a representative of the *idées fixes*, outrageous speculation, forced comparisons and incongruous generalizations prevalent in a rather high proportion of studies concerning the minority. Simson's enormous volume is of interest as a collation of some hundreds of years of Scottish writings and traditions about Gypsies, as interpreted through the filter of an early nineteenth-century proto-Gypsylorist.[3] In the main, Walter Simson's "investigation" of the Gypsies (or of those who could be retrospectively reinterpreted as being "of the tribe") is an exhaustive recounting of anecdotes or records of noted or hanged Gypsy robbers, thieves, coiners, extortionists, swindlers, smugglers and murderers. *History of the Gipsies* also lists titillating accounts of notable violent, thieving or insurgent Gypsy women of the previous 300 years. Simson's volume, and many of the sources upon which it was based suggest that the tradition of putative Gypsy crime or internecine strife appears to have constituted the only history of the minority that attracted the eighteenth- and early nineteenth-century Scottish researcher.[4] According to an article on long-ago crimes involving Scottish Gypsies written by Scott with the assistance of Thomas Pringle (1789-1834) for the influential Tory periodical *Blackwood's Magazine*: "bloody transactions appear to have been very frequent among this savage race in former times" (618). A reviewer dismissed Simson's style as "anecdotes" mixed with "wild speculation and so many

---

[1] Katie Trumpener. 1992. "The Time of the Gypsies: A 'People Without History' in the Narratives of the West". *Critical Inquiry*. 18.4: 869.

[2] "I pray you to proceed in your enquiries […]." Walter Scott to Walter Simson [April-May 1818] (Scott 1932-7, 285).

[3] *Gypsylorist* was a term applied to writers and adventurers associated with the influential Gypsy Lore Society and its journal, established in Britain in the late nineteenth century for the investigation of Romany culture and language.

[4] Certain of the anecdotes included in *History of the Gipsies* are obtained from acquaintances and Simson's own father, while others are gleaned from early accounts of criminal trials, *Scot's Magazine*, late eighteenth-century editions of *Ruddiman's Weekly Magazine*, and

unsupported assertions", though many of the author's most outrageous assertions were derived from "investigators" of the Gypsy such as Göttingen University ethnographer and historian, Heinrich Grellmann (1753-1804), author of the Orientalising *Dissertation on the Gipsies* (1783).

Grellmann's text purported to expose the Indian origins of European Gypsies through linguistic detective work, and the medieval and Elizabethan beliefs that "the tribe" originated in Egypt as a group of wandering pilgrims or were indigenous vagabonds ("counterfeit Egyptians") who "blacked up" in order to better resemble the stereotype of the "foreign" soothsayer were decidedly superseded by the rise of this hypothesis. Grellmann consolidated the exemplar of the heathenish, wild, asocial Gypsy, whose appetites were an inverse of, or in monstrous excess of, sedentary norms. The German ethnographer was not the first European scholar to publish a text devoted to Gypsies, or to suggest that "exotic" origin was discernible in their language. However, he wrote the earliest and best-known "standard work", the significance of which lies in its crystallisation of disparate stereotypes gleaned from earlier commentaries (Willems and Lucassen, 42). The *Dissertation* set the parameters of the subject, and studies in subsequent centuries often unashamedly paraphrased it. Grellmann was an ethnographer and historian based for most of his career at Göttingen University, the German enlightenment powerhouse, and he was academically active in an era in which the discipline of history was being institutionalized. He invented the category of "Gypsy" as has been understood since then: his work brought various itinerant groups "moving through different countries together under a single name, [...] and provided them with a collective history" (Willems, 17). Grellmann refined the previously obscure Oriental origin theory by suggesting that language proved that Gypsies were descendants of an Indian pariah group, with all the negative associations the analogy implied: Gypsies were filthy eaters, addictive, vulgar in dress, animalistic, lacking in willpower, instinctive, lazy, lustful and dishonest.

David MacRitchie stated in an 1889 *Journal of the Gypsy Lore Society* article that Irish tinkers "belong equally to the 'Irish' districts of Scotland" (355). The Scottish Gypsy is a more ambiguous figure than the English Romany Gypsy: although he (it is usually "he") is often constituted within the same discourse of Oriental origin, he is equally subject to the fashion for Celticism when linked to or collated with the Highlander and Scottish Tinkler, whose ancestry is generally (but not always) given as Irish. This ambiguity is underlined by the fact that the word "tinker" ("tinkler" is the Scots variant) has been variously identified as originating in Irish or Scottish Gaelic, Romani and English (MacRitchie, 355).[5] The potential for confusion in the overlapping meanings of the designations "tinker" and "Gypsy" is explicit in a reply to a questionnaire on Gypsies circulated to Scottish Sheriffs in approximately 1815 by John Hoyland from one John Blair, Sheriff Substitute for the County of Bute:

> I have to inform that the people generally known by the description
> of Gypsies, are not in use to come hither, unless abject, itinerant

Scott and Simson's own contributions to *Blackwood's* in the late 1810s. Scott offered Simson "scraps" given to *Blackwood's*, while William Blackwood supplied him with manuscripts. Scott to Simson [April-May 1818] (Scott 1932-7, 285; Simson 1865, 251).

[5] According to the OED, "Tynker" was both a trade name and a surname by 1265.

tinkers and braziers, generally from Ireland, may be accounted such. A few of them often visit us, and take up their abode for a time in different parts of the country, where people can be prevailed upon to give them the accommodation of an out-house or hut. (Hoyland, 93)

The "distinguished northern Poet", Scott, responded to Hoyland's questionnaire in his role of "Sherriff of Selkirkshire", and his testimony suggests that "Gypsy" and "tinker" were to be understood as equivalent and occupational terms.[6] Another informant, William Smith, notes that the contemporary Gypsies of Yetholm were formerly "called the Tinkers of Yetholm" (Hoyland, 98-9), suggesting that sometime around the turn of the nineteenth century, the designation "tinker", with its overtones of aboriginality, was replaced by that of "Gypsy", due to the gradual seepage into dominant discourse of Grellmann's model of Gypsy culture as a monolithic, mono-racial trans-European phenomenon; tellingly, one Scottish Gaelic gloss of "Gypsy" is *ceard-fiosachd,* "a fortune-telling tinker." Ostensible tinkers or smiths were later recast as "secret" Gypsies: during the Victorian period it became bizarrely fashionable among Gypsylorists to construct, retrospectively, John Bunyan as a Gypsy.[7]

One of the most striking features of the depiction of the Gypsy in Scottish writings is the veiled but nevertheless constant, implication that the Gypsy and the Highlander are both wild, colourful, but ultimately anachronistic figures. However, gradations of Otherness apply: Simson is careful to distinguish between the indigenous, righteous wildness of "the Gael" and the Oriental ("deceptive, demonstrative, fox-like") lack of civility of the Scottish Gypsy. In the following anecdote, the subtext of Simson's repeated stress on the ethnic and linguistic designations and markers of the parties involved is that such are the key to understanding the contrasting behaviour of the men concerned:

A [Scottish Gipsy] exchanged [a stolen black colt] for a white horse, belonging to a Highlander wearing a green kilt. The Highlander, however, had not long put the colt into the stable, before word was brought to him that it was gone. Suspecting the Gipsy of the theft, the sturdy Gael […] pursued him, like a staunch hound on the warm foot of reynard, till he overtook him […]. [T]he Gipsy was taking some refreshment in the same room with [Simson's informant, a respectable farmer], when the Highlander, in a storm of broken English, burst into their presence. The astute and polished Gipsy instantly sprang to his feet, and, throwing his arms around the foaming Celt, embraced and hugged him in the eastern manner,

---

[6] "A set of people possessing the same erratic habits, and practising the trade of tinkers, are well known in the Borders; and have often fallen under the cognisance of the law. They are often called Gypsies, and pass through the county annually in small bands, with their carts and asses. The men are tinkers, poachers, and thieves upon a small scale." (Hoyland, 93-4).
[7] Bunyan's father was, by occupation, a tinsmith, and this, and the seventeenth-century peripatetic preacher's vague references to his humble origins, were seized upon as "evidence" of undisclosed Gypsy descent.

> overpowering him with expressions of joy at seeing him again. This
> quite exasperated the mountaineer: almost suffocated with rage, he
> shook the Gipsy from his person, with the utmost disdain, and
> demanded the colt he had stolen from him. Notwithstanding the
> deceitful embraces and forced entreaties of the Gipsy, he was, with
> the assistance of a messenger, at the back of the Highlander, safely
> lodged in the jail of Cupar. (1865, 173-4)

The Gypsy resembles both the Other of the far-flung corners of the Empire, and untouchables within the British Isles: Walter Simson's editor, James Simson, considers that the supposed "subduing" of the behaviour of the lawless, "wild" Scottish Gypsy during the previous century mirrored that of the inhabitants of the Highlands, "where, in little more than a hundred years [...] the people, as a body, have emerged, from a state of sanguinary barbarism, into the most lawful and the most moral and religious subjects of the British Empire" (Simson 1865, 44). Scott's careful description of the architecture of a Scottish manor house "Sixty Years since" underlines the threat perceived to emanate from the Gypsy and the Highlander: "The windows were numberless, but very small [...]. Neither did the front indicate absolute security from danger. There were loop-holes for musquetry, and iron stancheons on the lower windows, probably to repel any roving band of gipsies, or resist a predatory visit from the caterans of the neighbouring Highlands" (Scott 1998, 35). Interestingly, in a letter to Simson, Scott warns him to be prudent in researching the language of the "vindictive" Scottish Gypsies lest he be exposed to "personal danger" (Scott 1932-7, 284). Walter Simson's editor, James Simson, cautions that the author's colourful account of the depredations of criminal Gypsies of the past are "illustrative of the Gipsies, in their wild state, previous to their gradual settlement and civilization" (Simson 1865, 123 fn.). The Gypsies "naturally" gravitate towards the romantic, but anarchistic past:

> As far as I can judge, for the few and short specimens which I have
> myself heard, and had reported to me, the subjects of the songs of the
> Scottish Gipsies, (I mean those composed by themselves) are chiefly
> their plunderings, their robberies, and their sufferings. [...] They
> appear to have been very fond of our ancient Border marauding
> songs, which celebrate the daring exploits of the lawless freebooters
> on the frontiers of Scotland and England. [...] The song composed on
> Hughie Graeme, the horse-stealer, published in the second volume of
> Sir Walter Scott's Border Minstrelsy, was a great favourite with the
> Tinklers. (Simson 1865, 306-7)

Like the routed Highlander, the Gypsy occupies the liminal areas of familiar cultural and physical territory: they "located themselves upon grounds of a flattish character, between the cultivated and uncultivated districts; having, on one side, a fertile and populous country, and, on the other, a heathy, boggy, and barren waste, into which they could retire in times of danger" (Simson 1865, 140).

In his response to Hoyland's questionnaire, Smith also comments that Gypsies are "universally" superstitious and the "Peculiar cast" of their features are "every where distinguishable", a view concurred with by Scott (Hoyland, 104; 109).

According to Simson: "The *Gitanos* in Spain, and the *Tinklers* in Scotland, are, in almost every particular, the same people," and Gypsies in "Scotland, England, and Ireland, are all branches" of the "continental tribes" (1865, 64; 69). "Mr Hoyland's account" furnishes proof, Simson claims in a February 1818 article for *Blackwood's Magazine*, "that the gypsies in Russia correspond exactly in language, manners, and habits, with those in Britain" (1818, 526). This trans-historical Gypsy emerges from the pages of travel narratives: Simson claims that his reading of earlier authors such as Richard Pococke, Edward Clarke, and Reginald Heber leads him to believe that Gypsies reveal "an hereditary propensity to theft" and are, "uniformly the same" in disreputable livelihood, "manners, habits, and cast of features," in "whatever country" they are found (1865, 72). Scottish historian Dr. Pennecuik's account of a late seventeenth-century Gypsy quarrel is compared to a Gypsy battle that takes place one hundred years later at Hawick, both events demonstrating, according to Simson, that "the nature of the Gipsies [remains] unchanged" (1865, 189). Hoyland offers relatively little detail or quotation from the data collected from the Scottish Sheriffs, and what is offered is often interpreted through the filter of earlier European authorities, to the extent that all local difference is universalised. Hoyland's vocabulary list is "extracted" from Grellmann's; the opportunity to collect Scottish Gypsy vocabulary afforded by his questionnaire is not availed of.

Grellmann's English-language translator, Matthew Raper, stated that his "chief aim in translating" the German ethnographer "was to give such of my Countrymen, who are unacquainted with the German language, an opportunity of learning from what part of the World, it is probable the Gipsies came among us" (Grellmann, n.p.). As previously noted, Grellmann's work instituted a Europe-wide craze for the subject that made him a touchstone for proto-Gypsylorism, and the ethnographer also appears to have inspired the Scottish *intelligentsia* to take notice of indigenous nomadic groups. In a contribution to the first number of *Blackwood's Magazine*, Scott and Pringle berated Scottish scholars for exploring far-flung exotica, while neglecting those which were under their very noses: "Men of letters, while eagerly investigating the customs of Othaheite or Kamschatka, and losing their tempers in endless disputes about Gothic and Celtic antiquities, have witnessed with apathy and contempt the striking spectacle of a *Gypsey camp*, — pitched, perhaps, amidst the mouldering entrenchments of their favourite Picts and Romans" (43). The late eighteenth-century investigation of Gypsies tutored the white European to "perceive" the minority: whereas "[p]eople not interested [in the population] travel through the East, Europe, and America, and never see a single Gypsy" (Sinclair, 198), those versed in the craze suddenly discovered "the tribe" in every corner of the world and under cover of a multitude of identities.

Scottish philosophy made a significant impression in the eighteenth century, not only on the English-speaking world but also on the Enlightenment in central Europe, and the impact was perhaps most greatly felt in Germany. Unsurprisingly, however, the Gypsy fad appears to have come to the attention of the Scottish *intelligentsia* through the works of German academics and literary writers. The melodramatic 1771 tragedy, *Goetz von Berlichingen*, which portrays a real-life predatory sixteenth-century German knight of that name, was written by Grellmann's contemporary, Johann Wolfgang von Goethe (1749-1832), and translated by Scott in 1799, and this may have influenced his (Scott's) vision of the noble but lawless Gypsy.[8] Moreover, Scott later borrowed scenes from *Goetz von Berlichingen* for his novels *Ivanhoe* (1819) and *Anne of Geierstein* (1829). Scott's "On the Gypsies of Hesse-Darmstadt in Germany," which appeared in *Blackwood's* in January 1818, was a contribution detailing the contents of a rare eighteenth-century German volume concerning the execution of a Gypsy Band at Giessen.[9] In the notes for his translation, Scott compares the history of the German Gypsies to that of the Scottish. Likewise, there is some indication that Grellmann was familiar with near-contemporaneous Scottish writing: the "Fergusson" indexed by the ethnographer as a source for his *Dissertation* may well be the eighteenth-century Scottish poet, Robert Fergusson (1750-74), whose vivid lyrics of the life of Edinburgh's poor anticipated Robert Burns. Scott appears to have been aware of the existence of Grellmann's *opus*; referring to Simson's researches on the Scottish Gypsy language, which he concludes are "Oriental, probably Hindostanee", Scott writes: "When I go to Edinburgh, I shall endeavour to find a copy of Grellmann, to compare the language of the German Gipsies with that of the Scottish tribes" (Scott 1932-7, 285). In a further letter to Simson, the novelist ponders on the "Oriental" cast of the Gypsy language: "I cannot determine, in my own mind, whether it is likely to prove really a corrupt eastern dialect, or whether it has degenerated into mere jargon" (Scott 1932-7, 283).[10] In *Guy Mannering* (1815), Vanbeest Brown (a.k.a. Harry Bertram), who has just of late returned from service in the East Indies, is astounded by the appearance of the Gypsy, Meg Merrilies: "'Have I dreamed of such a figure?" he said to himself, "or does this wild and singular-looking woman recall to my recollection some of the strange figures I have seen in our Indian pagodas?'" (1968, 154). As described, Meg's appearance ambiguously partakes of both of the tradition of the authentic Oriental Gypsy and the bogus exoticness of the "counterfeit Egyptian". Despite his interest in the modish Grellmann hypothesis, Scott ultimately gravitated towards the medieval theory of Gypsy origin in his writing; the 1829 Introduction to *Guy Mannering* states that the "degraded class who are called gipsies [...] are in most cases a mixed race, between the ancient Egyptians who arrived in Europe about the beginning of the fifteenth century, and vagrants of European descent" (1968, 11-2).[11]

The "lawless Gypsy" was doubtlessly a fashionable motif amongst late eighteenth-century Scottish writers. Robert Burns (1759-96) collected the song *McPherson's Rant (or Lament or Farewell)* and composed his own version,

---

[8] John Arden, personal interview, 11 Mar. 2002.

[9] Much material dealing with German literature appeared in the early volumes of *Blackwood's*, "particularly in the *Horae Germanicæ*, a series of twenty-seven numbers which extend from November, 1819, to August, 1828." (Strout, 14).

[10] Scott, who saw the Gypsy language as "a great mystery", seems to have had an intention of writing an account of the Gypsies himself, but was stalled by the difficulty of procuring "a few words of their language", and settled for donating the material to the newly-launched *Blackwood's*. The planned account of the Gypsies is probably a reference to Scott's intended article on the subject for the *Quarterly Review*.

[11] References to the Egyptian origin of Gypsies made after or in the knowledge of Grellmann's theory were generally presented in literary works: the associations of Egypt as a land of sorcery and archaic history are more allusive and deeply embedded in European culture.

although early Burns editors were inclined to claim it as the Ayrshire Bard's original composition. The ballad celebrates and was purportedly written by one James MacPherson, a renowned fiddler and the natural son of a Highland laird by a Gypsy woman, hanged in 1700 for being an "Egyptian" and a criminal.[12] Scottish tradition holds that the bold outlaw, a friend of Rob Roy MacGregor, a member of a proscribed Highland clan, played the stirring tune he had composed in the condemned cell on his violin, and then asked if any friend present would accept the instrument as a gift. When no one came forward, he indignantly broke the violin on his knee, and threw away the fragments, after which he calmly submitted to his fate.[13] The folklore surrounding MacPherson constructed him as the "wild-but-noble" Highlander-Gypsy of Scottish tradition: though a freebooter, no act of cruelty towards the widow, the fatherless, or the distressed was ever perpetrated under his command. Folklore relating to Burns himself avers that a tinker woman sheltered in the home of William Burns at Alloway on the night Robert was born, and prophesied the genius of the newborn baby (Simson 1865, 63). Burns's cantata, "The Jolly Beggars", also known as "Love and Liberty", originates in a pre-Grellmann understanding of the "tinker" or "caird" (if these labels, as used in the cantata, are taken to be equivalent with "Gypsy", as they often are in the Scottish context) as an occupational, rather than an ethnic term. The tinker describes himself as follows:

> My bonie lass, I work in brass
> A tinkler is my station:
> I've travell'd round all Christian ground
> In this my occupation [...]. (Burns, 188)

A further indication that the "tinker" or "caird" of "The Jolly Beggars" must be situated within an indigenous and pre-Grellmann paradigm is that he is placed amongst a motley procession of rogue literature stock types: an embeggared and maimed former soldier, his feisty "doxy" (mistress), a fool and an itinerant fiddler. The cantata, which is "clearly influenced by Gay's *Beggar's Opera*" (Burns, 182), is based on a scene of great jollity Burns witnessed in October 1785 at Poosie Nansie's hostelry at Mauchline, among a company who by day appeared to be miserable beggars.

Simson views the eighteenth-century Gypsies through the rose-tinted lens of childhood memory, and a Scott-inspired aura of romance: "The nomadic Gipsies in general, [...] have gradually declined in appearance, till, at the present day, the greater part of them have become little better than beggars, when compared to what they were in former times" (1865, 218). He elsewhere claims that in the distant, dashing past, they were said to donate to the poor some of what they robbed from the rich, and, in a back-handed compliment typical of his obtuse style, Simson praises the Gypsies of the previous century for only murdering each other rather than "having put to death natives of Scotland" (1865, 175). The author

---

[12] Most itinerant groups were subject to harsh if unevenly enforced statutes against mendicancy and nomadism from the medieval period until the end of the eighteenth century.

[13] For an account of the MacPherson tradition, see (Whyte, 24).

quotes from a manuscript given to him by William Blackwood detailing acts of "great kindness" Gypsies supposedly performed in the previous century on behalf of sedentary sympathisers (1865, 196). Like the Highlander idealised in post-Culloden Scottish literature, the authentic, wild Gypsy had only relatively recently disappeared: a 1774 edition of *Ruddiman's Weekly Magazine* article on the "blackmail[ing]" Gypsy Faa family mentions that they "continued to travel about in Scotland till the beginning of this century" (cited in Simson 1865, 237). Simson, whose volume appeared just under 100 years later, often implies that the real Gypsy disappeared in the era the *Ruddiman's* article was issued: according to the commentators of each successive era, the mythic noble Gypsy has only just receded into the recent past. In both Lady Morgan's *Wild Irish Girl* (1806), and Scott's *Waverley* (1814), set at the time of the second Jacobite rising of 1745, and concluding months after the battle of Culloden, that which is indigenous but, paradoxically, exotic, is allowed to enter the Romantic text only when it has become an apolitically "aesthetic" source of the sublime to the English visitor. After the putative victory of enlightenment and rationalism at Culloden, Gaelic and Jacobite identity is defused and transformed into an obsolete cultural resource to be mined by nostalgic writers and balladeers. By the time Scott wrote *Rob Roy* (1817), set in the period immediately preceding the Jacobite rising of 1715, Jacobitism had ceased to be a vital political force, and this had been the case even long before the death of the last Stuart claimant in 1807. The author had fostered Scots cultural nationalism by collecting the words of ballads in the three-volume *Minstrelsy of the Scottish Border* (1802-3), and the idealisation of outlaw Highlanders and Gypsies in his fiction was the logical outcome of his Tory nostalgia for the safely banished but heroic past. Scott portrays MacGregor as a perfidious outlaw who is, nevertheless, capable of acts of righteousness. Once his lawlessness and putative Jacobite sympathies appear to have been extinguished, the eighteenth-century Scottish Gypsy may be nostalgically and safely recollected. In a letter published in *Blackwood's Magazine* in 1817, Simson states that he is anxious "to see justice done the character (the devil must get his due) of a people, however savage and barbarous their manners may have been [...]. However numerous the vices may be that inhabit the dark breast of the swarthy gypsey, ingratitude and dishonour are not the most prominent" (1818, 282-3).

According to an article by Scott and Pringle: "the early eighteenth-century Scottish Gypsies were "the *Parias* of Scotland, living like wild Indians among European settlers" (49). Just as Jefferson insisted that the "Red Indians" should be forced to "modernise", Adam Smith (1723-90), author of *The Wealth of Nations* (1776), Professor of logic and moral philosophy at Glasgow University, and an originator of the eighteenth-century Scottish Enlightenment, held that primal tribal savages existed in earlier cultural time, a belief that justified the elimination of the "barbaric" elements of Scottish society.[14] Smith envisaged history as progressing through four economic periods: a hunter-gatherer stage, a nomadic and pastoral stage, a feudalist and agricultural stage and the final stage of manufacturing and commerce, which he believed that Scotland was then entering. According to the linear Smithian model of entwined historical and economic progress, the "nomadic" Gypsies lagged behind even the backward feudalism of

---

[14] Intriguingly, a bizarre tradition exists in Scotland to this day that during his childhood, the Gypsies stole Smith for a brief period. See (Scott 1968, 62).

the Highlands. Scott qualifies a note on superstitions associated with the Scottish Gypsy in *Guy Mannering* as follows: "These notions are not peculiar to the gipsies; but having been once generally entertained among the Scottish common people, are now only found among those who are the most rude in their habits, and most devoid of instruction" (Scott 1968, 423 n.). The "staunch Jacobite", Jean Gordon, a formidable Gypsy woman remembered by Scott's father, was the original of *Guy Mannering*'s heroine, Meg Merrilies; for the commentators of the Scottish Enlightenment and the authors who wrote in its wake, the Highlands and the Border districts, infested as they were with colourful Jacobites and their Gypsy sympathisers, constituted a space existing in earlier cultural time. The "pre-agricultural" nomadic mode of negotiating the landscape of the Gypsy, and his "Aryan" origin attesting to the distant source of modern European civilisation, ensured that, to general sedentary Western culture, the Gypsy functioned as a repository of all that contemporary civilisation had necessarily abandoned. After Maria Theresa, Empress of the Hapsburg lands, ordered Gypsies to settle in 1758, a 1761 proclamation commanded that the name "Gypsy" be replaced by that of "Ujmagyar" or "New Hungarian"; likewise, when Spain sought to assimilate its Gypsy population in the 1770s, those in charge of the policy recommended suppression of the term "Gitano" (Fraser, 158; 6). The European Gypsy was banished from the public realm just as the textual construct of the "Gypsy" decisively emerged in the spheres of European culture, linguistics and ethnology.

Scott's *Guy Mannering*, set mainly in the late eighteenth century, utilises a great deal of the hackneyed plot device of the highborn child whisked away by a Gypsy, eventually restored to its rightful social position, which has been commonly used in English language writing since at least Thomas Middleton and William Rowley's *The Spanish Gipsy*. Guy Mannering, a young Englishman travelling through Scotland, is hospitably received at New Place, the seat of Godfrey Bertram, Laird Of Ellangowan in the county of Dumfries, on the night of the birth of the Laird's son, Harry Bertram, thus beginning a long association between the two families. At the age of five, Harry is, as the erstwhile astrologer Mannering predicts, abducted by smugglers with the seeming connivance of the Gypsy, Meg Merrilies, only resurfacing many years later to claim his inheritance. The powerful Meg, perhaps Scott's most enduring and significant literary figure, also instigates the eventual restoration of the heir, due to the "ancient attachment" that existed between the Gypsies and the Laird of Ellangowan, despite his unjust treatment of the community. The romantic Gypsy of Scottish writing partly emanates from the symbiotic relationship of Scott with *Blackwood's Magazine*: accounts of the Border Gypsies are reproduced from various *Blackwood's Magazine* articles in Scott's notes, footnotes and the 1829 introduction to *Guy Mannering*. Scott did not sign his *Blackwood's* contributions, nor did he officially admit to authorship of the Waverley novels until 1827. Nevertheless, there would have been a certain degree of public consciousness of the identity of the author of both the novels and the articles,[15] and an awareness of the intertextual borrowings that ensued, particularly as Scott was referred to as "the anonymous author of Guy Mannering" in a contribution to the periodical relating to the ruthless and violent "Gypsey chief", Billy Marshall (Laidlow, 462).[16] Kenneth MacLeoy's contribution

---

[15] See (Austen, 404).

[16] Simson likewise lifts substantial quotations from articles and correspondence on Scottish

on the "noble" and "romantic" Highlander, Rob Roy MacGregor appeared in the second volume of *Blackwood's Magazine* in 1817, the same year that Scott's phenomenal *Rob Roy* was published;[17] the literary fad for Gypsies appears to have coincided with Edinburgh's period of literary supremacy. Scott, ill during 1817, dictated at least five articles throughout that year on the subject of Scottish Gypsies (three of which constitute one serialised piece entitled "Scottish Gypsies") to Pringle. The collaborators wrote of the original woman upon whom Meg Merrilies was based for the very first issue of *Blackwood's Magazine* in April 1817, constructing her as the quintessentially lawless but noble Gypsy of yore. The piece was reproduced verbatim as part of the 1829 introduction to *Guy Mannering*:

> My father remembered old Jean Gordon of Yetholm, who had great sway among her tribe. She was quite a Meg Merrilies, and possessed the savage virtue of fidelity in the same perfection. Having been often hospitably received at the farm-house of Lochside, near Yetholm, she had carefully abstained from committing any depredations on the farmer's property. But her sons (nine in number) had not, it seems, the same delicacy, and stole a brood-sow from their kind entertainer. Jean was mortified at this ungrateful conduct, and so much ashamed of it, that she absented herself from Lochside for several years. (Scott 1968, 12)

Scott continues that in the wake of the second Jacobite rising, Jean was murdered by a mob at a fair in Carlisle for her vociferous Jacobite views "soon after the year" 1746. In the same introduction Scott gives an admiring description of Jean's regal granddaughter, Madge Gordon (again, this account is reproduced exactly from Scott and Pringle's article in the very first issue of *Blackwood's Magazine*), "at this time accounted the Queen of the Yetholm clans", as a kind of underworld *doppelgänger* of Queen Anne (Scott 1968, 15). Scott and Pringle open the article by asserting that it is a "singular" phenomenon that "an Asiatic people should have resided four hundred years in the heart of Europe, subject to its civilized polity and commingled with its varied population, and yet have retained almost unaltered their distinct oriental character, customs and language" (Scott and Pringle, 43). With its secret self-government and inverted value-system, the Gypsy population constituted, to Simson, a sinister, submerged state within the law-abiding Scottish nation: "This system of Gipsy polity establishes a curious fact, namely, the double division and occupation of the kingdom of Scotland; by *ourselves* [my emphasis] as a civilised people, and by a barbarous community existing in our midst, each subject to its own customs, laws and government" (1865, 150). Simson's use of "ourselves" implies that no Gypsy could possibly have access to his volume, a statement subverted elsewhere in the book. His use of the term also contradicts his

Gypsies contributed to the magazine in the late 1810s for his *History of the Gipsies,* including his own contributions of that era.

[17] "[Rob Roy] was the strenuous opponent of every deed of cruelty or breach of faith, especially if committed upon those under pressure of misfortune; the poor, the orphan, the widow, were those for whom he stood boldly forward, and was the avowed champion" (MacLeoy, 149).

fear that many "respectable" families in Scotland unknowingly harbour "Gipsy blood" in their veins: the Gypsy is the Other of the Scottish gentleman, the anxiously externalised *doppelgänger* harboured within. Simson continues that even one drop of this blood ensures that the family concerned and all their descendants are "out-and-out Gipsies", regardless of any other genetic inheritance involved. The Gypsy parent, with or without the knowledge of the non-Gypsy partner, indoctrinates the offspring of any such union into Masonic Gypsy ways.

The class oppression intrinsic to the surveillance of marginalized population groups by those of higher social, economic and educational standing is often made manifest in Simson's accounts, where the witnesses to Gypsy affrays always appear to be, in his term, "gentlemen." Simson's grandfather, a very substantial "gentleman-farmer," was, by 1781, renting sixteen farms covering 25,000 acres of land in the Midlothian, Tweeddale, and Selkirkshire districts, and he occasionally allowed Gypsies to camp on his property into the late eighteenth-century. On one occasion, the author attempted to extract vocabulary from a "Tinkler" by reminding him that his (Simson's) grandfather had entertained the man's ancestors on his land (1865, 309 fn.; 311). Simson was a superintendent of quarantine at Inverkeithing, while Scott was appointed Sheriff-Depute of Selkirkshire in 1799, and awarded a baronetcy by the Prince Regent in 1818. The Scott and Simson families were members of the powerful class concerned with the monitoring of itinerant and criminal populations: according to Simson, a Gypsy named William Keith, who had been "concerned," with his brother Robert, in the murder of one of their own "clan", was apprehended on a farm occupied by Simson's grandfather in Tweed-dale, and one of those who "assisted at the apprehension of Robert Keith was the father of Sir Walter Scott," a writer to the signet (solicitor).[18] Moreover, Scott records in his reply to Hoyland that he instigated and played a part in the "extirpation" (a word that may be defined either as "rooting out" or "extermination") of the putatively ferocious Gypsies of previous years: "Formerly, [...] they were much more desperate in their conduct than at present. But some of the most atrocious families have been extirpated [...]. Mr. Reddell, Justice of Peace for Roxburghshire, with my assistance and concurrence, cleared this country of the last of them, about eight or nine years ago" (Hoyland, 94-5). The social status of the constellation surrounding *Blackwood's* underlines the fact that the average nineteenth-century contributor to the magazine is generally understood to have "championed a semi-feudal society, supporting a privileged, usually landowning class with certain self-imposed duties and responsibilities to the lower orders, and steadily supported all rural, as opposed to all urban, interests" (Houghton, 8). The political ideology implicit in *Blackwood's* attraction to the subject of the putatively anachronistic Scottish Gypsy may be the very reason the Whig *Edinburgh Review* showed absolutely no interest in the same topic throughout the 1810s.

---

[18] Both Scott and the "Ettrick Shepherd" (the poet and contributor to Scott's *Border Minstrelsy*, James Hogg [1770-1835]) refer to the murder concerned in pieces published in *Blackwood's Magazine*.

References

Austen, Jane. 1952. *Jane Austen's Letters*. Ed. R.W. Chapman. 2nd Ed. Oxford: Clarendon

Burns, Robert. 1993. *The Complete Poetical Works of Robert Burns, 1759-1796*. Ed James A. MacKay. Ayrshire: Alloway

Fraser, Angus M. 1997. *The Gypsies*. Oxford: Blackwell

Grellmann, Heinrich. 1787. *Dissertation on the Gipsies*. Trans. Matthew Raper. London: G. Biggs

Houghton, Walter E. 1966. *The Wellesley Index to Victorian Periodicals, 1824-1900*. Vol. 1

Hoyland, John. 1816. *A Historical Survey of the Customs, Habits, and Present State of the Gypsies: Designed to Develop the Origin of this Singular People, and to Promote the Amelioration of their Condition*. York: Alexander

[Laidlow, William]. 1817. "Some Account of Billy Marshall, a Gypsey Chief". *Blackwood's Edinburgh Magazine*. 1: 462-465

[MacLeoy, Kenneth]. 1817. "Memoir of Rob Roy MacGregor, and Some Branches of his Family". *Blackwood's Edinburgh Magazine*. 2: 149-155

MacRitchie, David. 1889. "Irish Tinkers and their Language". *Journal of the Gypsy Lore Society*. 2: 350.57

Scott, Sir Walter. 1968. *Guy Mannering*. London: Dent

Scott, Sir Walter. 1932-7. *The Letters of Sir Walter Scott*. Vol. 5. Ed. H.J.C. Grierson. London: Constable

Scott, Sir Walter. 1998. *Waverley*. Ed. Claire Lamont. Oxford: Oxford University Press

[Scott, Sir Walter and Thomas Pringle]. 1817. "Scottish Gypsies". *Blackwood's Edinburgh Magazine*. 1: 43-58; 154-61; 615-20

[Simson, Walter]. 1818. "Anecdotes of the Fife Gypsies". *Blackwood's Edinburgh Magazine*. 2: 523-27

Simson, Walter. 1865. *A History of the Gipsies*. Ed. James Simson. London: Sampson Low, Son, and Marston

Sinclair, Albert Thomas. 1908. "The Oriental Gypsies". *Journal of the Gypsy Lore Society*. 1.3: 197-211

Strout, Alan Lang. 1959. *A Bibliography of Articles in* Blackwood's Magazine*: Volumes I Through XVII, 1817-1825*. Lubbock: Texas Technological College Press

Trumpener, Katie. 1992. "The Time of the Gypsies: A 'People Without History' in the Narratives of The West". *Critical Inquiry*. 18.4: 843-884

Whyte, Donald. 2001. *Scottish Gypsies and Other Travellers*. Blackwell, Alfreton: Dawson

Willems, Wim. 1997. *In Search of the True Gypsy*. Trans. Don Bloch. London: Cass

Willems, Wim and Leo Lucassen. 1990. "The Church of Knowledge: Representation of Gypsies in Dutch Encyclopedias and their Sources". *100 Years of Gypsy Studies*. Ed. Matt T. Salo. Cheverly, MD: Gypsy Lore Society. 31-50

Rebels and Redcoats: Political Melodrama in the Kalem Company's Irish Films.[1]

Denis Condon

"What do you do with your old films when they are unfit for further use in picture theatres?" asked an anonymous reporter for the British film industry journal *The Bioscope* of "a leading member of the Trade" in February 1911. "'Oh!' was the reply, 'we sell them to a firm of leather dressers on the Continent. The celluloid is reduced by a chemical process and then used for coating the leather that is used for patent leather boots and shoes'" (Anonymous, 17). At the beginning of the 20th century, film was viewed as an ephemeral popular cultural product. Like greengrocers, film renters discarded stale produce to make way for the more marketable fresh batch that was being supplied, by the early 1910s, on a reliable basis a number of times a week by film "manufacturing" companies.

The Irish film historian Robert Monks has identified about 66 fiction films made in Ireland between 1896, when the cinematograph first showed projected moving pictures in Dublin, and the Censorship of Films Act 1923, one of the earliest pieces of legislation passed by the first Free State Dáil.[2] Of these, only 12 survive, six of which were directed by Sidney Olcott for Kalem and other U.S. film companies between 1910 and 1914. In 1910, a production unit of the Kalem Company consisting of Canadian Irish director Olcott, actress and scriptwriter Gene Gauntier, and cameraman George Hollister arrived in Ireland. A larger crew led by Olcott returned in the summers of 1911 to 1914, even after he and Gauntier left Kalem at the end of 1912. The films of the O'Kalems, as the Kalem unit in Ireland came to be called, are remarkable for a number of reasons.[3] Their 1910 emigration drama *The Lad from Old Ireland* was said to be the first film made by a U.S. film company outside America, and it was advertised as the first film to be shot on two continents and on the high seas. Their Irish output as a whole represents the largest body of films produced by a foreign film company in the country.[4]

This essay outlines the relationship between the theatrical genre of Irish

[1] Research for this paper was funded by the Irish Research Council for the Humanities and the Social Sciences, through a Government of Ireland Scholarship.
[2] See Monks (1996). Because of the ephemerality of films as cultural products at the time and the associated lack of reviewing, this figure represents an approximation, and its revision is contingent on ongoing research.
[3] The whimsical term 'O'Kalem' can only accurately designate the films made by Olcott, Gauntier, and their colleagues in the years 1910-12. Olcott and Gauntier left Kalem at the end of 1912 to found the Gene Gauntier Feature Players (the GGs) and returned to Ireland under that banner in 1913. When Olcott made his last films in Ireland in 1914, however, it was without Gauntier and for his own production company, the Sid Olcott International Feature Players. Once this is borne in mind, however, the term does provide a useful shorthand for referring to these films and filmmakers.
[4] Rockett (1996, 257). For a more detailed discussion of the O'Kalem films in relation to Irish tourism, see Condon (2002) and (2003).

political melodrama and the surviving O'Kalem rebel-and-redcoat dramas *Rory O'More*, *For Ireland's Sake*, and *Bold Emmett, Ireland's Martyr*. There are many similarities between the one-reel 1911 *Rory O'More* and the three-reelers made in 1913 and 1914 respectively, so much so that the later films might be considered versions of the earlier one.[5] Because of pressures of space, it will be necessary to draw examples mainly from *Rory O'More*, a short film that permits a view in miniature of much of what the O'Kalems achieved in their Irish history films. Politically, the O'Kalem films occupy similar ideological territory to Irish political melodrama. Like the stage melodramas, the films espouse a popular militant nationalism that focuses, in particular, on the events of the 1798 and 1803 rebellions. This is in marked contrast to the "constructive unionism" promoted, as Lionel Pilkington has recently shown, by the national theatre movement that was to find a home at the Abbey Theatre. That they delivered their political message while respecting the conventions of a popular form also clearly distinguishes the melodramas from their literary counterparts at the Abbey. In what follows, a brief discussion of the importance of Victorian melodrama in general to silent film precedes an elucidation of how the kind of popular Irish melodrama epitomized by Boucicault that played in Dublin and other cities affected the production and reception of the O'Kalem films.

For much of the 20th century, literary studies employed the term melodrama in a largely negative sense as the antithesis of high literary culture. It reemerged as an object of renewed analytical interest, first, in the late 1960s in theatrical histories that focused on it as a generic system and, second and seminally, in film studies in the 1970s, where it was employed primarily to discuss the post-World War II woman's film. The slipperiness of the term has prompted a number of critics to suggest that it is not a genre at all but a mode that is fundamental to popular culture in the West. What is relevant here, however, is how film adopted the defined conventions of a variant of Victorian melodrama, and a short description of how this theatrical form emerged gives an idea of why it was so readily adopted by early film.[6]

Melodrama first appeared in France and England in the eighteenth century, where royal edicts gave the monopoly on the production of spoken drama to two or three theatres. It is from this development that the terms legitimate and illegitimate theatre come. The "illegitimate" theatres or minor houses relied on a range of non-dialogue entertainments that drew on such forms as dumb show, pantomime, harlequinade, ballets, spectacles, acrobatics, clowning, busking, the exhibition of animals and freaks, and, particularly, musical accompaniment and song, from which the French term *melos-drame* (music drama) derives.

---

[5] Rockett (2001: 219) calls *For Ireland's Sake* a "version" of *Rory O'More*. While *Bold Emmett, Ireland's Martyr* has some interesting variations, it shares many of its narrative functions with the earlier films (for example, the rebel hero and his sweetheart, chase and capture by the redcoats, condemnation to death in court, and a climax involving a daring escape/rescue/reprieve).

[6] The literature on melodrama is vast. The account here is particularly indebted to the overview provided in Gledhill (1987), to Singer's recent book on sensational melodrama's translation from stage to screen (2001), to the works on Victorian melodrama in Britain and Ireland by Michael R. Booth (1965; 1977; 1981; 1991), and to Richard Pine (1985).

Prohibited from employing spoken dialogue, the minor houses concentrated on spectacle elaborated through intricate and varied costuming, exotic sets, spectacular enactments, and special effects; on performance traditions derived from dumb show, pantomime, harlequinade, tumbling, acrobatics, and balladry, and on music, including song with its verbal aspect. Words also formed a part of illegitimate theatre's heterogeneous entertainments through the employment of placards and banners, and, as Peter Brooks has pointed out, pantomime developed a large repertoire of non-verbal signs or "visible emblems" such as meteors, rainbows, lightning, spectres, crosses in flames, rising tombs, that immediately told spectators how to read the scene (63-4). By developing these traditional techniques, the minor houses had by the end of the eighteenth century evolved a complex theatrical *mise en scène*. When the economic potential of such forms brought them into the legitimate theatres, they melded with eighteenth-century sentimental drama's relocation of dramatic action from "feudal and aristocratic hierarchies to the 'democratic' bourgeois family" and the associated emergence of the types of hero, heroine, and villain. (Gledhill, 17)

By the early nineteenth century, a kind of theatre was already in existence that would later be particularly suited not only to adaptation by early and silent film but also to film's wholesale adoption of its conventions. There was, of course, direct adaptation, represented famously in the case of the Kalem Company by the location shooting of Dion Boucicault's Irish plays. A number of melodramatic conventions, however, lent themselves to wholesale adoption by silent film. Of the repertoire of non-dialogue features deployed by Victorian melodrama, the most important to silent film were its immediately identifiable stock characters, its gestural acting style, its expressive use of costume, setting, and music, and its incorporation of written words in the form of banners and placards.

The opening scene of *Rory O'More* offers a good example of how the film negotiates the conventions of Victorian melodrama. It is a clear instance of the establishment of melodramatic types in dumb show before the emergence of any real specificities of the historical situation in which the story is set. On the extant copy of the film, no opening titles or intertitles give a clue to who the characters are in the first one-shot scene, but their costumes, actions, and gestural acting establish them as stock melodramatic characters of hero, heroine, and villain. Before a picturesque waterfall, Rory kisses Kathleen before she exits right. Rory looks up joyfully then exits left. From behind a rock, the villain, who will soon be identified as the informer Black William, emerges laughing evilly, points first left then right, and exits left. While their costumes give some sense of the time frame, there is as yet no indication of the wider context of the action.

If this is the establishment of melodramatic character, the engagement with Irish politics is not long in coming in this single reel film that runs to about nine minutes. It consists of four sequences. The first begins by establishing the characters of Rory, Kathleen, and Black William, as discussed above, and goes on to reveal, through the use of a printed proclamation, that Rory is an Irish rebel leader for whose capture the British authorities have offered a substantial reward. The second concerns Rory's attempt to elude the authorities, helped by Kathleen, and his eventual capture by the redcoats, led to him by Black William. The third shows Rory's defiant court appearance and his receipt of the death sentence. The fourth concerns the local priest's sacrifice of his life in order to ensure Rory's escape from the gallows to America.

The film certainly includes a generic mix, with strong elements of the chase, a popular form of early film narrative, playing a major part. The dominant genre, however, is melodrama constructed around Ireland's historical resistance to British colonialism during the rebellions of 1798 and 1803. While there is no explanation here of the reasons for resistance (the later films do feature evictions – *Bold Emmett, Ireland's Martyr* – and crop burnings – *For Ireland's Sake* – by soldiers), the very fact that Rory is a melodramatic hero means that he must pursue his righteous struggle and win out against the forces of evil. By producing such films between 1911 and 1914, the Kalem filmmakers were aligning themselves with the contemporary armed resistance to British rule in Ireland. The only dialogue intertitle in the film is Rory's speech from the dock: "IF TO FIGHT FOR IRELAND BE A CRIME, THEN I AM GUILTY."

Because of its brevity, the film not only presents a basic narrative plot but also must be flexible in relation to melodramatic stock character. Michael Booth writes that the "stock character types of melodrama – hero, villain, heroine, old man, old woman, comic man, comic woman – are almost unvarying present in every play" (1965: 15-6). A subaltern figure, the comic man was often a friend or loyal retainer of the hero and is frequently responsible for saving the hero and/or thwarting the villain. As Booth puts it, "[t]he comedian – servant, artisan, or tradesman, usually a member of the working class and thus closely identified with this audience – is a friend or man-servant of the hero, and sometimes carries on the battle against villainy (though by comic means) in the absence or incapacity of his superior" (1965: 33). Rory represents the peasant as hero, conflating heroic and comedic roles. Marty, his equivalent in *For Ireland's Sake*, more clearly manifests the dual role of hero and comedian by engaging in battle with the villain but also providing the film's main moment of comedy, when he hides from the pursuing soldiers under Eileen's cloak.

The distinctions between hero and comedian had, in any case, long come under a degree of erasure in the most famous Irish melodramas. The comedian's capacity for heroic acts and the fact that the comic man in Victorian melodrama was frequently Irish created space for Boucicault to blur the line between comedian and hero in his full-length Irish stage melodramas. In *The Colleen Bawn* (1860), *Arrah-na-Pogue* (1864), and *The Shaughraun* (1874), Boucicault played peasants, who, while nominally comic characters, overshadow the supposedly central heroes. By the time of *The Shaughraun*, indeed, the role of the 'pleasant peasant' had expanded to such an extent that he steals the eponymous role from the heroine.[7]

In the last 25 years or so, serious critical attention has been devoted to the reconstruction of a subgenre of Irish political melodrama, a body of plays set at times of conflict between Britain and Ireland.[8] This scholarship has focused on works from the period from the 1860s into the early years of the Irish state by dramatists such as Boucicault, J. W. Whitbread, Hubert O'Grady, P. J. Bourke, and Ira Allen, plays particularly associated, in Ireland, with Dublin's Queen's Royal

---

[7] The term "pleasant peasant" is Joep Leerssen's (1996: 170-3). Under this heading, he explores the rhetorical strategies masked by the term "Stage Irishman".

[8] On Irish political melodrama, see Herr (1991), Watt (1991) and Pine (1985). See also Booth (1977) and Gibbons (1987).

Theatre, the justifiably self-proclaimed 'home of Irish drama' after Whitbread took over in 1884.[9] It has tended to identify Boucicault's Irish dramas, particularly the historically located *Arrah-na-Pogue* and *Shaughraun*, as the most significant early texts in this form. Comparing Boucicualt's and Whitbread's approach to British-Irish conflict, for example, Stephen Watt contends that:

> Boucicault's comic plays advance an optimistic, inherently conservative myth of reconciliation, while Whitbread's for the most part form a tragic, at times potentially emancipatory chronicle in which this opposition will inevitably continue. Equally important, both playwrights create dramas in which the status of native Irishness is elevated, offering effective counterrepresentations to especially loathesome [sic] Victorian caricatures of Irishmen. (1991: 63-4)

An earlier text that deals with the 1798 rebellion, and of obvious relevance here, is Samuel Lover's *Rory O'More: A Comic Drama* (1837). Lover's play is an adaptation of his novel *Rory O'More: A National Romance* (1836), which in turn, derives from his popular ballad.[10] First performed at the Theatre Royal, Adelphi, on September 29, 1837:

> [i]ts representation was a complete triumph. It was played for one hundred and eight nights in the first season, in London, and afterwards universally through the kingdom. The *Athenæum* remarked that Rory O'More, – a triple glory in song, story and drama, – was the greatest success of the day … (Symington, 47-8)

The play lacks many of the more critical scenes of the novel, such as the lynching of an alleged rebel sympathizer by a yeomanry captain and magistrate, the pronouncing of Rory guilty of murder even when the man who he is charged with having killed is produced in court, and the fact that Rory must leave Ireland because his identification as a United Irishman leaves him open to official harassment and possible extra-judicial execution. In common with the novel, however, it offers sympathetic central portrayals of its melodramatic hero de Lacy, a United Irishman reconnoitering in Ireland for a French landing, and its comedian and real focus, Rory, a peasant and rank-and-file member of the United Irishmen.

Many of the narrative functions of the O'Kalem film, however, do not derive from Lover's work. There is no court scene, for example, in Lover's play, and the court sequence that recurs in all of the O'Kalem rebel-and-redcoat films is not a distillation of the long and eventful court scene in his novel. Each film's court sequence serves to show that the judicial system is unsuited to weighing the subtleties of the interactions between Irish people and the British authorities and inexorably resorts instead to meting out summary justice. With the limited

---

[9] On the Queen's, see De Búrca (1983).

[10] Boucicault was well acquainted with *Rory O'More*: it was the second leading role that he played in his acting career, in Cheltenham in 1838. See Fawkes (1979: 19). A number of critics have pointed out the intertextuality between texts such as Lover's *Rory*, Charles Lever's *Jack Hinton: Guardsman*, Boucicault's Irish plays, and George Bernard Shaw's *The Devil's Disciple*. See Fawkes (1979: 155), Parkin (1987: 20) and Krause (1964: 39-42).

possibilities of the legal system exhausted, the way is clear for a climax involving a spectacular escape and/or a last minute reprieve. In both form and function, the court sequences more closely resemble the court scene in Boucicault's *Arrah-na-Pogue*.

This is just one instance of discursive similarity between the O'Kalem films and Boucicault's Irish plays. Another important case is their correspondence in allowing that at least some British soldiers can act honourably and, once again distinguishing it from Lover's work, in making the informer the real villain. Boucicault takes this to the point in the 1874 *Shaughraun* where the defeat of the land-grabbing Corry Kinchela and police informer Harvey Duff leaves the way clear for the British Captain Molineaux to marry the sister of the Fenian Robert Folliott. By 1911, such a symbolic reconciliation between Britain and Ireland was not imaginable. While it is possible in *Rory O'More* for a local commander to attempt to give Rory his freedom as a quid pro quo for Rory's rescue of one of his men from drowning and subsequently, to speak in his defence in court, the film ends with the rebel having to flee Ireland.

In its inability to represent *rapprochement* between Ireland and Britain, the film is closer to the work of Whitbread, written at a later historical juncture. Manager of the Queen's from 1884 to 1907, the English-born Whitbread wrote 15 plays on Irish themes, including *The Nationalist, Lord Edward Fitzgerald or '98, Sarsfield, The Insurgent Chief* (on Michael Dwyer), and *The Ulster Hero* (on Henry Joy McCracken).[11] A surviving daybill from a September 1901 production of his 1898 *Wolfe Tone*, one of the numerous cultural events marking the centenary of the 1798 Rebellion, at the Queen's by Kennedy Miller's Celebrated Irish Company describes the play as "illustrating the early adventures, romantic marriage, and stirring episodes in the life of this immortal figure in Ireland's history" (Herr, 172). This play begins by setting up the rivalry between Tone and Samuel Turner, a "Barrister, United Irishman and informer", for the affections of Susan Witherington, before moving to France, where Turner continues to pursue Susan, now Tone's wife, while seeking to undermine the alliance Tone attempts to build with Napoleon.[12]

The centrality of the informer as villain is a peculiarity of Irish political melodrama from the mid-nineteenth century. It is not the subaltern British soldier in Ireland but the traitor within that represents the most pernicious threat to Irish rebel hopes of emulating American rebels in throwing off the yoke of imperialism that the redcoats represent. Kevin Whelan has shown that it was the Catholic Church, in its attempt to wrest ideological control of the memory of 1798 from the Fenians, that focused attention on the weakness of the United Irishmen in the face

---

[11] He also produced a version, now apparently lost, of Lover's *Rory O'More*.

[12] From the dramatis personae of *Wolfe Tone* (Herr 171). Like the loss of many early films because they were considered ephemeral popular culture, the texts of many of the Irish melodramas of the late 19th and early 20th century are also believed to be lost. Those that toured in Britain, however, had first to be submitted to the Lord Chamberlain for approval, and these survive in the British Library. Herr reprints four Irish political melodramas from the Lord Chamberlain's Plays, Manuscript Collection, British Library: Whitbread's *Lord Edward, Or '98* (1894) and *Wolfe Tone* (1898) and Bourke's *When Wexford Rose* (1910) and *For the Land She Loved* (1915). Watt (1985) introduces the reprinting of the texts of O'Grady's *Emigration* and *Famine*.

of spies and informers. Part of the Church's wider battle with oath-bound societies, this struggle resulted in the emergence of the pairing of informing and clerical heroism. Franciscan friar Patrick Kavanagh's *A Popular History of the Insurrection of 1798*, first published in 1870 and going through nine further editions up to 1928, dominated discourse on '98 at the time of the centenary and through the foundation of the Irish Free State. Stressing the heroic role of Father John Murphy, Kavanagh argues that the spy-riddled United Irishmen deceived and abandoned the Irish people when fighting broke out.[13]

The O'Kalem's *Rory* follows this pattern, contrasting the heroic priest selflessly giving his life to save the rebel, while greed drives Black William to betrayal. Kevin Rockett contends that the priests in the later O'Kalem rebel-and-redcoat films show a decreasing pro-rebel stance because of difficulties that the O'Kalem filmmakers experienced from the local priest in Killarney. Rockett argues that Father Flannigan's motives for helping the rebel Marty to escape in *For Ireland's Sake* may be to leave an unchallenged clerical leadership in the community.[14] By the time of the 1914 *Bold Emmett, Ireland's Martyr,* the priest's role has diminished to the extent that he merely accompanies the condemned Con to the gallows, and it is left to Robert Emmett (as he is called throughout the film) and a British officer grateful for Con's assistance when he was wounded to save the rebel from execution.

The guile of the pleasant peasant, expressed most famously in the artful brogue of Boucicault's Myles-na-Coppaleen, Shaun the Post, and Conn the Shaughraun, was crucial to the international success of this form of Irish drama.[15] Because silent film was unable to reproduce the linguistic acrobatics of the peasant trickster, he drops out of sight in film, as is clearly shown by the relative unimportance of Myles to the O'Kalem *Colleen Bawn*. Reduced to the slapstick of the chase and signalled by costume and by inferred social relationships, both the pleasantness and peasantness, respectively, of Rory are features that rely on the audience's ability to read the intertextual signs. The trickster character also falls out of sight in filmic melodrama to some extent because he functions best in the theatre, where he develops in the interaction between the actor and the stage audience. If the villain worked the audience to a hissing frenzy by his dastardly acts, the trickster relied on comic timing to produce laughter and cheers. Indeed, it could be argued that film, by occupying the same space as melodrama and eventually supplanting it, played as large a role in killing off its performance tradition and participative audience as the decorous strictures of bourgeois literary

---

[13] Kevin Whelan (1996: 170-3).

[14] See Rockett, Gibbons, and Hill (1987: 10-1). Rockett has extended this argument to a larger group of U.S.-produced films in his more recent essay (2001: 219-22). This contextualization serves to highlight the wider discourse from which the O'Kalem representations of priests and other stock characters emerge and to downplay the role that the negative experiences of the O'Kalem crew with the local priest played in influencing those representations.

[15] Shane McMahon, the plain-speaking Trinity College porter turned French Army corporal who foils the informers' plot in *Wolfe Tone*, is a manifestation of this character in an urban setting. For an account of how class and nationalism intersect in a play performed in the centenary of the 1798 Rebellion in front of a predominantly proletarian audience in a theatre sited beside the entrance to Trinity, that bastion of the Ascendancy, see Morash (2002: 113-4).

theatre.

   In sum, an examination of the O'Kalem *Rory O'More* reveals, in general, early film's debt to Victorian melodrama and, in particular, the O'Kalem debt to Irish political melodrama. While all these texts espouse a decidedly nationalist ideology, the specific manifestation of the melodramatic dichotomy between hero and villain, good and evil, in the Irish context is played out on both stage and screen between the pleasant peasant, a development of the comic man of Victorian melodrama, and the informer, an Irish variant on the villain. While critics have, in the main, traced this genre from an originary point in Boucicault's internationally successful Irish plays, an investigation of the intertextual significance of Samuel Lover's earlier novel and drama *Rory O'More* suggests that at least the early O'Kalem films absorbed the Catholic Church's late-nineteenth-century representation of the heroic priest of the 1798 Rebellion. If silent film was eventually to replace the stage melodrama it liberally adapted and adopted, it was at the cost of losing stage melodrama's interactive performance traditions.

References

Anonymous. 1911. "Film Footwear". *The Bioscope*. 9 February: 17

Booth, Michael R. 1965. *English Melodrama*. London: Herbert Jenkins

Booth, Michael R. 1977. "Irish Landscape in the Victorian Theatre". *Place, Personality and the Irish Writer*. Ed. Andrew Carpenter. Gerrard's Cross: Colin Smyth

Booth, Michael R. 1981. *Victorian Spectacular Theatre 1850-1910*. London: Routledge and Kegan Paul

Booth, Michael R. 1991. *Theatre in the Victorian Age*. Cambridge: Cambridge University Press

Brooks, Peter. 1976. *The Melodramatic Imagination: Balzac, Henry James, Melodrama and the Modes of Excess*. New Haven: Yale University Press

Condon, Denis. 2002. "The Colleen Bawn Rock and Daniel O'Connell's Bed: Sights on the Kalem Company's Virtual Tour of Killarney". *NUI Maynooth Postgraduate Research Record: Proceedings of the Colloquium 2002*. 89-93

Condon, Denis. 2003. "Touristic Work and Pleasure: The Kalem Company in Killarney". *Film and Film Culture*. 2: 7-16

De Búrca, Séamus. 1983. *The Queen's Royal Theatre Dublin: 1829-1969*. Dublin: De Búrca

Fawkes, Richard. 1979. *Dion Boucicault: A Biography*. London: Quartet Gibbons, Luke. 1987. "Romanticism, Realism and Irish Cinema". *Cinema and Ireland*. Eds. Kevin Rockett et al. London: Croom Helm. 194-257

Gledhill, Christine, ed. 1987. *Home is Where the Heart Is: Studies in Melodrama and the Woman's Film*. London: BFI

Herr, Cheryl. 1991. *For the Land They Loved: Irish Political Melodramas, 1890-1925*. Syracuse: Syracuse University Press

Krause, David. 1964. "The Theatre of Dion Boucicault: A Short View of his Life and Art". *The Dolmen Boucicault*. Dublin: Dolmen. 9-47

Leerssen, Joep. 1996. *Remembrance and Imagination: Patterns in the Historical and Literary Representation of Ireland in the Nineteenth Century*. Cork: Cork University Press

Monks, Robert. 1996. *Cinema Ireland: A Database of Irish Films and Filmmakers 1896-1986*. CD-ROM. Dublin: National Library of Ireland

Morash, Christopher. 2002. *A History of Irish Theatre 1601-2000*. Cambridge: Cambridge University Press

Parkin, Andrew. 1987. "Introduction". *Selected Plays of Dion Boucicault*. Gerrards Cross: Colin Smythe. 7-22

Pilkington, Lionel. 2001. *Theatre and the State in Twentieth-Century Ireland: Cultivating the People*. London: Routledge

Pine, Richard, ed. 1985. *Dion Boucicault and the Irish Melodrama Tradition*. Dublin: Irish Theatre Archive

Rockett, Kevin, et al, eds. 1987. *Cinema and Ireland*. London: Croom Helm

Rockett, Kevin. 1996. *The Irish Filmography*. Dublin: Red Mountain

Rockett, Kevin. 2001. "Representations of Irish History in Fiction Films Made Prior to the 1916 Rising". *Rebellion and Remembrance in Modern Ireland*. Ed. Laurence M. Geary. Dublin: Four Courts. 219-22

Singer, Ben. 2001. *Melodrama and Modernity: Early Sensational Cinema and Its Contexts*. New York: Columbia University Press

Symington, Andrew James. 1880. *Samuel Lover: A Biographical Sketch*. New York: Harper

Watt, Stephen. 1985. "Introduction to O'Grady's *Emigration* and *Famine*". *Journal of Irish Literature* 14.1: 3-49

Whelan, Kevin. 1996. *The Tree of Liberty: Radicalism, Catholicism and the Construction of Irish Identity 1760-1830*. Cork: Cork University Press

Medieval Mendicancy: the Franciscan Experience in Ireland and Scotland in the Thirteenth Century

Niav Gallagher

According to Thomas Eccleston, the first Franciscan friars landed at Dover on Tuesday, 10 September 1224 (1858: 9). Within a few years the Order of Friars Minor had spread across England and into Ireland, Scotland and Wales. The intention of this paper is to examine the progression these friars made from poor dwellings outside the city walls, on the fringes of Irish and Scottish society, to centre stage in the larger political world. It will also look at the welcome they received from the populace and the established clergy, their involvement in local politics and, finally, their impact upon the communities of both countries.

Both the Scottish and Irish churches had undergone a period of reform, starting in the late eleventh century, and into this reformed church the Cistercians and the Augustinians were invited. These orders were greeted as a revival of the old ascetic monasticism, but by the end of the twelfth century they had fallen into some disarray. The newly formed mendicant orders filled the vacuum left by these old monastic orders and it was they who now attracted interest from the native populations. The Dominicans and Franciscans were established in England, Ireland, Scotland and Wales in the early decades of the thirteenth century and they differed from their monastic predecessors in several ways. These friars were itinerant and, therefore, not confined to the cloister. They were granted preaching and confessional rights, employed as papal envoys and taken as confessors by the wealthy and powerful. In many instances they were seen as usurping the existing clergy.

Francis intended his order, founded in 1209, to be the humblest members of society – unskilled, illiterate and mendicant – in other words, Friars Minor. Within a couple of decades this ideal had been subverted and friaries were founded, property was granted and places of learning were established. Within a few years of arriving in England, for example, the Franciscans had established a college at Oxford. Despite this, people welcomed the friars and the order expanded widely within the first century of its existence. This was aided by the lack of formal foundations. Friars were invited into a location and, usually, given derelict buildings outside the town walls. It might take years to establish a permanent friary and church but from such a humble foundation there would be a further expansion, leaving two or three of the brethren behind to maintain the Order's presence. In this way thirty-one friaries were established in Ireland in the thirteenth century, only two of which failed, and five were established in Scotland.

Agnellus of Pisa led the friars who landed at Dover in 1224. Eight companions, among whom were three English friars – Richard of Ingworth, a priest and preacher, Richard of Devon, and William of Esseby – accompanied him and Eccleston chronicled their rapid movement (Moorman, 72). These friars after remaining two days in Canterbury sent four of their number to London and, at the end of the month, Richard of Ingworth and Richard of Devon set out for Oxford. Here the Dominicans received them with kindness, Eccleston stating that "they ate in their refectory and slept in their dormitory, like conventuals for eight days"

(1858: 9). These friars then hired a house in the parish of St Ebbe from Robert le Mercer and, in the following year, left this and hired a house from Richard the Miller. "Within a year [Richard had] conferred the land and house on the community of the town for the use of the Friars Minor" (Eccleston, 10). Thus the pattern for expansion was established and by 1256 there were forty-nine English friaries, with 1,242 friars (Eccleston, 10).

The date for the arrival of the Franciscans in Ireland is a matter of some controversy but for the purposes of this paper I intend only to give an outline of the arguments that have been put forward. There is some debate that the Franciscans originally arrived in Ireland in 1214 and that their first foundation was at Youghal, in Cork. This earliest date originates in a belief that the first friars arrived from Compostella in Spain and Luke Wadding, seventeenth-century editor of the *Annales Minorum*, upheld this theory, saying this tradition was confirmed by Francesco Gonzaga, author of *De Origine Seraphicae Religionis Franciscanae*, which was published in 1587 (1731-41: 225). Gonzaga claimed that "this province of Ireland…did [not] derive its origin from any other, but had as its founder one of the companions of the seraphic father, Francis, who, crossing thither from Compostella, built some monasteries on the island and at length died there with the greatest reputation for holiness" (Cotter, 12). This, however, is only one of several dates that have been proposed and 1224 (O'Donnell, 1-2), 1231 (Jennings, 15) and 1232 (Mooney, 2) have all been put forward as the original date, with varying degrees of confidence. Donagh Mooney, a seventeenth-century historian of the Order, presented 1214 as a possible date but ultimately dismissed it, eventually citing 1231 as the date that the friars first arrived, a date which he states he obtained from an ancient and unnamed manuscript he consulted (Jennings, 15). Canice Mooney, a more recent historian of the order, believed that the tradition could not be so easily dismissed, stating that "Irish pilgrims were in the habit of visiting the shrine of St James at Compostella, and some of them, meeting the friars there, may have inspired them to send a few of their members to Ireland" (Mooney, 68). Yet these historians have produced little or no evidence upon which to base their claims. Cotter points out that James Ware, for example, used late fifteenth-century Observant sources upon which to base his claim (Cotter, 14-5). Youghal became one of the most prominent houses in the Observant reform of the fifteenth-century and there is some debate that later Franciscan historians, as part of this reform, wished to further the reputation of the house and so willingly accepted this "tradition". The second piece of evidence that seems to dispute Youghal's pre-eminence is Eccleston's account of the Franciscans in England. He chronicled the arrival of the friars, their numbers, the establishment of the college at Oxford and he testified that the Irish province was of English provenance. He has been judged accurate in other parts of his account, and there is little reason to believe that this is the exception. In conjunction with this is the silence of contemporary records on the existence of Youghal until 1290. In this year, shipwrecked goods, being kept in the friary for safe-keeping, were stolen and this is the first time that Youghal is mentioned in extant records. While several Irish houses are known to have been founded long before they appear in the records, it does seem unusual that this first foundation would be excluded from a series of royal grants made, starting in 1233 (Sweetman, 298) and naming, in all, thirteen Irish houses. Finally, Youghal does not fit in with the pattern of Franciscan settlement. The friars, as mendicants, were reliant upon alms for their survival, and it seems far more likely that the first Franciscans in Ireland would have arrived at Dublin.

Regardless of when the Franciscans arrived in Ireland the Irish province was formally established at the general chapter of the Order in Assisi in May 1230. Richard of Ingworth was named as the new province's first minister (Fitzmaurice and Little, xi.). There is some merit to the argument that Franciscans were present in Ireland before the province was established, but their first mention in extant records is in a royal grant. On 13 January 1233 royal alms of twenty marks were granted to the custodians of the Friars Minor in Dublin – Geoffrey de Turvill, Archdeacon of Dublin, and Robert Pollard, citizen of Dublin – for the repair of the friars' church and house in Dublin (Sweetman, 298). In July 1236 Maurice Fitzgerald, justiciary of Ireland, and the same Geoffrey de Turville, were ordered to pay to the Friars Minor of Dublin, fifty marks of the king's gift in aid of the construction of buildings which they have commenced in that city (Sweetman, 488). Other entries in the records chart the growth of the order in Ireland. For example in 1237 the treasurer and chamberlains of Dublin were ordered to provide thirty-five marks to enlarge and better the building of the house of the Franciscans of Waterford, and the like sum in the following year which the king ordered to be applied in purchasing tunics (Sweetman, 361). In 1245, on the Feast of All Saints, the king ordered the payment of twenty pounds for purchasing 100 tunics for the Franciscans of Ireland. It came to light that this would not suffice and an extra five marks was paid (Sweetman, 416). In this grant the houses of Dublin, Waterford, Drogheda, Cork, Athlone and Kilkenny were named. Youghal is notable by its absence.

The accepted belief is that the Franciscans moved outwards from England and into Scotland and Ireland. As already mentioned Richard Ingworth was named as provincial minister of the newly formed Irish province in 1230, and he travelled there soon after. In Scotland however, Franciscans did not move north of the Tweed until 1231. In that year the *Melrose Chronicle* reports that "the Friars Minor now came into Scotland for the first time"[1] and this date is also given by Fordun in the *Scottichronicon* (Skene, 59). Although the friars were established in Berwick from this date, there was no regular friary established there until May 1244, when David de Bernhame, the Bishop of St Andrews, consecrated its church and cemetery (Bryce, 6). From Berwick the friars moved to Roxburgh, between 1232 and 1234. Shortly after this they came into conflict with the established clergy. The friars had marked out a piece of ground for use as a cemetery and requested its consecration under the terms of the papal bull *Ita vobis*. This bull, promulgated by Gregory IX in 1227, granted friars permission to bury members of the Order in their own churches and cemeteries and was seen as a serious encroachment on the rights of the established clergy (Bryce, 6). The *Lanercost Chronicle* records under the year 1242 that there was a regular friary in the royal burgh of Haddington.[2] Certain

---

[1] See *The Church Historians of England*, Volume IV, Part 1: Containing the Chronicles of John and Richard of Hexham; The Chronicle of the Holyrood; The Chronicle of Melrose; Jordan Fantosme's Chronicle; Documents respecting Canterbury and Winchester, translated by Rev. Joseph Stevenson, (London, 1854), 176.

[2] See *Chronicon de Lanercost, 1201-1346*, (Edinburgh, 1839), 49-50.

"ministers of evil," the chronicler tells us, foully burned Patrick of Galloway, Earl of Atholl, to death in his lodgings in 1242.[3] He tells us that the perpetrators of this outrage were the Bissets and that the body of the murdered earl was "carried to the place of the Friars Minor of that town, unlamented, and buried there."[4] This burial tells us that, not only had the friars been there long enough to establish a cemetery, but also that they were going against the provisions of *Ita vobis*.

By 1266 there were four foundations in Scotland – Berwick, Roxburgh, Haddington and Dumfries. In this same period twenty friaries had been established in Ireland. This huge variance between the two countries is hard to explain as English friars made their initial expansion into Ireland and Scotland at a similar time. Yet within a few years of arriving in Ireland, there were friaries at Dublin, Kilkenny, Waterford, and Cork, while in Scotland, within the same period, there were foundations at Berwick and Roxburgh only. This pattern is repeated if the number of Dominican friaries is studied. In the thirteenth century twenty-four Dominican houses were established in Ireland, in Scotland the number was eleven. Perhaps the Irish populace was more receptive to these new orders, or the enthusiasm of the Anglo-Irish ensured that foundations accompanied fortifications. Certainly in Scotland it was mostly the Gaelic-Scots who were responsible for inviting the Franciscans to a region, after the initial foundation at Berwick, and all the Scottish foundations in the thirteenth century were in royal burghs. The names associated with the early houses in Ireland, on the other hand, are noteworthy for the minority of native Irish names. Henry III claimed to be the founder of the house at Dublin, the Marshall family were involved with the friary at Kilkenny and Hugh Purcell is credited with inviting the Franciscans to Waterford. Cork has traditionally been linked to several possible founders, only one of whom, Dermot MacCarthy, is native Irish.

A possible explanation for this variation in numbers is that the Scottish friars found themselves embroiled in controversy almost from their inception. The Irish province had always been seen as independent of the English provincial minister. The Scottish houses were not so lucky. As there were only two houses north of the Tweed for several years, it seemed only logical to include them in the custody of Newcastle (Bryce, 7). For the next century the Scottish friars laboured to rid themselves of this English domination and possibly this diverted their energies from one of expansion to one of consolidation.

About 1233 the Scottish friars appealed to Elias, recently elected Minister General, and in him they found a sympathetic ear. A mandate was issued directing that "the English province be divided into two Provinces, the one to be styled the Province of Scotland, and the other the Province of England as heretofore" (Eccleston, 31-2). This division was effected about 1235 (Bryce, 7). Eccleston tells us that Brother Henry de Reresby, having been Vicar of the Warden of Oxford, was appointed first provincial minister of this newly-formed Scottish province, but was prevented by death from taking it up (Eccleston, 25). John de Kethene, who had been guardian of London, was appointed to replace him and he became the first provincial minister of the Scottish province. Not content with escaping the jurisdiction of Newcastle, de Kethene then set about incorporating all houses north of York into his province and during his ministry the Scottish

---

[3] See *Chronicon de Lanercost, 1201-1346*, 49-50.

[4] See *Chronicon de Lanercost, 1201-1346*, 49.

province included all houses as far south as Nottingham (Fitzmaurice and Little, 5).

This desire to maintain an individual identity manifested itself in several ways, some reasonable, some not so. For example, a re-script of the minister general ordering that the Brethren personally do their own washing was ignored by the Scotland province until they received a copy addressed to themselves (Edwards, 7). It seems also that the Scottish province was more eager to be identified with the province of Ireland, independent since its inception, than with that of the English. During the visitation of Friar Wygmund in 1238 the Scottish friars objected, claiming that they had already been visited by the Provincial of Ireland on behalf of the Chapter General (Bryce, 8).

However the fate of the Scottish province was linked to that of Brother Elias and, at the General Chapter held at Rome in 1239, Elias was deposed and replaced by Albert of Pisa, Provincial Minister of England (Bryce, 8-9). This chapter also reduced the number of provinces Elias had created, and among those abolished was that of Scotland. John de Kethene was transferred to Ireland where he replaced Richard of Ingworth as provincial minister, and the Scottish convents were returned to the custody of Newcastle (Bryce, 9-10).

The Scottish friars attempted to reassert their independence and to this end enlisted the help of the Scottish king, Alexander III. The friars proposed an independent Scottish province and backed-up their request with a petition from Alexander III to Pope Alexander IV. He approved their request and wrote to the Minister General on behalf of "the illustrious King of Scotland," stating that king's desire to have "the counsel and advice of religious and God-fearing men, and especially of the friars...as the support of his tender years." To aid the king in this endeavour, the pope requested that the Chapter "provide for the appointment of a Provincial Minister in that kingdom without delay" (Bryce, 9-10). The request was refused and the Scottish friars took matters into their own hands, electing Brother Elias Duns, the uncle of Duns Scotus, as their Vicar-General. It appears that although nominally attached to the English province, there was a *de facto* independence established after 1260 and in 1296 there was a compromise between the English friars and their rebellious Scottish counterparts – although officially part of the English province, Scotland would be independent of the customs of Newcastle. This is not unlike the compromise reached concerning the Scottish church as a whole in the twelfth century, when it was declared a special daughter of the Roman see. This declaration of *Ecclesia Scoticana* marked the emergence of an independent Scottish church but one that had no metropolitan of its own. In a similar vein the Scottish friars had no official independent status, but were a *de facto* province until the situation was finally concluded in 1329 when the Scottish friars obtained a definite Vicar of the Minister General, and were wholly separated from their English brethren (Cowan and Easson, 9).

The Irish province was not free of controversy either, but this manifested itself differently. Franciscans in both countries experienced similar difficulties when dealing with the local clergy but in Ireland there was an added dimension. As well as being unwelcome by certain religious and clergy, there was also a division within the order that gradually defined the nature of the foundations established there. In Ireland Anglo-Irish friars and native Irish friars began to divide along racial lines until, by the end of the century, warnings were being issued regarding the treachery of the Irish brethren. Friar Nicholas Cusack, Bishop of Kildare from 1279 to 1299, wrote to Edward I informing him of "secret counsels…and poisonous colloquies which certain insolent religious of the Irish tongue…hold with the Irish and their princes" (Grannell, 10-1). He warned that secret meetings were being held in which rebellion was being instigated. He advised that religious of Irish sympathies should be removed from convents in dangerous districts, and that only good and select Englishmen, with English companions should be sent among the Irish in future (Fitzmaurice and Little, xxii).

About the same time Friar Malachy, a doctor of theology and a prominent preacher, compiled his treatise on the seven deadly sins, the *Venenum Malachiae*. This also reveals a strong anti-Irish bias. Ireland, he tells us, was blessed in not having any poisonous animals, however there was present that poison which God allowed to be injected into human nature.[5] Malachy also had a poor opinion of the sexual morals of the Irish, especially Irish women, and one of his biggest complaints was on the spend-thrift hospitality of the natives. He felt the Irish showed excessive generosity, but only in order to impress.

A more contentious issue, seen by many as the ultimate illustration of this racial split within Ireland, is an incident reported in two chronicles under the year 1291. In that year, according to the *Annals of Wygornia* and Bartholomew of Cotton's *Historia Anglicana*, a provincial chapter held in Cork resulted in the deaths of sixteen friars. The Worcester annalist tells us that "On 10 June at Cork in Ireland, there was a general chapter of the Friars Minor where the Irish friars came armed with a papal bull: a dispute having arisen regarding this, they fought against the English friars; and after many had been killed and wounded…the English at length gained the victory by the help of the city.…" He adds that "papal bulls are disastrous to the friars, and turn gentle and mild men into fighters" (Howlett, xiv). The Norwich monk adds slightly more detail telling us that "The minister general of the Order of St Francis, making visitation throughout the world, came to Ireland to visit there and in his general chapter, sixteen brothers with their brethren were slain, several were wounded and some more imprisoned by action of the king of England" (Luard, 1859: 431). There are several reasons why the validity of this incident is contested, and the first argument is based on terminology. The Worcester annalist referred to a general chapter in Cork, when it was a provincial chapter – a small semantic difference but huge in terms of Franciscan government. The second issue is that of timing. The Norwich monk claimed that the minister general, Raymond Gaufredi, was in attendance but records show that Gaufredi only arrived in Ireland in September, some months after the chapter. It is possible that this visit took place in response to the violence in Cork but Gaufredi had made a visitation of England in August, and it has been suggested that Ireland was the next logical stage in this visitation (Cotter, 37). The third issue is lack of evidence. For example, no bull has yet been uncovered which might explain the conflict. In conjunction with this is the lack of evidence in contemporary Irish sources. The *Kilkenny Chronicle* and Friar John Clyn both refer to the happening in just two words – *Capitulum Cork*. Likewise Luke Wadding makes no mention of it in his *Annales Minorum*, and the *Annals of the Four Masters* seems unaware of such an event. Finally the two sources that do

---

[5] "*Sed proth dolor venenum qoud negauit ei deus aranea bestiali et in terra permisit regnare in humana natura …*"

record the event must also be called into question. Both were Benedictine Abbeys and relations between friars and monks in England were strained at this time. Perhaps the monks were only too eager to record unfounded rumours relating to the Franciscans!

One piece of evidence that may vindicate their accounts, however, is a patent letter issued on 17 September of that year. In it Edward I expressed a desire that "peace and concord may prevail among the brothers of the Order of the Franciscans in Ireland". To this end he commanded that the "justiciary and sheriffs, bailiffs and ministers in that country ... assist Brother Reymund, general minister of that order, and the other brothers commissioned in his place, that they may freely when need be, correct the excesses of the brothers according to the discipline of their order, and restrain those who rebel against it (Sweetman, 422). Obviously there was some cause for concern within the order in Ireland, and it is possible that an incident in Cork could have prompted Edward to write such a letter. However it was about this time that Friar Nicholas had reported the treasonous and rebellious actions of the native Irish friars, and this letter might have been a response to those warnings. Nevertheless, two seemingly independent chronicles and a royal letter concerning the behaviour of Irish Franciscans prevent an outright dismissal of this event in Cork.

The readiness of members of the clergy to denigrate the Franciscans is common to both Ireland and Scotland at this time. Certainly there was a large amount of jealousy on the part of the established clergy. Matthew Paris gives some indication of why this might be when describing the friars' entry into Scotland: "A party of Minorites, taking advantage of being within the territory of a great abbey for the purpose of preaching would, on some pretext of illness or the like, stay for the night. Under cover of darkness they would erect a wooden altar, place it on a small consecrated stone slab brought for the purpose and celebrate mass. Having thus gained ecclesiastical footing, they would hear confessions, say masses, and ultimately even despatch messengers to Rome to obtain substantial concessions. These would often be yielded by the monks from fear of a scandal and from dread of the power already gained by the Order at the court of Rome itself" (Eccleston, xii). No wonder the friars were greeted less than enthusiastically. John Spottiswoode, in his 1655 *History of the Church of Scotland* went further, adding that "these Orders not being known before in this church, by their crafty insinuations with people, and the profession they made in leading an austere life, did supplant the credit of the priests, drawing to themselves all the force and credit of the spiritual ministry, and were upheld by the popes, whose designs they studied especially to advance (1972: 43).

In 1245 Innocent IV issued his bull *Nimis iniqua*. This bull was to "restrain all persons from oppressing the Friars Minor." It then outlined some of the difficulties facing the order where "Many prelates and others of the church wish to hear friars' confessions and impose penance on them, object to friars being buried in their churches, or to their having cemeteries or bells, extort taxes, rents and tithes from them, and claim the offerings given to them by the faithful; and that they may subject them entirely to their power, they wish to impose on them "priors" according to their own will." In response to this the pope nominated conservators of the rights of the friars.[6] As already mentioned, the Franciscans of Roxburgh

---

[6] See *Bullarium Franciscanum*, I, 372-4; Bliss, 226.

found themselves in disagreement with the monks of Kelso upon their arrival there, and the *Liber de Calshou* gives an account of the dispute. The case was brought by Herbert Mansuel, Abbot of Kelso, and Friar Martin, *Custos* of the Friars Minor in Scotland, before Bishop William of Glasgow. The bishop recognised the rights of the friars as granted by *Ita vobis* and the *Liber de Calshou* reports him as declaring himself "Satisfied that the Friars Minor are privileged to bury their whilom brethren, and none others ... [and] that the said cemetery be consecrated at the aforesaid place ... under the provision that the rights of the monks of Kelso over their churches should suffer no prejudice".[7]

The Franciscans were in competition, not only with the established parish clergy but also with the other mendicant orders. In both Ireland and Scotland there are instances of the Franciscans and Dominicans being unwilling or unable to share a town or location. According to one source Basilia, daughter of Mailer de Bermingham, was displeased when her husband, Stephen de Exonia, invited the Franciscans to Strade about 1250. She invited her father to a great feast there and then announced, in front of all their guests, that she would neither eat nor drink until the Franciscans were expelled and replaced with Dominicans (Cotter, 20). Similarly, the Franciscans visited Elgin in Scotland about 1284 and were received there by the Bishop of Moray with an invitation to settle in the diocese. According to the *Registrum Episcopatus Moriavensis* William, earl of Ross, granted "certain lands ... to the bishop and chapter of Moray, in pure and perpetual alms, for the sustenance of the Friars Minor, who for the time being should be dwelling or should dwell in the future at Elgin in their house near the cathedral".[8] However, because the Dominicans were already established in the town, the Franciscans declined the bishop's offer and it seems that this was expected. Provision had been made that, should the Franciscans not remain, an annual rent be given for the sustenance of two Chaplains in the cathedral church there (Edwards, 26).

It was not just the clergy who viewed the Franciscans as a threat. In the first wave of expansion of the Order it was easy to find recruits, some of whom joined against family wishes. The English author of the *Liber Exemplorum* records an incident in 1258. This English friar was living in the Dublin house at the time that David de Burgh, younger brother of Walter de Burgh, Earl of Ulster, joined the Order. According to the author Walter reacted violently to this, and stormed the friary with knights, soldiers, and his satellites. David was forced from the house, but one of the earl's men fell to his death from the walls of the friary, and another died violently soon after (Little, 117). In a similar incident one of the leading historians of the Order, Salimbene de Adam had to fend off attempted abductions by his family. He recorded that "all his life my father sorrowed over my entrance into the Order of the Friars Minor, and would not be comforted, because he had no son left to him as an heir" (Baird et al: 13).

Despite the negative reception the friars received among the parish clergy, members of the hierarchy, both clerical and secular were only too eager to employ the friars. For example Edward I, when adjudicating the matter of the Scottish throne, asked the minister general to give an opinion regarding the rival claims of Bruce and Balliol. They decided in favour of Bruce. On 4 April 1296, after the

---

[7] See *Liber S. Marie de Calchou, Registrum Cartarum Abbacie Tironensis de Kelso* 1113-1567 (Edinburgh, 1846), 321, no. 418.

[8] See *Registrum Episcopatus Moraviensis* (Bannatyne Club), 281.

capture of Berwick, it was Friar Adam Blunt, Warden of the Roxburgh friary, who delivered Balliol's renunciation of fealty and allegiance to Edward. According to the author of *Scottichronicon* the letter was badly timed and Edward responded sarcastically, "What folly! If he will not to me, I must to him" (Bryce, 19-20). The Scottish friaries continued to remain centre stage for most of the War of Independence and, in the fourteenth century firmly allied themselves to the nationalist cause. By 1335 Edward III felt obliged to deal with Scottish friars in much the same way that Nicholas Cusack had recommended Irish friars be dealt with. In the border areas Scottish friars were removed and replaced with English ones, probably only "good and select Englishmen, with English companions" as Nicholas had advised.

The arrival of the Franciscans into Ireland and Scotland signalled a new era in church reform. The missionary zeal and genuine poverty of the friars moved the people of both countries to welcome them, and within a period of eighty years thirty-one houses had been established in Ireland, and five in Scotland. The Franciscan not only moved into the towns and colleges, but also into the political arena as advisors, confessors and messengers, sometimes to their detriment. The higher up the hierarchy the Order moved, the further behind were left the ideals that Francis had instilled in his friars – that they would be the most minor of all. By the end of the century the order had seen one of their members become archbishop of Canterbury – John Pecham – and another become Pope – Nicholas IV. They had established a college at Oxford and been involved at some of the highest levels of political debate. By the end of the century Robert Grosseteste, Bishop of Lincoln would seem to be vindicated in his praise for the Franciscans. Writing to Gregory IX in 1238 he warmly praised them, saying: "Your Holiness may be assured that in England inestimable benefits have been produced by the friars; for they illuminate our whole country with the light of their preaching and learning" (Luard, 1861: xxii).

References

Baird, Joseph L., Guiseppe Bagliri and John Robert Kane, eds. 1986. *Chronicle of Salimbene de Adam*. New York: Medieval and Renaissance Texts and Studies

Bliss, W. H. 1893. *Calendar of Papal Entries in the Papal Registers relating to GB and Ireland: Papal Letters*. Vol. 1. 1198-1304. London

Bryce, William Moir. 1909. *The Scottish Grey Friars*. Volume I. Edinburgh and London

Cotter, F.J. 1994. *The Friars Minor in Ireland from their Arrival to 1400*. Ed. Roberta A. McKelvie. New York

Cowan, Ian B. and David Easson, eds. 1976. *Medieval Religious Houses, Scotland*. London: Longman

Eccleston, Thomas Eccleston. 1958. *De Adventu Fratrum Minorum in Angliam* in J.S. Brewer, ed., *Monumenta Franciscana*. Vol. 1. London

Edwards, John. 1907. "The Grey Friars and Their First Houses in Scotland". *Transactions of the Scottish Ecclesiological Society, 1906-7*. Aberdeen

Fitzmaurice, E. B. and A. G. Little, eds. 1920. *Materials for the History of the Franciscan Province of Ireland 1230-1450*. Manchester

Howlett, Richard, ed. 1882. *"Bullae papales sunt fratribus exitiales, Qui quondam mites, faciunt nunc praelia, lites"*. *Monumenta Franciscana*. Vol II. London

Grannell, Fergal. 1976. *The Franciscans in Wexford*. Wexford

Jennings, B., ed. 1934. "Brussels MS 3947: Donatus Moneyus Provincia Hiberniae S. Francisci". *Annalecta Hibernica*. 6 (1934): 15

Little, A. G. 1908. *Liber Exemplorum Ad Usum Praedicantium*. 117. Aberdeen

Luard, Henry Richards, ed. 1859. *Barthlomei de Cotton monachi norwicensis historia Anglicana*. Rerum Britannicarum Medii Aevi Scriptores. London

Luard, Henry Richards, ed. 1861. *Roberti Grosseteste, Episcopi Quondam Lincolniensis Epistolae*. London

Mooney, Canice. 1951. *Racialism in the Franciscan Order in Ireland, 1224-1700*. Louvain: University of Louvain

Moorman, John. 1968. *A History of the Franciscan Order from its Origins to the Year 1517*. Oxford: Clarendon Press

O'Donnell, Fr. Terence. 1951. *The Franciscan Abbey of Multyfarnham*. Multyfarnham

Skene, William F. 1993. John of Fordun's *Chronicle of the Scottish Nation*. Volume I. Llanerch Publishers

Spottiswoode, John. 1972. The *History of the Church of Scotland 1655*. Yorkshire

Sweetman, H. S., ed. 1875. *Calendar of Documents Ireland 1171-1251*. London

Wadding, Luke. 1731-41. *Annales Minorum*. Vol.I 1208-1220. Rome

Ireland, the Popish Plot and "British" History, 1678-81

John Gibney

This paper is about the Popish Plot, the outbreak of mass paranoia in England that followed the claims of Titus Oates in September 1678 about an imminent Catholic plot (with French assistance) to assassinate the King, Charles II, and re-impose Catholicism across the Stuart dominions. More specifically it is about the connections between Ireland and the Popish Plot, which tend to be overlooked by Irish historians, being deemed worthy of only cursory treatment.[1] Equally, in the work of English historians Ireland receives only a fleeting mention in relation to the Popish Plot, but even if the plot (and subsequent Exclusion Crisis) are implicitly deemed matters for English history alone, the gap can be bridged if the concept of 'British' history is brought into play.

The notion that Ireland, England, Scotland and Wales have interacted down through the centuries is an obvious point to make to the Irish, and presumably to the Scots and Welsh. Its introduction to English historiography is belated, yet cannot be accepted uncritically. 'British' history unfortunately remains overstated but under-researched: witness the emphasis on discrete historical episodes (such as the Civil Wars) and the continual use of a deeply misleading term: there were two islands at stake here. The subtleties of such interaction may have been overridden by the novelty of the concept, but the discrete and differing historical experiences of each country can be complemented rather than supplanted by the existence of another, broader level of shared experience.[2]

The relation of the Popish Plot to Ireland illustrates this; and by viewing it within such a framework its broader relevance becomes apparent. The plot had internal dynamics within Ireland, yet in other ways it reached beyond it. Its obvious religious dimension inevitably caused concern amongst Irish Protestants, exacerbated in turn by uncertainties over the religious inclinations of the viceroy James Butler, duke of Ormond. Religion also saw Ireland utilised as an essential part of the argument to exclude the Catholic James, Duke of York, from the succession to the three Stuart kingdoms. The aspects of the plot outlined here do not amount to a comprehensive account, and involve one obvious chestnut of

---

[1] Thomas Carte, *History of the life of James, Duke of Ormond*, (Oxford 1851), iv, 542-638, and Richard Bagwell, *Ireland under the Stuarts*, (Dublin 1916), iii, 127-40; J.G. Simms, 'The Restoration, 1660-85' in T.W. Moody et al, (eds.), *A New History of Ireland, vol. III: Early Modern Ireland, 1534-1691*, (Oxford, 1976), 432-3; David Dickson, *New Foundations: Ireland 1660-1800*, (Dublin, 2nd ed. 2000), 19-21; J.C. Beckett, *The Cavalier Duke: A life of James Butler, first Duke of Ormond 1610-88* (Belfast, 1990), 115-22; S.J. Connolly, *Religion Law and Power: the making of Protestant Ireland, 1660-1760*, (Oxford, 1992), 24-32

[2] Tim Harris, 'The British dimension, religion, and the shaping of political identities during the reign of Charles II' in Tony Claydon & Ian McBride (eds.) *Protestantism and National Identity: Britain and Ireland, c. 1650-c.1850*, (Cambridge, 1998), 131-56; Jane Ohlmeyer, 'Seventeenth-Century Ireland and the New British and Atlantic Histories', *American Historical Review*, vol. 104, no. 2 (April 1999), 446-62; T.C. Barnard, 'British History and Irish History' in Glenn Burgess (ed.), *The New British History: Founding a Modern State, 1603-1715*, (London, 1999), 201-37.

'British' history (high politics), but they do demonstrate two essential facets of the relationship between the two islands; firstly, interaction was a concrete, everyday reality that may not need a concept to be understood; secondly, and less obviously, that interaction was a two-way street.

The first aspect is the effect of an English problem upon Irish Protestants. The heterogeneous Protestant community in Ireland had generally accepted the restored monarchy, only to be immediately confronted with the problem of their Catholic neighbours. The massive land transfers of the 1650s had been at the expense of Catholic landowners, and the subsequent land settlement of the 1660s was still open to challenge in the late 1670s; understandably, Catholics wanted their land back. Uncertainties about the intentions of that dispossessed Catholic community readily combined with the memory of the disastrous events of mid-century to ensure that Protestant fears remained and were easily revived. Protestants in Ireland were drastically outnumbered, and the ambiguous attitude of the English government to Catholicism both at home and abroad were bound to be causes for concern; the 'English in Ireland' remained acutely aware of their own difference.[3] Finally, the Protestant community in Ireland possessed something their English co-religionists lacked; the sense and conviction that in 1641 their Catholic neighbours had attempted to slaughter them wholesale.[4]

In England Catholics served as bogeymen but in Ireland they were the neighbours. If so, it was inevitable that suggestions of a Catholic plot would provoke alarm in Ireland, especially as Oates's original allegations referred to a rising by 35,000 Irishmen, armed by the Pope and assisted by the French.[5] The immediate response of the Irish government to these disclosures was to arrest a number of figures implicated by Oates, most notably the titular Catholic Archbishop of Dublin, Peter Talbot, and to issue a series of proclamations ordering the banishment of Catholic clergy, the disarming of the Catholic laity, the exclusion of Catholics from towns and the imposition of the oaths of allegiance and supremacy, amongst other measures.[6] That some of these proclamations made specific reference to the activities of Jesuits and a plot to kill the King was an open statement in itself, and could not have gone unnoticed.[7] But aside from this, little more was done. This would prove to be the problem.

Rumours and reports of dubious Catholic activities came into Dublin from throughout the country prior to Christmas,[8] amplified from Munster by the detailed missives of Roger Boyle, Earl of Orrery.[9] But given the general lack of hard evidence, Ormond was inclined to discount such fears as a whole, and did not pursue an active policy against Catholics: his analysis did not require one. His conviction was that there was little to fear, though he was aware that the fears of

---

[3] Barnard, 'British History and Irish History', 202-3

[4] T.C Barnard, 'The Uses of 23rd October 1641 and Irish Protestant Celebrations', *English Historical Review*, vol. 106 (1991), 889-920

[5] *CSP. Dom., 1678*, 426-7

[6] Bagwell, *Stuarts*, iii, 127

[7] National Library of Ireland, ms. 1793, f. 24, 26

[8] 'Examination of Marcus Cra[?] of Meath, 23 Oct. 1678', (Bodliean Library, Carte ms. 38, f. 715); Anglesey to Ormond, 23 Nov. 1678 (*HMC Ormond MSS*, new ser., iv, 242-3)

[9] Orrery to Ormond, 3 Dec. 1678 (*HMC Ormond MSS*, new ser., iv, 260-1); same to same, 7 Dec. 1678, (ibid., 265-8); same to same, 10 Dec. 1678, (ibid., 270-4)

Protestants would be laid at his door; if no rebellion was stirring stringent action was superfluous, but such inactivity would leave him open to accusation, as it did. Yet if he was to take action purely to defend himself, he ran the risk of provoking the very rebellion he sought to prevent. True, he conceded, the Irish vastly outnumbered the Protestant community, and could yet attack them, but they knew that retaliation would inevitably follow.[10] The real danger, in his view, was from the French, for whom the Irish would merely be a useful if incidental tool; harsh measures such as the purges and internments proposed by Orrery were both unrealistic and provocative, for even a small insurrection might attract the attention and involvement of the French.[11] Therefore his government advocated a lenient attitude, but for cogent reasons. And to deflect mounting criticism the analysis of the government, and an account of its conduct, was presented to the House of Lords by his son Thomas Butler, earl of Ossory, in March 1679.

This account stated a number of things: that Ormond had not delayed the implementation of his orders (as was seen by the swift arrest and interrogation of Peter Talbot). It cited the various proclamations issued, the preparations to raise militias, the suppression of 'mass-houses', and the confiscation of Catholic weapons. True, many of those Irish previously expelled from corporate towns had returned. But they were allowed back by those English who had required their services. Ormond himself had acted as guarantor for the purchase of extra weapons, and military arrangements were as good as current resources allowed. Finally, it stated the key principle that had guided the government over the preceding months: Ireland and England were too different to be subject to the same laws and policies; the disproportionate numbers of Catholics vis-à-vis Protestants was the most immediate discrepancy, and in any case there were other means of ensuring Ireland's security. Prudence and leniency marked out a wiser course than outright repression, and for the time being there was no reason to alter this position.[12]

Ormond's analysis remained constant throughout the period. But even as reports of the plot began to die down and lose credence, as early as April 1680, it was being re-invigorated for other purposes; it was too useful to discard.[13] Traditionally Ormond has been lauded for his prudence in keeping Ireland quiet at this time. But this was a judgement based upon hindsight, and some contemporaries held a very different view of the Duke and his policy.[14]

Prudence might not equate zeal, and the second aspect of the plot under discussion is the vigorous effort to procure Ormond's dismissal. The prime allegation against him was his alleged partiality and favour towards Catholics; a strange suggestion, for Oates had claimed that Ormond was to have been

---

[10] Ormond to Sir Robert Southwell, 6 Nov. 1678, (*HMC Ormond MSS*, old ser., ii, 279)

[11] Ormond to Ossory, 30 Nov. 1678 (*HMC Ormond MSS* , new ser., iv, 254); Ormond to Sir Cyril Wyche, 20 Nov. 1678 (*HMC Leybourne-Popham MSS*, 242-3)

[12] 'An account of the present state of Ireland, presented by the Lord Butler of Moor park to the House of Lords, March 31st 1679', *HMC Ormond MSS*, new ser., v, 15-20)

[13] Daniel Hignott to Sir John Percival, 23 April 1680 (*HMC Egmont MSS*, ii), 94; Petitions of Sir Thomas Southwell, Sir John Fitzgerald, Col. Piers Lacy, 23-3 March 1681 (*HMC Rep. 11, app. 2*, 270-1); Connolly, *Religion, Law and Power*, 30-2

[14] T.C. Barnard, 'Introduction: the Dukes of Ormond' in Toby Barnard & Jane Fenlon (eds.), *The Dukes of Ormond, 1610-1745*, (Woodbridge, 2000), 46

murdered along with the King, and it was the lack of Catholic qualities that had contributed to his previous dismissal from the same post in 1669.[15]

The simple reality for any Irish viceroy was that his post was gained, maintained and lost by the vagaries of English politics, and this remained applicable to Ormond in 1678. Charles II's pro-French flirtation was ending by the late 1670s and so Ormond's Anglican principles were coming back into vogue. His immediate task on arriving in Ireland in 1677 was to prepare for a parliament. His overall priority was to provide for Ireland's defences, which required money, which in turn required the calling of parliament, which was unlikely to be tractable without anything to show for it; such as full confirmation of the estates held by so many since the 1650s. For Ormond this was the sweetener, but for many in Ireland and the English government it was the sticking point, conceding as it seemed to do automatic favour to Catholics and closing the restoration land settlement permanently.[16] More immediately, he also had to deal with the army and its disastrous finances. Any attempt to do this would require an investigation into the somewhat murky revenue establishment, which in turn meant investigating the undertaking of Richard Jones, earl of Ranelagh, in the early 1670s, thereby exposing its irregularities.[17] Ranelagh perceived the danger of a potential prosecution, which may explain why in early October, just after the first plot disclosures, it was reported that he and his associates planned to smear Ormond as a Catholic.[18] Any attempt to discredit Ormond would be useful to Ranelagh; it would also prove useful to others, and criticism of Ormond's predilections and policy was the obvious avenue to take.

His conduct in the 1640s and 1660s had ensured that Ormond was hated by many Catholics (coward and traitor being the watchwords here).[19] Yet despite his Cavaliers reputation, the first duke stood out among the Butlers as virtually the only Protestant of the family. His survival at the head of a predominantly Catholic network of family and clients ensured he was not militantly opposed to Catholicism at this stage in his life, viewing it largely in political terms.[20] But such associations ensured vulnerability, as Ormond's own scepticism about the plot combined with his lenient policy towards Catholics to provide a basis for an attack. Such attacks on his character predated the plot, and continued throughout the period of it, taking a variety of (often inventive) forms, ranging in a spectrum from mild toleration of Catholics to outright conspiracy with the French.[21] He had

---

[15] James McGuire, 'Why was Ormond dismissed in 1669?', *Irish Historical Studies*, vol. 18, no. 71 (March 1973), 295-312

[16] James Ernest Aydelotte, 'The Duke of Ormond and the English Government of Ireland, 1677-85', (Ph.D, Iowa, 1975), i, 30-98

[17] Sean Egan, 'Finance and the Government of Ireland, 1660-1685', (Ph.D, TCD, 1983) ii, 85-94

[18] Longford to Ormond, 8 Oct. 1678 (*HMC Ormond MSS*, new ser., iv, 214-5)

[19] Eamonn O'Ciardha, ''The Unkinde Deserter' and 'The Bright Duke': contrasting views of the Dukes of Ormonde in the Irish royalist tradition' in Barnard & Fenlon, *The Dukes of Ormond*, 180-3

[20] Raymond Gillespie, 'The religion of the first Duke of Ormond' in Barnard & Fenlon, *The Dukes of Ormond*, 111-2

[21] Longford to Ormond, 5 Aug. 1679 (*HMC Ormond MSS*, new ser., v, 167-9); Ossory to Ormond, 3 April 1680, (ibid, 297)

supposedly permitted Catholics to retain weapons, had slandered loyal Protestants, gladly suppressed evidence, and like his unfortunate mentor Thomas Wentworth, earl of Strafford, had allegedly sought to raise a Catholic army to travel to England 'to set up arbitrary government'.[22] Indeed, his previous stint as viceroy supposedly began with 40 Catholic priests in the country and ended with 10,00 who had let the rest in, and why?[23] Last but not least it was suggested he had secretly reverted to his families' traditional religion.[24] Such claims were rebutted by Ormond, who nonetheless remained acutely aware of them. Yet such attacks became an integral part of both Irish and English politics at this time, which begs the question of who was after him, and why? In Dublin he remained vulnerable, though he could marshal family and friends in London to defend his interests and keep him informed. The King assured him of his support,[25] though Ormond probably had no illusions about the reason; at this juncture Charles would need a powerful and loyal servant in Ireland, to keep the island in line. Ormond was especially paranoid about Orrery,[26] possibly with good reason,[27] but the most significant attacks seemed to stem directly from London.

Certainly Ranelagh had tangible reasons to smear Ormond (and was ably assisted by his wife).[28] Indeed, he sought to harness burgeoning disquiet about Ormond in the House of Commons to his purposes.[29] Ormond's predecessor Arthur Capel, earl of Essex, also proved an enemy, perhaps aware of the possibility of returning to his old station should Ormond be removed.[30] But most significant was Anthony Ashley Cooper, earl of Shaftesbury, who roped Ormond into his project to exclude York from the succession.

Shaftesbury was perceived as a threat by both Ormond and his allies; they were, after all, old adversaries.[31] But the essential purpose for his attack upon Ormond was acutely perceived by the Papal internuncio in Brussels; the assumption was that Ormond was in league with York and the French, and the object was not merely to see him dismissed but to ensure his discrediting and destruction: he was too powerful and influential, which might ensure that Ireland would go royalist and back the monarchy if need be.[32] The exclusion of York from the succession was Shaftesbury's priority, but the removal of Ormond was bound to be useful; the reasons for Charles' support were the same reasons for

---

[22] 'Articles against the Duke of Ormond', *CSP Dom., 1680-1681*, 98; 'A coppy of som discovery of ye plott', NLI ms. 13,014

[23] Anonymous to Ormond, 25 Jan. 1681 (*HMC Ormond MSS*, new ser., v, 560-3)

[24] Ormond to Arran, 1 Jan. 1681, (ibid., 543-4)

[25] Arlington to Ormond, 8 Aug. 1679, ibid., 175; Coventry to Ormond, 9 Aug. 1679, (ibid., 177-8)

[26] Ormond to Sir Cyril Wyche, 20 Nov. 1678 (*HMC Leybourne-Popham MSS*, 242-3)

[27] Coventry to Ormond, 20 Sept. 1679 (*HMC Ormond MSS*, new ser., v, 210-1)

[28] 'A-. B-' to Ormond, 13 May 1679, (ibid., 95-7)

[29] Ossory to Ormond, 26 April 1679, (ibid., 70-1)

[30] Ossory to Ormond, 25 March 1679, (ibid., 1-2)

[31] Ossory to Ormond, 22 March 1679 (*HMC Ormond MSS*, new ser., iv, 366-7); Ormond to Ossory, 30 April 1679 (*HMC Ormond MSS*, new ser., v, 73); K.H.D. Haley, *The First Earl of Shaftesbury*, Oxford (1968), 187-9, 199-200.

[32] Tanari to Secretariate of State, 27th April 1680, Cathaldus Giblin (ed), 'Catalogue of material of Irish interest in …Vatican Archives', *Collectenea Hibernica*, vol. 3 (1960), 75

Shaftesbury's assault; any attack on the Stuarts would surely be eased by the removal of arguably their most powerful and loyal servant. Indeed, when the Irish informers patronised by Shaftesbury began to recant in early 1681, and admit to perjury, those to be specifically perjured for treason were the Queen, York and Ormond.[33] Ormond's difficulties stemmed from his record of loyalty to the Stuarts, during the nascent Whig-Tory conflict in England over the critical issue of the Stuart succession. The fundamental argument for exclusion was the presence of a Catholic threat in waiting, encouraged by the presence of the current heir to the throne. The most immediate form of this, as promoted by Shaftesbury, was the spectre of Catholic Ireland waiting to burst into rebellion, as it had done in 1641. It is this that allows consideration of a third issue: propaganda.

From late 1680 Shaftesbury promoted a number of highly dubious Irish witnesses to travel to London and swear to the existence of a plot in Ireland.[34] Their testimonies were published, slipping into a genre of work that took as its cornerstone the inevitable savagery of the Catholic Irish. Dubious attitudes towards the Irish were nothing new, but how they existed in the humble medium of the pamphlet is the subject at hand. The following survey is more impressionistic than comprehensive, but from a number of discrete and differing popular works a number of salient and corresponding points can emerge.

The hyperbole of such works can be taken for granted, stressing as they did 'how indefatigable and courageous those hellish bloodhounds are in their endeavours and practices, in contriving and executing of all manner of wickedness, though to the hazard of their lives and fortunes, to bring to perfection their most horrid and 'Matchivilian'(sic) designs',[35] which in 1641 at least had been 'not to leave a drop of English blood in Ireland, and so consequently not the least spark or glimpse of gospel and pure Protestant religion'.[36] This had been done at the instigation of the Pope, with the ultimate intention of capturing all three kingdoms. More significantly, the plot was nothing new; it was part of a pattern stretching from the reign of Mary Tudor, via Philip of Spain's attempts to marry her sister, through the rebellion in Ireland of James Fitzmaurice Fitzgerald (dealt with by the combination of the Lord Deputy, Sir Humphrey Gilbert and God), and the St. Bartholomew's Day massacre, the Spanish Armada and the Gunpowder Plot culminating in Ireland on 23 October 1641.[37] The rebellion of that year occupied a special place in the Protestant imaginations of both islands. That English readers should be reminded of this in 1679 speaks volumes in itself.

Certainly this writer was not hide-bound by geography; nor was the Whig pamphleteer who pointed out that 'a Tory is a monster with an English face, a French heart, and an Irish conscience'.[38] That conscience had, in English eyes, been amply testified to in the past; and the general principle of which it was a part remained constant. Within the assumed framework of Catholic intentions, the

---

[33] Ormond to Arran, 1 March 1681 (*HMC Ormond MSS*, new ser., v, 592-3)

[34] Haley, *Shaftesbury*, 569-99

[35] *A true and perfect narrative of the manner and circumstance of apprehending that notorious Irish priest, Daniel Mac-Carte...*,(London, 1681), 1

[36] *A brief account of the several plots, conspiracies and hellish attempts of the bloody-minded papists...* (London, 1679), 29

[37] Ibid., 10-3

[38] *The character of a Tory*, (London, 1681), 1

published testimonies of the informers were disturbingly consistent and specific. The similarity was at a more general level, irrespective of their intricacy. The salient elements were the existence of a long-standing plot for a rebellion in Ireland, involving members of the Catholic gentry and clergy and to be implemented with French assistance, with the restoration of the Irish to their estates providing a partial incentive for their involvement. The plot was itself directed at all three kingdoms, and at the Protestants therein: the implicit (occasionally explicit) purpose was the destruction of those Protestants, which was stated to be the ultimate goal of the Papacy, backed as they were by French muscle. Attempts to silence witnesses and potential informers with either violence or money were also a common theme (some were luckier than others) and indeed, occasionally Catholics might attempt to disguise such claims as Protestant malice. But at the heart of the plot was the Papal design to destroy Protestants; this was the purpose. The alleviation of Irish suffering was merely the inducement to such slaughter.[39]

Admittedly, the consistency in many may stem from the coaching the witnesses almost certainly received. Nonetheless they outline what many feared and suspected; in January 1681 parliament concurred on the existence of precisely such a plot as this.[40] But works such as these were bound to have a resonance in Ireland; the Irish Protestant community had its own particular perspective on the events of 1641 that was both echoed and regurgitated in such works.[41] The plot saw an outburst of pamphlet production in Ireland (often reprints of London editions), and such narratives could overlap with oral culture to ensure, at least for a time, the vindication of their perpetual vigilance.[42]

Ireland lacked the public participatory elements of anti-Popery prevalent in England throughout this period. But this is suggestive of the differing perspectives on the problem. True, the 1641 rebellion had an enormous impact upon England at the time. Throughout the Restoration 1641 retained a special position in the

---

[39] For examples see: *A narrative of the late Popish Plot in Ireland, for the subjugating thereof to the French King*, (London, 1680); *The information of Hubert Boark, gent., touching the Popish Plot in Ireland*, (London, 1680); *The information of Eustace Comyn...*, (London, 1680); David Fitzgerald, *A narrative of the Irish Popish Plot...*, (London, 1680); *The narrative of Mr. John Fitzgerald...*,(London, 1681); *The examination of Edward Fitzharris, relating to the Popish Plot...*, (London, 1681); *The several informations of John Macnamara...touching the Popish Plot in Ireland...*, (London, 1680); Florence Weyer, *The honesty and true zeal of the King's witnesses vindicated...*, (London, 1681)

[40] 'Debate in the House of Commons concerning the Irish Plot', 6th January 1681, *A collection of the Parliamentary Debates in England...to the present time* (London, 1739), ii, 38-45

[41] Aidan Clarke, 'The 1641 rebellion and anti-Popery in Ireland' in Brian MacCuarta (ed.) *Ulster 1641: aspects of the rising* (Belfast, 2nd ed. 1997), 139-57; Barnard, 'The uses of 23rd October 1641 and Irish Protestant celebrations'

[42] James Kelly, *Gallows speeches from Eighteenth-Century Ireland*, (Dublin, 2001), 21-22

mentality of English Protestants, even if it did gradually become depoliticised, and reduced to a less contentious if equally emotive level.[43] The essential point was this: in a country without any substantial internal Catholic threat, whose European flank was dominated by increasingly hostile Catholic powers, the susceptibility to a plot such as was posited by Oates required at least something to give it credibility. Ireland did so; it was the kingdom that posed the most immediate, plausible and unsurprising threat to England. More abstracted and less immediate than that perceived by Protestants in Ireland, but nonetheless there. The English themselves were deeply aware of this, despite the fact that efforts were made by rival polemicists to ridicule and downplay that alleged threat. For example:

> 'Great stores of wild Irish, both civil and wise,
> Designed to join with the pilgrims of Spain,
> Many thousands being ready all in good guise,
> Had vow'd a long pilgrimage over the main,
> To arm well this host,
> When it came on our coast,
> Black bills, forty thousand, are sent by the post,
> This army lay privately on the sea-shore,
> And no man e'er heard of them since or before'[44]

No one may have seen this army. But outbreaks of anti-Irish hysteria during the Glorious Revolution seven years later suggests that, assuming that anyone had read the verse, nobody had believed it.[45] The fear that Ireland provided had remained; that was enough.

Simply put, a wider awareness is the key to what has been sketched here. An English crisis deeply unnerved Irish Protestants. The resultant policies of Ormond in response were deemed inadequate by many in both islands. Finally, such fears were perceived and manipulated in turn, tapping into a pre-existing if inchoate pattern of thought about Ireland to employ the island as a Whig argument. This seems evident; it does not require the repetition of a concept of 'British' history to be understood. Geography would seem sufficient. True, Ireland was effectively subordinate to England at this time. On the other hand, had there not been some awareness of Ireland at a popular level in England, the fabrication of an 'Irish Plot' would have been pointless. Irish politics in many ways derived from London; English fears from Ireland. It is a two way process. This is admittedly a sketchy and narrow survey of a handful of obvious themes, but the unfortunate reality for anyone who would emphasise the 'British problem' (and those words are their

---

[43] Arthur Alfred Forbes, 'Mentalities in Restoration Britain and Ireland, 1660-1678: Anglo-Irish relations from the Restoration to the Popish Plot', MA, NUI, 1995, 6-29; Jonathan Scott, 'Englands Troubles: Exhuming the Popish Plot' in Tim Harris, Mark Goldie & Jonathan Scott (eds), *The politics of religion in Restoration England*, (Oxford, 1990), 122-3
[44] 'A new narrative of the Popish Plot' in Walter Scott (ed.), *A collection of scarce and valuable tracts ... belonging to the late Lord Somors*, (London, 1809-15), viii, 63-4
[45] G.H. Jones, 'The Irish fright of 1688: real violence and imagined massacre', *Bulletin of the Institute of Historical Research*, vol. 55 (1982), 148-53

undoing) is that both islands and their constituent peoples always interacted, whether in the tangible arena of politics and influence, or the more inchoate realm of awareness and prejudice. This is not a particularly exciting conclusion; but conclusion it is, and unfortunately it must be emphasised. The blunt reality is that the history of that interaction between the two islands remains largely unwritten, despite profusions of good intentions. How that situation may change over time is, of course, another matter entirely.

Fightin' Dominies and Form: Politics and Narrative in Some Modern Scottish Novels of Education[1]

Scott Hames

Most cultural criticism of Scottish education takes its "Scottishness" as the main object of concern, leaving aside primary questions of authority, knowledge and freedom[2] (see Johnston and Mackenzie; Harrison; Humes and Bryce). This seems curious when we consider that the revival of interest in national intellectual traditions has been stimulated largely by champions of Scottish generalism – a philosophical "broad course" of reflection on human nature and society. Students of George E. Davie might be expected to take a theoretically circumspect approach to the politics of the school, but most cultural discussion of Scottish education is oriented toward the discourse of "democratic intellectualism", in which the purpose and methods of education are contested in mainly sociological terms (Beveridge and Turnbull, 77). This is not an essay on the politics of education from the standpoint of Scottish culture and history, but a formalist inquiry into how modern Scottish literature has raised more radical, self-critical questions about education and authority than the cultural nationalist discourse seems to recognise. As I will show, structural, writerly problems about representing the authority of knowledge, and questioning the power of writing itself, have occupied postwar Scottish novelists in striking ways. In an essay situating the work of James Kelman within national literary traditions, Alan McMunnigal and Gerry Carruthers identify Patrick Doyle, the protagonist of *A Disaffection*, as "a type much dealt with in Scottish literature, a teacher within a much vaunted schools system whose professional life is in crisis" (61). I will discuss three instances of this type, but not with a view to establishing what is peculiarly Scottish about this sub-genre – this I leave to the cultural historians. Instead, I mean to examine how a few Scottish writers have approached formal problems concerning narrative authority in dramatising the power-knowledge relations of the school.

Of course, these relations of authority extend much more broadly throughout society. At the risk of launching a supposedly radical inquiry into educational authority with a blithe appeal to the experts, the following two quotations sketch the connection between politics, education, and narrative I mean to explore. The first is by Antonio Gramsci, who notes in the *Prison Notebooks* that "every relation of 'hegemony' is necessarily an educational relationship" (350). The second is by the Brazilian educational theorist Paulo Freire, who observes that "a careful analysis of the teacher-student relationship at any level, inside or outside

---

[1] I would like to acknowledge the support of the British Council's Overseas Research Studentship Scheme.

[2] When more radical Scottish educational thinkers are acknowledged in this discourse, it is often by way of charting the progress of reform: "The current generation of teachers and headteachers would certainly disagree with the critics [Patrick Geddes, A.S. Neill, R.F. Mackenzie] and claim that modern schools are much less oppressive places where pupil achievements are celebrated and the richness of learning in all its forms is recognised and encouraged" (Humes and Bryce, 115). The disparity between this (undoubted) progress and

the school, reveals its fundamentally *narrative* character" (71). As a form of symbolic 'educational' production, narrative fiction tends to reflect these relations of power and knowledge, perhaps most clearly in terms of narrative technique. The following brief excerpt from William McIlvanney's *Docherty* suggestively illustrates how the "teacher-student" narrative relationship applies not only to classroom novels. In this scene the miner Tam Docherty has asked his teenage son, Conn, to "see the sense o' goin' oan at the schil" (163), and Conn is struggling to convey the reasons why he bitterly hates his schoolmaster, his school, and the whole humiliating ritual of education as he knows it. Conn fails to salvage a rational argument from "the lethargy of [his] long-established attitudes" on the subject, and he is meant to: the narrator reports that Conn is "incapable [...] of proving his right to [his judgments] with words", and so obligingly expresses Conn's authentic convictions *for him*. This is necessary because the basis of Conn's views seem to him "so irrational as to be anonymous forces" (163). But for all that, the narrator relates:

> [T]hose convictions nevertheless represented areas of real experience for Conn. They related to truths he had earned for himself, no matter how incapable he was of proving his right to them with words, to the fact that nothing he was taught at school took the slightest cognizance of who he was, that the fundamental premise underlying everything he was offered there was the inferiority of what he had, that the vivid spontaneity of his natural speech was something he was supposed to be ashamed of, that so many of the people who mouthed platitudes about the liberating effects of education were looking through bars at the time, that most teachers breathed hypocrisy, like tortured Christians trying to convert happy pagans, that the classroom wasn't a filter for but a refuge from reality. (163-4)

This tirade covers a familiar argument about the liberating (or not) effects of education, but I'm more interested in the narrative mode used to deliver the argument. The quotation continues: "[Conn's] indignation came in a welter of incoherent images, a mob of reasons that drowned reason, and the only expression of it all he could achieve was a dogged, sullen silence" (164). Critics have already seized upon the ironic gap separating the message of *Docherty* from its make-up; here, in a passage decrying the alienation that results from having one's own way of speaking inferiorised, the character is not allowed to speak at all – worse, he is deprived of the capacity even to *think* fluently. It is as if Conn's language has been dignified at the expense of his subjectivity: without a prior grasp of rational self-awareness – of knowing *why* he thinks what he thinks – he has no hope of explaining the basis of his hatred in *any* language. It then falls to the Olympian narrator to provide the lucidity and rhetorical force the argument calls for, and the effect is of McIlvanney drawing polished thought-bubbles toward the clouded head of a puppet-character. We could probably summarize this petard-hoisting approach to *Docherty* by amending McIlvanney's diatribe to read "political novels" in place of "school/education". That is: for all its ennobling intent, the

---

the aspirations of A.S. Neill, for example, is stark: "I am trying to form minds that will question and destroy and rebuild" (102).

"fundamental premise underlying everything [we] are offered [in the novel] is the inferiority of what [the characters] have".

But catching the writer out is not my point. I want to examine three novels about politically out-of-step schoolteachers by way of demonstrating how their various approaches to the politics of education are reflected in formal problems about textual authority, narratorial self-judgment and "writing power". The teacher-protagonists in each of the three novels I'll be discussing – Muriel Spark's *The Prime of Miss Jean Brodie*, George Friel's *Mr. Alfred M.A.* and Kelman's *A Disaffection* – are indeed revealed to be "looking through bars" when they mouth their respective platitudes about the emancipating, civilizing and repressive effects of education; it is where their authors stand in relation to those same confining bars, involved as writers in kinds of formal discipline ("breathing hypocrisy" or otherwise) that I wish to explore. These writers, and their teachers, seem guided by the form of educational reason whose procedures marry the techniques of government with the production of truth (Foucault 1977, 184). Michel Foucault sees the school as a clear case of the "techniques of the self" being linked to techniques for the direction of others: "[In] educational institutions, we realize that one is managing others and teaching them to manage themselves" (1991, 369-70). I will explore how these novelists portray the *reflexive* ethical narrative in which the self-suspicious teacher examines his or her own intellect and conscience as objects of knowledge, by way of "monitoring the quality of his own ethical self-formation" (Jones, 60). I will show how these teachers' authority in the classroom, like their relative textual autonomy, is produced by "reciprocal effects" which prevent the formation of coherent political narratives – Miss Brodie is a freethinking "born Fascist" (Spark, 125), Mr. Alfred finds himself defending a society he has already withdrawn from, and Patrick Doyle is an anarchist anchorite, a "Fightin' Dominie" of the mind, but never the real world. But first, some background.

According to Dave Jones's "Genealogy of the Urban Schoolteacher", during a period of transition in the mid-nineteenth century, following the failure of the self-regulating, utilitarian "monitorial" school system, it became necessary to cede authority to individual teachers "whose function altered from that of a mechanical instructor to one of a moral exemplar" (60). Before being invested with this new authority, the Good Teacher was subjected to monastic discipline, and taught to accept an ethic of service. "In this new training [...] which aroused and heightened self-awareness, the virtues of morality and humility were consistently opposed to the corrosive vices of intellect and arrogance" (61), and schoolteachers were taught to know their place in the society they were being trained to reform (66). Elevated from the status of overseers and technicians of the classroom's "engine of instruction" – as Jeremy Bentham had conceived it – urban teachers were endowed with a form of managerial authority, but also made subject to that authority: trained to worry about their own fitness for the task, and to internalise the technology of surveillance by keeping tabs on themselves from the perspective of an inspector. Foucault would say the modern teacher wields – and is subject to – a diffuse form of disciplinary authority which combines "the deployment of force [with] the establishment of truth" (1997, 184). I want now to see how this self-governing authority fits into teachers' personal ethical narratives of education, and how, in turn, these are represented formally in the novels.

Writing Discipline

Muriel Spark's Miss Jean Brodie has a considered understanding of her role as a teacher, and imparts her theory of education with typical forthrightness:

> 'The word "education" comes from the root *e* from *ex*, out, and *duco*, I lead. It means a leading out. To me education is a leading out of what is already there in the pupil's soul. [...] Now Miss Mackay has accused me of putting ideas into my girls' heads, but in fact that is her practice and mine is quite the opposite. Never let it be said that I put ideas into your heads. What is the meaning of education, Sandy?'
> 'To lead out,' said Sandy ... (36-7)

Sandy's robotic reply is, of course, heavily ironic: Miss Brodie doesn't just put ideas into her girls' heads, effectively she *is* the directing "head" of the corporate "Brodie set"[3]: she does her pupils' thinking for them, and perfectly embodies the well-proportioned sensibilities she hopes to instil. This unprompted vindication of Miss Brodie's teaching methods *to the subjects of those methods* is a nice example of the reflexive manoeuvre of self-government mentioned above, by which the teacher inspects herself as a knowledge-object of which she herself is the manager – or, we could as easily say, as a character in a story of which she is also the narrator. This ritual of truth is of little pedagogic value; the conclusion to Miss Brodie's demonstration is as pre-ordained as the content of her pupils' souls, and we are not surprised when she emerges from the imagined inquest justified as ever.

The lesson the Brodie set *will* take away from the episode is to do with discipline: they have learned a technique for monitoring their own righteousness, and producing their own correctness. Some of her pupils learn this lesson in do-it-yourself rectitude more readily than others, and make unexpected use of it. Miss Brodie's patrician mode of self-narration becomes a powerful sort of weapon in the inept hands of Sandy and Jenny, who grasp from Miss Brodie's incautious "embroidery" of her love history that all such stories are up for grabs, not predestined in the slightest:

> This was the first time the girls had heard of Hugh's artistic leanings. Sandy puzzled over this and took counsel with Jenny, and it came to them both that Miss Brodie was making her new love story fit the old. Thereafter the girls listened with double ears and the rest of the class with single. (72)

From then on the girls use their position as subjects *within* the Brodie fable to foment a kind of narrative rebellion against its totality: they re-narrate Miss Brodie's mythologized love history, countering its fixity, innocently wrecking its propriety and setting a precedent, in Sandy's case, for "betraying" one kind of narrative authority with another. Their imaginative re-writing of the Brodie myth,

---

[3] "Sandy looked back at her companions, and understood them as a body with Miss Brodie for the head" (30).

"The Mountain Eyrie", re-casts the tragic chronicle of their teacher's love life to comic effect. The fictionalized "love correspondence" of Miss Brodie registers the utter failure of the teacher to inculcate an "innate sense" (46) of bourgeois decorum; the letters abound with bungled euphemism and groaning clichés. What they also show is that the stamp of Miss Brodie's narrative style has been deeply impressed upon the girls. They don't really appreciate what they're saying, but they know very well how it ought to sound: "If I am in a certain condition I shall place the infant in the care of a worthy shepherd and his wife, and we can discuss it calmly as platonic acquaintances" (73). The letter concludes by congratulating Mr Lowther "warmly upon [his] sexual intercourse, as well as [his] singing" (74). This tone of rudderless, reckless propriety is the best possible mimicry of Miss Brodie's example: what has sunk into the girls' habits of thought is not any substantive lesson about how to behave in a moral or even "well-mannered" way, but this aura of restraint in self-presentation: the ring of correctness.

Sandy in particular understands that Miss Brodie's ceremonial confessions are about producing truths in a way that insulates her from judgment:

> Sandy was fascinated by this method of making patterns with facts, and was divided between her admiration for the technique and the pressing need to prove Miss Brodie guilty of misconduct. (75)

The sort of discipline Miss Brodie demands of her Set parallels Spark's own "penchant for strict authorial control" (McIlvanney, 189); and so a three-tier narrative structure is established in which it becomes possible for the rebelling pupils Sandy and Jenny to retaliate against the totalizing Brodie fable, in which they figure as mere puppets. But is any such reversal possible in the gap between Miss Brodie, and the author? The point of Sandy and Jenny's rewriting of the Miss Brodie myth is to show that, in fact, she does not exercise power over her students, properly speaking; she fosters discipline, a rigorous self-regulation which relies on suspicious introspection, rather than visible force. It operates by means of anxiety: do I possess an "innate sense" of the proper distance to prop open a window (46)? Have I correctly ascertained the supremacy of Giotto over da Vinci (11)? This authority, as the girls show, is constitutively unstable: might the textual authority which the narrator holds over Miss Brodie be similarly limited, and open to the same reciprocal "betrayal"[4] as that between Sandy and Miss Brodie? With Sandy's mindless rehearsal, Spark is apparently setting Miss Brodie's well-meaning despotism up for a fall; and yet we can't quite be sure of the distance between Spark's own, highly orchestrated narrative style, and Miss Brodie's "magnificently organized" cast of mind. Perhaps Spark's God-like narrator will punish Miss Brodie for "her excessive lack of guilt", for "the general absolution she had assumed to herself" (85) and for "electing her self to grace" (109). The perceptive Sandy "smells" the hubris of Miss Brodie (109) and relishes the Calvinist prospect that it is "God's pleasure to implant in certain people an erroneous sense of joy and salvation, so that their surprise at the end might be the nastier" (109). But then, it seems the God-like narrator is not beyond the reach of Brodie's influence: the close resemblance of the teacher's clipped tones and the style of the omniscient narrator is most striking in a filmic cut-away scene which conflates the truth-making voice of impartial reportage in the novel, with Miss Brodie's own,

---

[4] " If you did not betray us, it is possible that you should have beeen betrayed" (126).

extremely correct habits of speaking:

> Miss Brodie sat in her defeat and said, 'In the late autumn of nineteen
> thirty-one – are you listening Sandy?'
> Sandy took her eyes from the hills.
> In the late autumn of nineteen thirty-one Miss Brodie was away from
> school for two weeks […]. (56)

It seems Miss Brodie does not only put thoughts in her pupils' heads, she is able somehow to put words into the mouth of the God-narrator. Is this a case of the narrator being "stamped" with Brodiesm in the way Sandy's letters are, or is Spark here mimicking Miss Brodie's overbearing preamble, by way of highlighting its officiousness? Perhaps Spark's narrator is straightforwardly exercising power over the character – making Miss Brodie a pawn to be travestied. Or is this the teacher somehow answering back, stirring her self-regulation to rebellion, her reflexive "technique of the self" overtopping itself to challenge for narrative self-rule? If the novel is an indictment of a God-playing teacher, is the moral point that Miss Brodie has been shown to act too much like a Sparkian narrator – ordering her pupils about in a "magnificently organized" cult of personality; or is Miss Brodie instead punished for getting above her station, narrating herself into a position of *excessive self-government*, for not "knowing her place" in a textual world she should only have managed, but never ruled?

The Writing and the Wall

Writing is, of course, central to what Foucault would call the "power-knowledge relations" of the school. In the classroom, the register and the examination stand as emblems of a documentary regime which "places individuals in a field of surveillance and situates them in a network of writing [which] engages [pupils] in a whole mass of documents that capture and fix them" (1977, 189). The place of this coercive "power of writing" outside the classroom is at issue in George Friel's 1972 novel *Mr Alfred M.A.*, originally entitled "The Writing on the Wall". As critics have already noted, the novel's interest lies not in its central action but in how it treats language and boundaries, violence and communication (Burgess, 236). The school's code of discipline is compared to a language early on, when the protagonist, himself a failed poet, muses on the place of corporal punishment in a tough urban school: "'It's like the language of a country,' said Mr Alfred from his lonely corner. 'You've got to speak it to be understood'" (425). Friel returns to this image of the classroom as a battlefield throughout his work,[5] and his lesson is always the impossibility of making an honorable peace. Mr Alfred describes his own writing in diplomatic terms:

> He had called his poems *Negotiations for a Treaty*. He meant a treaty
> with the reality of philosophers, politicians, economists, scientists
> and businessmen. […] The poet would insist on his right to live in the
> independent republic of his imagination. But he would let reality be
> boss in its territory if it gave up all claims to invade and conquer his.

---

[5] See, in particular, the story "A Friend of Humanity" in the collection of that title.

If it didn't he would organize his own resistance movement. (434-5)

The angelic figure who seems to provide a link between Mr Alfred's private utopia and the bleak reality of his job is Rose Weipers, a girl pupil for whom he develops a dubious affection. The questionable arrangement by which Rose fetches the teacher's lunch and sits in his lap in exchange for a kiss on the forehead and a weekly half-crown comes to light through an anonymous letter to the head teacher. It is described as "a rambling piece of vernacular prose without punctuation. Some words were badly misspelled. But the errors were so uncommon they seemed to arise from the writer's desire to support anonymity by bogus solecisms" (503). The letter's accusations of "indesent praktises" (505) are baseless, but when Mr Alfred is questioned "he felt guilty enough of what he was charged with":

> There came into his mind the Gospel text that whosoever looketh on a woman to lust after her hath committed adultery with her already in his heart. He didn't like that text. He thought it unfair. But he knew how he had often looked on Rose. So the anonymous letter could claim the support of the Gospel for what it said about him. (509)

These two pieces of writing – one malicious, counterfeit, and profane, the other divine, true, and sacrosanct – have the effect of a sort of textual pincer movement, and force Mr Alfred into open confrontation with a world of threatening signs.

The battle takes place over the public writing of graffiti, a form of inscrutable language in the novel which does not communicate so much as simply occupy public space, laying claim to territory in the same way Mr Alfred's hoard of quotations lays claim to his own education. The mysterious "YA BASS" signs, unlike Mr Alfred's endless allusions,[6] function not by dialogic reference to other writing, but declare their origins through insistent self-reference: the author's name is often all that differentiates one sign from the next. They are essentially untraceable signatures, whereas Mr Alfred is endlessly citing other writers, referring across the chasm of his own failure. In the novel's hallucinatory climax, Mr Alfred is conquered by the demonic figure of "Tod", a self-publicising anarchist *graffito* who Mr Alfred elliptically calls Coriolanus (564), perhaps referring to that traitor's yearning to "stand / As if a man were author of himself" (5.3.36-7), and who appears exactly opposed to the bureaucratic "power of writing" Mr Alfred enforces. The first act of Tod's revolutionary "Action Group" has been to scatter the library catalogues, to undo the "documentary regime" on which relational literary authority depends. This figure of an immensely destructive, anarchic power of writing seems to cry out for the civilising linguistic discipline Mr Alfred represents – but Tod's unaccountable place in the text makes

---

[6] Friel shares Mr Alfred's penchant for allusion: the teacher's affection for Rose Weipers strongly recalls the figure of Rose La Touche, an adolescent girl John Ruskin tutored and mentored "before deluding himself that she ought to be his wife. Rose fled in horror from the proposal, triggering first in her, and then in the spurned Ruskin, a violent mental collapse" (Schama 236). See also Bell's *Ruskin*. Likewise, an intimation of *Mr Alfred M.A.'s* essentially Arnoldian approach to education – he too is a civilizing inspector-apostle – is contained in his name.

him as slippery and ubiquitous as his graffiti, and thus beyond the reach of a narrative power which operates by compulsory visibility. Not even the omniscient third-person narrator – who has for a single instant been a visible "I" itself (478) – can "capture and fix" the place of Tod in the sea of quotations Mr Alfred gushes forth, like an exploded card-catalogue. Friel's own smugly allusive, endlessly punning style is at stake here, too, and the novel's conclusion is haunted by the prospect of communicative breakdown following the loss of a shared literary heritage. Tod exults in his success: "You're all on the way out. All you literary bastards. It's the end of the printed word. Everything's a scribble now" (568). There can be no self-governing republic of the imagination without an orderly and well-stocked cultural commonwealth to draw upon. As he descends into hysterical ravings Mr Alfred faces the prospect of total defeat in the war of culture versus anarchy, and places the blame squarely on the undisciplined, "child-dominated" school: "Taught them language. And the profit on it is. Caliban shall be his own master. [...] What the inspectors want. Do-it-yourself poetry. Mathew Arnold was an inspector too. What would he say now?" (580). Literature is Mr Alfred's "refuge from reality", and hence the writing isn't just *on* the wall, as in the novel's original, cautionary title, it *is* the wall. Confusing the authority of knowledge with his own, professional authority (see Freire, 73), Mr Alfred's education makes up the protective "bars" which shield him from a menacing, lawless society which has forsaken the civilizing power of the word.

Being Fenced in by the Teachers

The last teacher I want to mention has a much higher opinion of what he would probably rather call the "non-hierarchical classroom", but a much more pessimistic sense of his part in the repressive, policing function of school. Patrick Doyle is a lad o' pairts turned Fightin' Dominie, who maintains a slender hope that he can have a liberating effect on his pupils, if only he weren't handcuffed by awareness of his complicity in their suppression. If Miss Brodie does not recognize her involvement in social control, Patrick sees very little else – he does not look *through* bars so much as directly and fixedly *at* them. The following passage shows him indulging his taste for bluff self-censure:

> P for Patrick Doyle Esquire, a single man, a bachelor; a chap with little or no responsibilities. A teacher who has become totally sickened, absolutely scunnered. A guy who is all too aware of the malevolent nature of his influence. He is the tool of a dictatorship government. A fellow who receives a greater than average wage for the business of fencing in the children of the suppressed poor. (67)

This self-portrait is narrated in the idiom of objective bureaucratic authority – as if Patrick were filing a report on himself as a schools inspector, from inside another layer of Bentham's monitorial machine. Patrick's surveillance of his own ethical formation has malfunctioned: with brutal – if somewhat ostentatious – honesty, he finds himself guilty of Conn's second charge, of "breathing hypocrisy". Patrick does not quite repent this sin, but does conclude that he has no business setting an example for children. Or rather, that the only thing he *is* qualified, and indeed obliged to teach children is this very technique of unforgiving self-criticism. Like Miss Brodie, it is important for Patrick to objectify this confessional knowledge, to make an informative "pattern of facts" with it. He actually drills his first-year students in his corruption, and has them recite their parents' stupidity in entrusting them to his care:

> Now, all of yous, all you wee first-yearers, cause that's what you are, wee first-yearers. You are here being fenced in by us the teachers at the behest of the government in explicit simulation of your parents viz. the suppressed poor. Repeat after me: We are being fenced in by the teachers
> We are being fenced in by the teachers
> [...]
> in explicit simulation of our fucking parents the silly bastards
> Laughter.
> Good, good, but cut out that laughing. You're here to be treated as young would-be adults under terms that are constant to us all; constant to us all. Okay then that last bit: viz. the suppressed poor!
> viz. the suppressed poor!
> Cheering. (25)

This regimented harangue calls its own structure into question, and the sermonic lecture crumbles into comic irony. But inside the teacher's own head, holding to a standard of honest self-criticism has more unsettling implications. Eating dinner with his parents, Patrick is unable to stop examining himself, searching out hidden motivations. He sees all things through a veil of detached suspicion:

> How is it all contained? The heads craned over the plates, the three people eating, this man and woman and man, while within the limits of each an intense caterwaul. We are alone! We are isolate beings! The good Lord alone
> Fucking bastards.
> And of course Patrick, going in for a bath to avoid being alone with his da.
> Pardon?
> And of course Patrick, going in for a bath to avoid being alone with his da.
> Is that possible?
> Fucking right it is ye kidding! (114)

That "Pardon?" makes us doubt whether this questioning is strictly internal to Patrick's mind, or whether he's addressing some inquisitorial third-person narrator. The mixed form allows Patrick to examine himself in the very way he would examine a pupil. During the same meal he examines his dinner:

> The fish was a dead animal. It had lain there upon the plate open for inspection, eager to impress s/he who is about to partake. Just please devour me. I'm as good as the next thing you'll catch. [...] I'm a good

wee fish. Courageous and heroic. Its body sliced open for examination by the education authority. Give it a tick. A plus. Five out of ten. Fine for a Glasgow table but don't send it south to the posher restaurants of England. (114)

We see the extent to which Patrick has internalised the teacher's "marks out of ten" power of writing, power of ticking. In the novel's endgame Patrick, like Mr Alfred, finds himself pursued by police in surreal circumstances. He imagines his own status as an object of surveillance to affirm his guilt, thereby freeing him from the duty of self-inspection:

> There was a pair of polis across the street who needless to report were observing him quite openly and frankly and not giving a fuck about who was noticing [...]. They had appeared at the very thought of insurrection [...]. The polis watching him now in a serious and suspicious manner. About to give chase. Catch the bastard, there he goes. He had started running now instead of later once they were gone and that was daft and really stupid because they would worry as to his veracity or something after that [...] daft, fucking daft, but too late, if he was to pause to see what they were doing because them taking that as the sign of guilt, of criminality, of his being suspicious, a suspicious being [...]. Yes Doyle is dangerous, dangerous to himself. He is dangerous to himself and thus to the weans he teaches on that daily basis. (336-7)

The novel's despairing coda, "Ah fuck off, fuck off" (337) is not directed at the police, but at the unrelenting, self-policing mindset of the teacher. Exhausted by his own doubleness, Patrick's "last words" evoke Joseph K. lying in the quarry, almost relieved after another police-chase (126-7) to at last be sentenced, if not judged. This double-barreled imprecation is also directed at the reader: whereas K.'s dying self-accusation "Like a dog!" is uttered "as if he meant the shame of it to outlive him" (128), Doyle demands that the curtain fall before he does, and that we shut the book unable to know whether his story exceeds Kelman's narrative. His final "technique of the self" is a revolt against the forces, textual as well as political, which pervert his knowledge – and self-knowledge – to managerial ends.

Conclusion: Freedom and Form

In a famous passage from *Émile*, Jean-Jacques Rousseau councils the wise teacher to "let [the pupil] always think he is master while you are really master. There is no subjection so complete as that which preserves the forms of freedom; it is thus that the will itself is taken captive" (100). In their structured allocation of knowledge and authority within limited "forms of freedom", such educational relationships are both political and narratological in ways Gramsci and Freire would surely recognise. These novels demonstrate three Scottish writers' keen awareness of how the precepts of "educational reason", and the textual procedures by which it is justified and practiced, work to "capture and fix" not only pupils, but teachers as well. Muriel Spark allows Miss Brodie to narrate herself into the position of a secular God before allowing a dissenting pupil to expose her hubris: but perhaps she does so because the teacher has risen above her station, like a pupil who talks back, testing the limits of the teacher's authority. If Miss Brodie is an emblem of domination in the guise of freedom, the figment of "Tod" represents illiteracy and barbarism posturing as "cultural revolution" (565) for George Friel. Mr Alfred grasps that there can be no private self-narration without a dialogic public code to support its transactions, and fears that philistine social atomism threatens the collective fund of cultural signs on which every "independent republic" of the mind invisibly depends. Fearful, defensive and bewildered, Mr Alfred sees his students through gaps in a garrison wall, savages bent on destroying what they cannot possess. Patrick Doyle advocates a more existential sort of discipline, and attempts to implant in his pupils a subjectivity which takes itself as the first object of doubt. He hates himself for "performing the fencing-in job on behalf of a society he purports to detest," but his example of remorseless self-suspicion internalises these very procedures of control-by-inspection. Though his libertarian posture would be the most baldly opposed to Rousseau's doctrine, it is Kelman's character who seems the most thoroughly traduced by an illusion he apprehends, but cannot evade. His efforts to resist and unmask the disciplinary regime end up expanding its sphere, tightening its grip, and destroying his own freedoms. Patrick Doyle, the great demystifier, seems to be "looking through bars" even before he opens his eyes.

According to the educational historian James Scotland, one of the distinguishing features of the Scottish tradition is a kind of formalism, "a stress on verbalism, on the magical powers of words" which can be traced to the national system's Presbyterian inspiration (266). Another characteristic impulse is militant educational democracy (265), which makes the school "a battleground of political principle" (266). By attention to the formal dimension of how educational thinking is transmitted *within* Scottish culture in these novels, I hope to have shown how a few modern writers raise radical questions about education, authority and knowledge in ways germane to both of these traditions, if not to the conventional discourse of nationalist intellectualism.

References

Bell, Quentin. 1978. *Ruskin*. 2nd Ed. London: Hogarth Press
Beveridge, Craig and Ronald Turnbull. 1989 *The Eclipse of Scottish Culture*. Edinburgh: Polygon
Burgess, Moira. 1998. *Imagine a City: Glasgow in Fiction*. Argyll: Argyll Publishing
Foucault, Michel. 1977. *Discipline and Punish*. Trans. Alan Sheridan. London: Penguin
Foucault, Michel. 1991. *The Foucault Reader*. Ed. Paul Rabinow. London: Penguin
Freire, Paulo. 2000. *Pedagogy of the Oppressed*. Trans. Myra Bergman Ramos. 30th Anniversary Ed.New York: Continuum
Friel, George. 1992. *A Friend of Humanity*. Edinburgh: Polygon
Friel, George. 1999. *Mr Alfred M.A.* [1972] in *A Glasgow Trilogy*. Edinburgh: Canongate

Gramsci, Antonio. 1971. *Selections from The Prison Notebooks*. Ed. and Trans. Quintin Hoare and Geoffrey Nowell Smith. London: Lawrence and Wishart

Harrison, Cameron. 1997. "How Scottish is the Scottish curriculum?" *Education in Scotland: Policy and Practice from Pre-school to Secondary*. Ed. Margaret M. Clark and Pamela Munn. London: Routledge. 156-69

Humes, Walter and Tom Bryce. 2003. "The Distinctiveness of Scottish Education". Tom Bryce and Walter Humes. Eds. *Scottish Education*. 2nd Ed. Edinburgh: Edinburgh University Press. 102-11

Johnston, Derek and Malcolm L. Mackenzie. 2003. "The Politics of Scottish Education". Tom Bryce and Walter Humes. Eds. Scottish Education. 2nd Ed. Edinburgh: Edinburgh University Press. 86-98

Jones, Dave. 1990. "Genealogy of the Urban Schoolteacher". *Foucault and Education: Disciplines and Knowledge*. Ed. Stephen J. Ball. London: Routledge. 57-75

Kafka, Franz. 1992. *The Trial* [1925] in *The Complete Novels*. Trans. Willa and Edwin Muir. London: Minerva

Kelman, James. 1999. *A Disaffection*. [1989]. London: Vintage

McIlvanney, Liam. 2002. "The Politics of Narrative in the Post-war Scottish Novel". *On Modern British Fiction*. Ed. Zachary Leader. Oxford: Oxford University Press. 181-208

McIlvanney, William. 1975. *Docherty*. London: Allen & Unwin

McMunigall, Alan and Gerry Carruthers. 2001. "Locating Kelman: Glasgow, Scotland and the Commitment to Place". *Edinburgh Review*. 108: 56-68

Neill, A.S. 1986. "Notes on Education". *Edinburgh Review*. 73: 100-2

Rousseau, Jean-Jacques. 1993. *Émile*. Trans. Barbara Foxley. London: J.M. Dent

Scotland, James. 1969. *The History of Scottish Education*. Vol. 2. London: University of London Press

Shakespeare, William. 1997. *Coriolanus*. Ed. Greenblatt et al. New York: W.W. Norton & Company

Spark, Muriel. 1965. *The Prime of Miss Jean Brodie*. London: Penguin

"Completely Inaccessible": James Kelman, the Booker Prize and the Cultural Politics of Subaltern Representation

Richard Harris

The 1994 Booker prize was awarded to James Kelman for *How Late it Was How Late*, a novel which deploys a sustained, high modernist, interior monologue to represent the consciousness of its protagonist Sammy, a Glaswegian *lumpenproletarian* subject. The decision was by no means unanimous, nor was the award conferred graciously. It was awarded only after an unprecedented degree of acrimony, backroom horse-trading and a second round of voting. Among the panel of judges, the most virulent opposition to Kelman's novel came from Julia Neuberger. Richard Todd reports that Neuberger was "implacably opposed to the choice [...] claiming she had felt outmanoeuvred during the lengthy discussions prior to the judges final decision" (65). Julia Llewellyn Smith, writing in *The Times*, observed:

> Kelman has woken up to a chorus of outrage. The previous evening his fifth novel *How Late it Was, How Late* won the Booker Prize, but the tributes and glory, the comparisons with Kafka and Zola, have been buried in carping and quibbling: the news that Julia Neuberger, one of the judges, considered the choice "a disgrace" and the book "completely inaccessible for most people". (17)

A general article about feuding Booker judges on the BBC news website, singles out 1994 as a vintage year for bad feeling: "Julia Neuberger, [...] one of the judges in 1994, went so far as to call that year's winning book, *How Late it Was, How Late* by James Kelman, 'crap'". Now this belligerent outburst would seem odd if it originated from a more quotidian member of the judging panel for this prestigious event; the fact that it was the urbane and intellectually sophisticated Neuberger renders it positively extraordinary. She is Oxford and Harvard educated, an ex-Chancellor of the University of Ulster, holds eight honorary doctorates, is an author and broadcaster, and is a member of umpteen foundations, trusts, councils and boards including, significantly, the Booker Prize Foundation. What prompted this influential and authoritative figure, an academic acting in an official capacity, to react to the work of an author of Kelman's standing[1] in such an inappropriate and unprofessional fashion?

Critical reaction in certain areas of the British quality press to Kelman's win was ideologically congruent with Neuberger's. Gerald Warner fulminated in *The Sunday Times*:

---

[1] There is nothing ambivalent about Kelman's stature within the present cultural and academic constellation. Compared to, say, Irvine Welsh, who as Geoff Huggan (413) observes, enjoys a sort of self-reflexive subcultural 'outsider' status, Kelman is an establishment/canonical figure: his novel *A Disaffection* was shortlisted for the Booker Prize in 1989, and he has taught at the Universities of Austin and Glasgow. *How Late it Was* has been taught at Sheffield as a compulsory part of the undergraduate English literature degree for some years now.

> He [Kelman] fails to recognise that, in reality, what he is describing is not properly a 'culture', but the primeval vortex of undevelopment that precedes culture. If the literary gurus who consider his work 'daring' had any real instinct for adventure, they would unfashionably proclaim that there is a good cultural case to be made for Kelman's people remaining taboo (20)

And here is Simon Jenkins in *The Times*:

> The award of the Booker Prize to Mr Kelman is literary vandalism. Professor Bayley must have known in his heart that a dozen authors this year were more merit-worthy [...] none of whom even made the shortlist. I can only assume that the judges were aspiring to some apogee of political correctness. They greeted Mr Kelman as an inversion of the norm, a Jilly Cooper of the gutter, a Barbara Cartland of the Gorbals. They wanted to give awfulness a break. Here was a white European male, acceptable only because he was acting the part of an illiterate savage. Booker contrived both to insult literature and patronise the savage [...] This book is literature's answer to the Turner Prize. (20)

The curious logic that underpins the above synechdochic collapse of Kelman's novel into the sphere of a feared and loathed avant-garde art is echoed in Harry Ritchie's favourable review of *How Late it Was* for *The Sunday Times*:

> Kelman has a unique voice and style, and one that makes me sympathise for once with art pundits facing the dilemma that the pile of rubble or scribbled mess on the canvas might as easily be the creation of a child as an alleged genius [...]. Since the Second World War, there have been very few writers who have put literary critics in such a tizz. Kelman's own brand of avant-gardism has escaped suspicion of critics who in former years might well have pooh-poohed Beckett or BS Johnson as con-artists, for the simple reason that many middle-class English critics have been cowed by Kelman's militantly working-class, Scottish material. (7)

Note here the implication of an infantilism, which is somehow connected with Kelman's class position, and which has the same ideological pedigree as Neuberger's, Jenkins' and Warner's overtly hostile reactions. Clearly, this affair is more complex than it first appears, and there has been a limited acknowledgement of this from the sphere of left/liberal academic criticism. Geoff Gilbert, for example, called it an "extraordinary moment" and suggested that "there was something about the terms in which Kelman was discussed that interfered with the closed circuits of consecration and commodification" (220). Nicola Pitchford considers the controversy to be "representative of how the idea of English national identity continues to be articulated [...] through concepts of 'high culture'. This entanglement results invariably in a number of discursive and ideological contradictions" (694). However, little is made of this affair in the only book length work on the Booker prize, Richard Todd's *Consuming Fictions*, and *How Late it*

Was is significantly something of a marginal presence in this work. Given the extraordinary events and media furore that surrounded the 1994 award, the reader might reasonably expect a chapter devoted to it, but it is barely mentioned. Commenting on the unprecedentedly low sales of *How Late it Was*, Todd merely says that "the novel has proved the least commercially successful Booker winner since before 1980" (114). Obviously, to see the reaction by Neuberger and the others as simply the outraged sensibilities of *haute bourgeois* arbiters of taste is to treat it as a surface appearance, an abstraction, a static, frozen moment: it is clearly *mediated* by deeper and far more complex historical and ideological forces.

When I first read *How Late it Was* I was studying something called 'working class writing' and I was greatly impressed by Kelman's aesthetic and political strategy. Instead of the usual straightforward Edwardian realism or naturalism that is the traditional vehicle for narrating proletarian experience, this novel mobilised a European high modernism to gain access to the consciousness of its protagonist – here was an attempt to represent life at the margin that owed more to Kafka, Proust and Joyce than it did to Robert Tressall or Alan Sillitoe. But when the Booker controversy happened I began to think about the political and ideological problems that freight attempts to represent subaltern subjectivity. What struck me most was the nature of the reaction of the judges and the press, the language in which this reaction was deployed, and the fact that these people, who carry a certain professional cachet, were seemingly blind, or more appropriately deaf, to the luminous technical and formal achievements of this novel at the expense of its class content. I turned to Gayatri Spivak's essay 'Can the Subaltern Speak?' (1988) because what seemed to happening was a working out, at the institutional and ideological level, of some of the assertions that she makes in this text. Spivak argues that western and/or postcolonial intellectuals such as Foucault and Deleuze are wrong to assume that, given the opportunity, the oppressed can speak and know their condition. She suggests that there is something of a "not speakingness" structurally inscribed into the very notion of subalternity itself, that if the subaltern could speak – not just 'utter' – in a way that mattered to 'us' (who are on the right side of the international division of labour) then by definition this would not be subaltern.

I think it is right to call *How Late it Was* a novel that deals with the condition of subalternity, especially if the word subaltern is restored to its original Gramscian meaning – literally 'second-in-line,' or economically dispossessed. With the advent of globalisation, the international division of labour that Spivak speaks of is far more fluid than before, so the north/south centre/periphery model is losing its original spatial coordinates. Michael Hardt and Antonio Negri observe that under globalisation "the spatial divisions of the three worlds have been scrambled so that we continually find the First world in the Third and the Third in the First" (xiii). Kelman's novel narrates this reconfiguration. Since the 1970s the British working class has been fragmented into two broad groups: skilled and self employed workers with strong ideological links to the middle classes and a dispossessed or 'underclass'. In 1994 Mari Marcel-Thekaekara, an Indian aid worker, visited Glasgow's Easterhouse estate and was horrified by the level of deprivation she witnessed there. In a *Guardian* article she wrote: "Malnutrition in

Britain! Even we were amazed" (p.3). John Beverly suggests that the condition of subalternity presents itself to 'us' as something like the Lacanian category of the Real, "that which resists symbolisation, a gap-in-knowledge that subverts or defeats the presumption to 'know' it" (p.2). This perspective provides an insight into why *How Late it Was* proved so traumatic, so inaccessible and so *unreadable* to the middle class literary elite and why it interfered with the smooth self-congratulatory running of the Booker prize mechanism and forced its liberal multi-culturalist mask to slip. Kelman's ultimately political mobilisation of class stages an irruption of the Real, and, despite the reservations expressed by Spivak, it manages this on the terrain of the aesthetic and mimetic, at a remove of two levels of representation. *How Late it Was* is not a *testimonio*[2] written by Kelman, who is, in any case, not (now) a subaltern subject but in the same position as the intellectuals that Spivak questions in her essay. In writing this novel he is both speaking *for* (the terrain of politics) and speaking *of* or re-presenting (the terrain of art) a subaltern condition, and these are the two senses of the word 'representation' that Spivak argues get run together when western intellectuals speak for subaltern groups. In my opinion, it is precisely Kelman's militant 'running together' of these two modes of representation which creates a valid recovery of a subaltern voice.

Spivak's essay contains many useful insights. She asks if, in taking on this condition of "not speakingness" postcolonialism might be a specifically first-world, privileged, and institutionalised discourse that classifies and surveys the East in the same measure as the actual modes of dominance it seeks to dismantle? This is an important question, especially in the light of the trend within academic postcolonial criticism which suggests that globalisation may provide the world's subaltern classes with potentially emancipatory opportunities – the chance to 'speak' as it were. The best known example of this notion to emerge in recent years is Hardt and Negri's *Empire*. Although not postcolonial criticism as such, certain strands of their argument encapsulate its generally optimistic spirit:

> We insist on asserting that the construction of Empire is a step forward in order to do away with any nostalgia for the power structures that preceded it and refuse any political strategy that involves returning to that old arrangement, such as trying to resurrect the nation-state to protect against global capital. We claim that Empire is better in the same way that Marx insists that capitalism is better than the forms of society and modes of production that came before it. Marx's view is grounded on a healthy and lucid disgust for the parochial and rigid hierarchies that preceded capitalist society as well as on a recognition that the potential for liberation is increased in the new situation. (79)

Hardt and Negri's project is an attempt to rethink the beleaguered Marxist project to take account of a new, emergent regime in capital accumulation – the shift from production capital to neoliberal finance capital, and its attendant cybernetic

---

[2] Sammy Samuels is not a Rigoberta Menchu, for example, but the fictional protagonist of a novel – which is itself the archetypal bourgeois art form.

revolution – so the register in which it is written is speculative, philosophical, optimistic, almost dreamily utopian, though underpinned by a materialist dialectics of a certain kind. However, much postcolonial theory originating from this set of assumptions often verges on an unproblematic celebration of the conditions produced by newly globalised capital. This can be observed in the notions of hybridity, transnationality, disjuncture, and border crossings promulgated by theorists such as Anthony Appaduri and Homi Bhabha.
According to Kanishka Chowdhury, Appadurai claims:

> The world that we live in now seems rhizomic, even schizophrenic, calling for theories of rootlessness, alienation and psychological distance between individuals and groups, on the one hand, and fantasies (or nightmares) of electronic propinquity on the other. This new global order, argues Appadurai, is characterized by disjuncture and scapes: the critical point is that the global relationship among ethnoscapes, technoscapes, and financescapes is deeply disjunctive and profoundly unpredictable, […] the global flow of images, news, and opinion now provides part of the engaged cultural and political literacy that diasporic persons bring to their spatial neighbourhoods.

Chowdhury counters this with the assertion that the world in this regime of global capital is only random, chaotic and disjunctive on a *manifest* level; globalisation exists in order to make the latent system of surplus extraction ever more efficient. There is empirical evidence to support this: the gap between rich and poor is growing larger and capitalists are making ever greater profits. Furthermore, this postmodernist celebration of multiple subjectivity and fluidity is complicit with neoliberal capital, since it is exactly the kind of subjectivity that the new regime requires of its workers so it can de-skill and re-skill and move them around the globe efficiently. Julian Stallabrass points out that the focus on schizophrenia, fragmentation and instability at the expense of a coherent subjectivity forecloses the possibility of producing coherent political strategies for a better future (11).

Moreover, Appaduri's celebration of the utopian potential inherent in the flow of electronic images and digital information ('technoscapes' in his terminology) strikes me as extremely problematic, for two reasons. Firstly his argument only has force if it ignores a number of material facts: 2.5 billion people live on less than two dollars a day, and 25 percent of the world's population does not even have access to electricity, let alone computers and televisions. Secondly, given that there must be subalterns in the southern hemisphere who do have access to the digital world, the amount of leisure time they have to avail themselves of it must be extremely limited; for example the Maquila Solidarity Network reports that workers in the ZIP Choloma, one of many free trade zones in Honduras, work a basic 11 hour day with extra compulsory overtime. This dismissal of a politics of fixed subjectivity and apparent blindness to the real material conditions suffered by the genuinely dispossessed is also a feature of Homi Bhabha's related formulation of hybridity, which I will gloss as a celebration of the disruptive and subversive potential of the migrant in the metropolis, a valorisation of openness and of the postcolonial subject always in the process of being made and remade. In his introduction to *Nation and Narration* he writes:

> [T]he margins of the nation displace the centre; the peoples of the periphery return to rewrite the history and fiction of the metropolis. [...] The bastion of Englishness crumbles at the sight of immigrants and factory workers. (7)

But do they and does it? For Bhabha, Salman Rushdie's *The Satanic Verses* is the paradigmatic articulation of the migrant's "empowering condition of hybridity", yet, as Chowdhury affirms:

> In short, hybridity, though potentially disruptive of homogeneous narratives, is inevitably implicated in the capitalist commodification of culture [...]. We have to remember that the truly voiceless, the subaltern worker, does not find space in Rushdie's world. Are Rushdie's cosmopolitan protagonists similar to the millions of migrant workers who traverse the globe in search of economic survival? No!

But Kelman's protagonists definitely are. A brief consideration of the role played by 'work' in the life of Sammy, the protagonist of *How Late*, should illustrate this. During a key scene in the novel Sammy attends the benefits agency, and some of his history emerges as he is subjected to an interrogative process:

> Yer a construction worker to trade?
> Well no to trade, I'm a labourer – semi skilled [...].
> What was yer last job?
> Community work provision.
> And before that?
> Oh christ now ye're talking ... eh ... it was down in London; 11 year ago. (95)

These scraps and traces of work, atomised and removed from community in this exchange do not even provide a folk memory of the historic potential of organised labour that informs traditional British working class narrative. During the period of time which demarcates the 'present' of *How Late it Was*, Sammy's only moment of active participation in the economy is his feeble attempt at trading in stolen goods, the stolen dress shirts bought from the traditional 'bloke in the pub'. This is itself an extremely attenuated reproduction of the ideological complex that conflates a fetishisation of individual freedom with a fetishisation and teleologisation of profit, and serves to naturalise the rapacities of global capitalism. As this scene progresses it also emerges that Sammy could have been a professional footballer:

> Christ I used to live for the game myself . If I had took my chances [...] the scouts were up an aw that. I blew it.
> What happened?
> I just blew it. I was silly. What about yerself? (97)

There is no more potent symbol of escape and salvation in traditional working class narrative than the figure of the professional sportsman, and whereas a novel like *This Sporting Life* will centre on this fetishisation to foreground a tragic waste of potential, here it is evoked by Sammy in a sudden burst of passion – "Christ I used to live for the game" – only to be relegated to the margin of the text and subordinated to the novel's dominant narrative trope: "I just blew it. I was silly". 'Silliness' and 'stupidity' are the terms that Sammy uses to articulate the aleatory nature of his existence, his Heideggerian 'thrownness' into absurd and gratuitous being, the frightening arbitrariness that determines his experiences as a helpless object entirely at the mercy of random events. The 'silliness' begins early in the novel when he knows the two men he approaches for money are policemen and likely to be unsympathetic, yet he still approaches them, inexplicably kicks one of them, and subsequently receives a beating. In keeping with the logic that structures this trope, no proper explanation is proffered for his blindness, nor does he seem particularly surprised or bothered by it. In the most illustrative examples, it transpires that Sammy's two terms in prison are the result of what he calls 'stupidity': he gets four years in jail when he is nineteen for pointlessly going on the run with a wanted criminal, then seven years as a result of getting caught trying to drive away from a botched robbery in a getaway car, even though he can't drive. Here is the reality of hybridity for the true subaltern subject, stranded and drifting in a global, but horizonless and perpetual present. Significantly, the novel is bereft of an 'ending': Sammy just moves somewhere else.

To conclude, Rushdie is emblematic of the institutional ideology that underpins the Booker prize – he was the author for whom the Foundation invented a Booker of Bookers, awarding this honour to *Midnight's Children*. On the other hand, Kelman's novel – which, ironically, could be called a 'hybrid text' because of its fusing of working class realism with European modernism – generated that extraordinary hostile response. There is, then, a further irony in the fact that the Booker Prize sells itself as a carnival of postcolonial multicultural hybridity, a celebration of the fact that the English language no longer belongs to the metropolis. But as I suggested earlier, all that is really changing is the nature of capital itself. Consider the origins of the prize: Booker PLC is a giant Agribusiness multinational with origins in the sweated labour – sugar plantations of Demerara – that set up the prize to advertise its withdrawal from overt colonial exploitation. The sponsorship of the literary prize is therefore a logical and ideological move intended to create a certain image and to shore up a desired public perception of Booker PLC which is symbiotically related to its diversification into areas of cultural production and immaterial labour. The company now exploits the cultural capital of the ex-colonies, rather than simply its raw materials and material labour. At a deep-structural and ideological level, nothing has changed – the prize constitutes a legitimising regime which is administered from London, the metropolitan centre of the old empire. This is absolute: the *entire* panel of judges for the 2001 award came from London. The sale of the prize to the Man group, which markets financial services – is a further indication of the ascendancy of speculative finance capital and its penetration into culture. It is ironic that these theories of hybridity, transnationalism and diversity are emerging now when, as Julian Stallabrass puts it "corporate control of the means of expression has reached an all time high and keeps climbing" (10).

References

Beverly, John. 1999. *Subalternity and Representation: Arguments in Cultural Theory*. Duke University Press

Bhabha, Homi K. 1990. "Narrating the Nation". Homi K. Bhabha. Ed. *Nation and Narration*. London: Routledge. 1-7

Chowdhury, Kaniska. 2002. "It's All Within Your Reach: Globalization and the Ideologies of Postnationalism and Hybridity". *Cultural Logic*. 5.1. Accessed at http://eserver.org/clogic/2002/chowdhury.html

Gilbert, Geoff. 1999. "Can Fiction Swear? James Kelman and the Booker Prize". Rod Mengham. Ed. *An Introduction to Contemporary Fiction: International Writing in English since 1970*. Cambridge: Polity. 219-34

Hardt, Michael and Antonio Negri. 1999. *Empire*. Cambridge, MA: Harvard University Press

Jenkins, Simon. 1994. "An Expletive of a Winner". *The Times*. 15 Oct: 20

Kelman, James. 1995. *How Late it Was, How Late*. London: Minerva

Llewellyn Smith, Julia. 1994. "The prize will be Useful. I'm Skint". *The Times*. 13 Oct: 17

Ritchie, Harry. 1994. "Out of Sight". *The Times*. 27 Mar: 7

Spivak, Gayatri C. 1988. "Can the Subaltern Speak?" Cary Nelson and Lawrence Grossberg. Eds. *Marxism and the Interpretation of Culture*. Basingstoke: Macmillan. 271-313

Stallabrass, Julian. 1996. *Gargantua: Manufactured Mass Culture*. London: Verso

Todd, Richard. 1996. *Consuming fictions : the Booker Prize and Fiction in Britain Today*. London: Bloomsbury Publishing PLC

Warner, Gerald. 1994. "Time for a Disaffection From Literary Slumming". *Sunday Times*. 25 Sept: 8

Why National Tale and Not National Novel? Maturin, Owenson, and the Limits of Irish Fiction

Jim Kelly

What I want to suggest is not so much that Irish fiction is in some way limited, as that it has suffered a dearth of critical analysis due to criticism's limited embrace of what constitutes fiction. This is not said as a prologue to some clichéd postmodern position that would see all types of narrative, perhaps even all acts of language, as necessarily fictive in nature. Rather, I propose that if criticism of Irish fiction has been historically limited, it is so because it has taken a too rigidly formalistic stance, seeing the classic realist novel as the normative standard of prose fiction. Irish fiction is then judged against this standard, variously applauded or derided for its inability to conform to certain generic specifications. Criticism of Irish fiction, I would suggest, has suffered from what Clifford Siskin calls "novelism", that is, the "habitual subordination of writing to the novel" (Siskin, 172). So a hugely important study of Irish fiction of the early nineteenth century, Thomas Flanagan's *The Irish Novelists, 1800-1850*, concludes by saying that "[the] history of the Irish novel is one of continuous attempts to represent the Irish experience within conventions which were not innately congenial to it" (334). Flanagan's work appeared in 1959, two years after the publication of Ian Watt's seminal *The Rise of the Novel: Studies in Richardson, Fielding and Defoe*. Watt's emphasis on what he termed "formal realism" (9) can be seen to have influenced Flanagan's approach to the fiction of the early nineteenth century. While his is a perspicacious reading of the writers surveyed, there is an undercurrent of unease, a realisation that working within the formalist straightjacket necessarily precludes much literature from serious discussion. Flanagan, of course, was not the first to suggest that the term "Irish novel" might function as a type of oxymoron. Such a view has a long genealogy. Sean O'Faolain famously stated that there was no such genre (Kenny, 51), and a recent article in *The Irish Times* proved that such a view has a long shelf-life when it was suggested that "the big, steady, realist Irish novel is as far away as ever" (O'Toole, 12).

I would argue that such a view encapsulated in the above remark crystallises what is the main problem with criticism of the Irish novel; the proposition of the steady, realist novel as the normative category of prose fiction, the only suitable form for a "national narrative". One might say, the steady, realist, English novel. Criticism should move, as Aaron Kelly says, from "analyzing Irish fiction [as] failed novels to radically decentred and nonhegemonic fictions" (129), as long as this does not entail slipping into what Gerry Smyth sees as "the post-colonial fairy-tale which tells of the Big Bad Wolf of English realism versus the playful, subversive, anti-realist nature of Irish story-telling" (20). After all, in order to construct a 'counter-tradition' of anti-mimeticism, one necessarily pre-supposes a Great Tradition against which it defines itself. It is therefore dangerous to construct a meta-narrative of Irish fiction that takes as its basis some teleological belief that literary history is a linear progression towards the ultimate manifestation of Joyce. The plaintive cry asking why Ireland in the nineteenth century could not produce a Jane Austen can easily become a triumphal essentialist cry explaining why only

Ireland in the twentieth could produce a Flann O'Brien.

Caught between these two antinomies of a realist or anti-realist tradition, how are we to assess Irish fiction? I would suggest that what is needed is a methodological approach that returns Irish fiction to its place within a wider network of literary and cultural production. This might sound suitably vague. I agree with John Kenny when he insists on the need "to resist the prohibition by formalist genre theorists of correlations of the novel with its immediate social contexts" (45). By re-viewing Irish fiction in what has been traditionally seen as its foundational moment, that is, the early nineteenth century, we can assess the ways in which Irish writers negotiated their place within a variegated marketplace, profoundly aware as they were of their texts' places within a market which both consumed, and as I will argue, in Maturin's view, produced, cultural commodities. This has the added benefit of examining Irish fiction's interactions with a British and, indeed, a European, market at a formative time in the critical formation of what would become the big, steady, English realist novel.[1] After all, Irish fiction of this period was not unique in being somewhat outside the mould of realist fiction. Jane Austen is hardly representative of her time, and indeed was not particularly popular during this period.[2]

Writing in 1826, Thomas Moore was optimistic about the opportunities that Ireland had in the field of cultural, specifically fictional, production. In an article in the *Edinburgh Review* Moore wrote:

> At present Ireland bids to be the great mart of fiction; and as, from what we have just said, it may be concluded that the character of her people will bear working, somewhat better than her gold mines – we may indeed expect a sufficiently abundant product from that quarter. (359)

The placing of novelistic production within terms borrowed from a discourse belonging to political economy was hardly a revolutionary proposition from Moore. Indeed, to emphasise the materialist contours of fiction is to reproduce previous concerns. As Kathryn Sutherland has pointed out, "the general complaint against the mechanisation and commodification of literature is as old as the printing press itself" (118). What I want to suggest is that in Maturin's fiction, and particularly in *The Wild Irish Boy* (1808), there was a direct engagement with the difficulties that this materialist bias against novels entailed when those novels were involved in the constitution of national narratives. The portrayal of an Ireland that was defined as, in terms of culture and (implicitly) morality, historically anterior to a more consumerist Britain was problematised, for Maturin, by its presentation in a form that was bound up in the latter position. The use of different terms by authors to describe their works is indicative of the connotations that the term novel carried, as neither Sydney Owenson nor, indeed, Maria Edgeworth, labelled their Irish fictions as "novels", both preferring the more neutral (and less

---

[1] See Brown, *Institutions*; Ferris *The Achievement of Literary Authority*; Lynch and Warner, *Cultural Institutions of the Novel*; and Garside "The English Novel in the Romantic Era".

[2] Part of the interest in Austen's work was sparked by Walter Scott's review of *Emma* in 1815. If Jane Austen invented a type of English fiction, who invented Jane Austen?

morally and commercially suspect) term, "tales".[3]

The first thing to note about *The Wild Irish Boy* is its title, recalling Owenson's 1806 novel (I use that term deliberately) yet performing an important gender reversion, which can be linked to what Jacqueline Pearson has called its "politico-cultural enterprise of masculinizing the novel" (625). Maturin's work, however, instantly refers to another novel from 1806 when the dedication is addressed to the Earl of Moira, recalling the dedication to the Countess of Moira which occurred in the infamous *roman-à-clef, A Winter in London*, by Thomas Surr, a work which, incidentally, appeared under the imprint of Richard Phillips, Owenson's publisher. It is also important to note that the full title of Surr's fiction was *A Winter in London; or, Sketches of Fashion: A Novel.*[4] Maturin's novel melds the plot of Surr's novel to Owenson's. Surr's novel portrays a culture clash between old and new money, the marriage at the end of the novel representing a compromise of dyadic oppositions. In a scene that would be replayed in the national tale, Surr presents two contrasted estates:

> On each side of the eminence [Montagu] saw a park and mansion: but in nothing were they similar to each other. On his right the ivy-mantled towers of Beauchamp Abbey bounded the view of a thickly wooded domain, where huge oaks, the growth of centuries, waved over long dark terraces of grass, which the mower's scythe had never visited for years; grottoes of shell-work, surmounted with ill-formed images of stone, now green with moss; hermitages with straw-thatched roofs; fountains which leaden Cupids guarded; and caves dug deep in gloom, formed all together a display of the taste of other times, and made up a scene, which, while it impressed the thought "that grandeur once dwelt here," at the same time told to the beholder the tale of its desertion [...] When the eye turned to the left, a scene so different presented itself [...] the mansion of lord Roseville, combining, in a most masterly style of composition, all the magnificence of an Eastern palace with all the elegance of an Italian villa. (I: 106-8)

The inevitable resolution will see a marriage between the two estates, marrying old and new money, sublime and beautiful, aristocracy with emergent middle-class. Surr wrote, to quote Peter Garside, "[novels] pitched to the prurient curiosities of an urban middle-class audience" (43). While ostensibly critical of "this little nation of shopkeepers" (II: 143), there is also a celebratory streak running through Surr's work, praising the extent to which what had previously been thought marvellous had been normalised through a consumerist revolution:

> No longer let the descriptions of entertainments recorded in the Arabian Nights be regarded as fabulous, when the nobility, and even

---

[3] *Castle Rackrent* first appeared as "An Hibernian Tale", *Ennui* and *The Absentee* as "Tales of Fashionable Life", and *Ormond* as "A Tale". Owenson's fiction adopted the now generic category of "National Tale", or "An Irish Tale".
[4] Thomas Skinner Surr *A Winter in London* (London, 1806)

the merchants of London, can charm away the hours of winter with such fêtes as these. (II: 215)

The Wild Irish Boy continues to make a series of connections between Owenson's novel and Surr's, implicitly upsetting the self-categorisation as "National Tale" that occurs in the former. The contrast between Irish and English in *The Wild Irish Girl*, was, for Maturin, not so much a pedagogical device to inculcate an ignorant British readership of Ireland, as a blatantly populist and simplistic positioning of national differences. The fact that it could be both at the same time eluded him. In other words, Maturin set about proving that the National Tale was a novel after all, and as such, it was subject to the same material exigencies that caused the novel, in its most commercial form, to be seen as the ultimate example of commodified literature in the period.

The emphasis on commodities in Maturin takes on, at the same time, some of the trappings of a colonialist position, as Maturin points out the extent to which the colonial culture's self-representations are largely tailored by a metropolitan audience. Through its allusiveness, *The Wild Irish Boy* forces us to read it as explicitly caught up in a colonialist dialectic that involves the aesthetic distantiation of the periphery from the core, a process that is implicitly bound up in the subsequent production and consumption of a blanched version of the periphery's culture by that same core, operating under the rubric of a bourgeois political economy. That the Arabian Nights no longer seem fabulous is precisely because they have been normalised through the ability of the London audience to recreate them. Joep Leerssen has termed this "auto-exoticism" (35-38), although the degree of agency that he gives to Irish writers might be over-stressed. Whereas Leerssen saw Irish writers as 'selling' an exoticised Ireland, he neglects to look at the consequences of a fashionable world that was all too ready to buy up those images.

Maturin's preface to his *The Wild Irish Boy* is important, and worth quoting at length:

> This novel from its title purports to give some account of a country little known. I lament I have not had time to say more of it: my heart was full of it, but I was compelled by the laws of this mode of composition to consult the pleasure of my readers, not my own…He who would prostitute his morals, is a monster, he who sacrifices his inclination and habit of writing, is – an author. (I: x)

Maturin does a few things here. Firstly, the work is declared as a novel. Then, the success of Owenson's pedagogic purpose in *The Wild Irish Girl* is questioned, as Ireland after that work remains "a country little known" even though *The Wild Irish Boy* presupposes an audience for Owenson's novel. Ireland is presented as a subject unsuitable to "the novel". The author is presented as slave to the demands of the audience. The suitable materials for a novel, "a lounge in Bond Street…a masquerade with appropriate scenery" (I: x), are exactly those that Surr capitalised upon to such a commercially successful degree.

Maturin seems to collude, therefore, with a critical position that seems to suggest that "Ireland" and the term "novel" are somehow mutually exclusive. *The*

Wild Irish Boy, however, manages to subvert this. What I would argue is that Maturin's presentation of Ireland as suited to a process of cultural commodification renders the term "novel" much more appropriate than "tale". To recall Moore, Maturin presents Ireland as the "great mart of fiction". The novel, indeed, becomes the genre most suited to carrying the national narrative. Powerful signifiers of national identity are reduced to the level of interior decoration:

> I hardly know which to prefer for this cabinet; orange drapery to correspond with the antiques in the cornice ... or dark green, as the chimney-piece is of verde-antico. I believe we must consult Hope. (III: 315-316)

The "Hope" referred to by Lady Montrevor is Thomas Hope (1769 – 1831), whose *Household Furniture and Interior Decoration* (1807) is repeatedly referred to in the work. While Hope's work was immensely popular and influential, for Maturin it represented the extent to which colonised cultures provide the raw (cultural) materials for domestic metropolitan consumption. Hope's book took part in the general vogue for Egyptian furnishings and fabrics of the early nineteenth century, a fashion that was the result of an increased awareness of Egyptian artefacts due to the military conflict in the Nile basin. Hope based much of his research on Vivant Denon's *Travels in Upper and Lower Egypt...during the campaigns of Napoleon Bonaparte*. The English translation of Denon's text appeared in 1803, and apart from its value to antiquarian studies of Egypt, it also contained, in the words of the translator, a display of "[the] dreadful licence of lust, rapine, and slaughter, the French troops were allowed to indulge in" (Aikin, vi).

For Maturin, military domination was followed by the domestication of the vanquished culture, represented in *The Wild Irish Boy* as the craze for furnishings from Egypt. One of the characters, Lord Montrevor, plans to decorate his Irish residence according to "Hope's exquisite system of decoration"(II: 193), a scheme that will involve decorating a room that looks onto the Shannon in 'aquatic' fashion. A powerful demarcation between "modern" Ireland and some anterior cultural space in Connaught becomes simply another part of a neo-classically arranged apartment; "mirrors placed opposite the windows shall multiply the reflections of the water"(II: 194). Maturin has one character comment acerbically on "the fashionable rage for borrowing all the embellishments of our drapery, and apartments, and fetes, from the recent local scenery of some national victory"(III: 309). Such a comment has hidden implications for the popularity of reproductions of Irish artefacts after the publication of *The Wild Irish Girl*.[5]

The Wild Irish Boy's most direct reference to Owenson's novel, apart from the title, comes during a masquerade when a Lady M. makes a triumphant entry as "*Glorvina, in the Wild Irish Girl*"(III: 356), floating into the assembly "with a glittering train around her". Such a reference not only comments on Owenson's habit of appearing as a Glorvina figure, but also points out both the artificiality and commercial reproducibility of a powerful Irish national icon. This does to Glorvina what Walter Benjamin said mechanical reproduction did to the work of

---

[5] For the craze for "Glorvina" objects after the publication of *The Wild Irish Girl* see Claire Connolly "The Wild Irish Girl as Media Event", 98-115.

art: "[It] detaches the reproduced object from the domain of tradition. By making many reproductions it substitutes a plurality of copies for a unique existence" (215). The erasure of "unique existence" is also tied in with military subjugation. The masquerade at which Lady M. makes her appearance is decorated with paintings of the Inca chieftain Ataliba (Athaluapa):

> The first [apartment]…was decorated with paintings representing the most striking passages of Peruvian history; the first interview of the unfortunate Ataliba with the Spanish troops; the magnificence of his train and procession; the car enamelled with pearl and diamond…from which he was dragged by the hands of the Spanish soldiers. (III: 348-349)

Apart from the subtle emphasis on both Ataliba's and the fake Glorvina's "train", this passage refers to a particularly charged footnote in *The Wild Irish Girl* in which Owenson compared the insurrection against the Spanish to the events of 1798. Maturin saw the presentation of Ataliba as a decoration as a removal of the actual historical figure from a level of agency into a static aesthetic realm. An obvious parallel with this would be Walter Scott's nostalgia for Jacobitism, which allowed an aestheticisation of a volatile political situation only after that situation is normalised, and the Highlands are militarily subjugated. The classic instance of this in *Waverley* is the painting of Waverley and executed Jacobite chieftain Fergus MacIvor at the end of the novel, where, as James Buzzard points out, Fergus is "translated…from deliberative historical agent into static symbol" (48).

Maturin therefore proposes that after the military subjugation of 1798 Ireland is reduced to the status of a colony providing *cultural* commodities as opposed to actual material commodities. Glorvina is robbed of her national associations and becomes another fashionable accessory to the fashionable crowd. Pearson is right to note that Owenson, for Maturin, becomes a sort of dress-designer, but it is important not to downplay the significance of this. Dress, while ostensibly presenting national character as, literally, materially based, may in itself become the only signifier of difference. The paintings of Peruvian history that Maturin has his London masquerade decorated with end with one depicting the present state of the country:

> In another part of the room, the paintings represented the modern state of South America, views of the country and sketches of the inhabitants, in all the varieties of the mingled, the native, and the Spanish costume. (III: 349)

Reproducing the comforting teleological drift of Owenson's novel, where Irish and English eventually unite and ride into the Whiggish sunset, the painting also questions any essentialist notion of national character, as differences are based on 'costume' rather than on any overt racial characteristics.[6]

---

[6] Considering that two years after the publication of *The Wild Irish Boy*, Latin America would be convulsed by the wars of independence, Maturin's reduction of national difference to what clothes one wears takes on an added irony, as now the reproductions are shown to have a political agency of their own.

Another text that becomes important for Maturin, as other critics have noted, is Maria Edgeworth's *Belinda*, which, again, advertised itself as a "Moral Tale". While Pearson has suggested that *The Wild Irish Boy*'s hero, Ormsby Bethel, is modelled on Edgeworth's Clarence Hervey, there is a more direct correlation made between Bethel and Mr. Vincent, the Creole landowner who very nearly marries Edgeworth's eponymous heroine. In a highly intertextual move, Bethel is characterised by the phrase "*il y' a infiniment l'air d'un heros do Roman*" (Maturin, I: 236), a phrase which Edgeworth has ascribed to Mr. Vincent. Bethel and Vincent are both outsiders from the colonies, both lacking a certain self-control (both gamble excessively), and both woo an Englishwoman. Mr. Vincent is rejected, while Bethel marries. The linking of Bethel with Vincent, and by implication Ireland with the West Indies, is a move to synchronise the two characters within an imperial discourse while opposing them in the manner in which they provide commodities for the metropolitan market. The West Indies had appeared in Surr's novel as a source of material wealth, but Maturin's point about Ireland is that it is a provider of cultural resources.

Therefore, we have in *The Wild Irish Boy* a series of replications of Irish culture, replications whose symbolic significance is undercut by their status as consumer productions. Such an outlook is bleak for the Romantic artist, and would seem to suggest that Maturin provides a proto-Marxist historical materialist reading of Owenson, and, indeed, Irish culture in general. However, it is possible, despite this, to see in *The Wild Irish Boy* a positioning of literature that is not tied to a simplistic base/superstructure model of cultural production. The move towards economic determinism is countered by the stress laid on the constitutive role that literature has in forming the individual subject, in both a pedagogical institution such as Trinity College, and in the private domestic sphere. In one of the many digressions in the novel, Maturin asks whether "the study of English literature...[would] be of more consequence to them [i.e. students of Trinity], as men and citizens" (I: 118) than science. Of course, one notices here the contiguity of the terms men and citizens. Pearson notes the opposite extreme of reading, that is, the dangers inherent in women's reading (629). Significantly, Bethel's wife is seen to have morally and intellectually progressed once she has thrown away her "French books" and replaced them by Walter Scott's *The Lay of the Last Minstrel*. The kind of reading that Glorvina in *The Wild Irish Girl* indulges in must be replaced and that replacement involves implicitly removing a female-authored, novelistic account of national character, by a male-authored, poetic one.

Of course, that does not resolve Maturin's problems. Even Scott's text can be used as a dress-design to the fashionable crowd. The fact that Maturin could only deconstruct any idea of a transcendent national character in *The Wild Irish Boy* without replacing it with any programmatic alternative may indicate why he saw this novel as a failure.

In terms of its place within Irish fiction, we might see *The Wild Irish Boy* as arguing against the impossibility of its own, or any fictional representations, within a meta-narrative which would in itself be a fiction, a story grafted onto a bewildering multiplicity of exchanges and transactions. Tradition in *The Wild Irish Boy* is a matter of which tailor one visits on Saville Row. For Maturin, Bond Street, not Bards, have created Ireland. Yet even though this might seem bleak, the very fact that Maturin could engage in this debate through the medium of the "novel" might suggest that what is lacking in Irish fiction is not so much the fiction as the willingness to engage with works that in themselves test the assumptions that narratives, be they in the form of novels, poetry, or otherwise, make. Maturin may not have written "sober, realist, novels", yet very few other writers in his period did either, and the very use of such terms suggests that it is the critic, not the imaginative writer, who has limited the field of vision. In an intelligent review of some of the difficulties facing analyses of Irish fiction, David Lloyd offers a conclusion that is at once both potentially liberating and yet somewhat regressive:

> We are only just beginning to forge the theoretical terms in which the atypicality of the Irish novel can be analysed but, to borrow a line from Tom Dunne, it may be that we are approaching a 'less coherent but in more ways more interesting' theory of the novel. (155)

A statement one might welcome, if only for the unfortunate use of the term "atypical". After all, Maturin's point was that Irish fiction was not so atypical after all. It may be that a greater integration of Irish fiction within critical surveys of other writing that was being produced elsewhere in the North Atlantic archipelago might help us move away from seeing such fiction as deficient and instead really begin to disable the fetishisation of "sober, realist" novels.[7] Perhaps then we will see such critical myopia for the fiction that it is.

References

Aikin, Arthur. 1803. "Translator's Note". *Travels in Upper and Lower Egypt in Company with Several Divisions of the French Army, during the Campaigns of General Bonaparte in that Country*. By Vivant Denon. Trans. Arthur Aikin. London. vi

Benjamin, Walter. 1999. "The Work of Art in the Age of Mechanical Reproduction".*Illuminations*. Ed. Hannah Arendt. Trans. Harry Zorn. 1970. London: Pimlico Press. 211-45

Brown, Homer O. 1997. *Institutions of the English Novel: From Defoe to Scott*. Philadelphia: University of Pennsylvania Press

Buzzard, James. 1995. "Translation and Tourism: Scott's *Waverley* and the Rendering of Culture". *Yale Journal of Criticism*. 8.2: 31-59

Connolly, Claire. 2000. "The Wild Irish Girl as Media Event". *Colby Quarterly*. 26.2: 98-115

Ferris, Ina. 1981. *The Achievement of Literary Authority: Gender, History and the Waverley Novels*. Ithaca: Cornell University Press

Ferris, Ina. 2002. *The Romantic National Tale and the Question of Ireland*. Cambridge: Cambridge University Press

Flanagan, Thomas. 1959. *The Irish Novelists, 1800-1850*. New York: Columbia University Press

Garside, Peter. 2000. "The English Novel in the Romantic Era: Consolidation and Dispersal". Eds. Peter Garside and Rainer Schowerling. *The English Novel 1770-1829: A Bibliographical Survey of Prose Fiction Published in the British Isles*. Vol. 2. Oxford: Oxford University Press. 15-105

Kelly, Aaron. 2001. "Reproblematizing the Irish Text". *Critical Ireland: New*

Voices in Literature and Culture. Eds. Aaron Kelly and Alan A. Gillis. Dublin: Four Courts Press, 124-31

Kenny, John. 2000. "No Such Genre: Tradition and the Contemporary Irish Novel". *New Voices in Irish Criticism*. Ed. P. J. Matthews. Dublin: Four Courts Press. 45-51

Leerssen, Joep. 1996. *Remembrance and Imagination: Patterns in the Historical and Literary Representation of Ireland in the Nineteenth Century*. Cork: Cork University Press

Lloyd, David. 1993. "Violence and the Constitution of the Novel". *Anomalous States: Irish Writing and the Postcolonial Moment*. Dublin: Lilliput Press. 125-62

Lynch, Deirdre and William B. Warner, eds. 1996. *Cultural Institutions of the Novel* London: Duke University Press

Maturin, Charles Robert. 1970. *The Wild Irish Boy*. Ed. Robert Lee Wolff. 1808. New York: Garland Press

Moore, Thomas. 1825-26. "Irish Novels". *Edinburgh Review*. 63: 359

O'Toole, Fintan. 2001. "Writing the Boom". *Irish Times*. 25 January

Pearson, Jacqueline. 1997. "Masculinizing the Novel: Women Writers and Intertextuality in Charles Robert Maturin's *The Wild Irish Boy*". *Studies in Romanticism*. 36.4: 635-50

Siskin, Clifford. 1999. *The Work of Writing: Literature and Social Change in Britain 1700-1830*. Baltimore: John Hopkins University Press

Smyth, Gerry. 1997. *The Novel and the Nation: Studies in the New Irish Novel* London: Pluto Press

Surr, Thomas Skinner. 1806. *A Winter in London*. 3 Vols. London

Sutherland, Kathryn. 1987. "Fictional Economies: Adam Smith, Walter Scott and the Nineteenth-Century Novel". *ELH*. 54.1: 97-127

Trumpener, Katie (1997) *Bardic Nationalism: The Romantic Novel and the British Empire* Princeton, NJ: Princeton University Press

Watt, Ian. 2000. *The Rise of the Novel: Studies in Richardson, Fielding and Defoe*. 1957. London: Pimlico

Súil Eile, Dúil Nua (another perspective, a new desire): Short Films in the Irish Language since the Advent of TG4

Ruth Lysaght

Since the mid-1990s, there has been a dramatic growth in indigenous film-making in Ireland, and this rising tide has also lifted the currach of Irish language ventures. *Oscailt* and *Lasair*, the film and digital initiatives of the Irish language television station TG4 (with An Bord Scannán, the Irish Film Board), are evidence of the recent resurgence of interest in the Irish language as a cultural entity. This renaissance is linked to changes in the way we see national, cultural and ethnic identity throughout the world. In the short films of the *Oscailt* scheme, a new vision, or version, of Irish is posited, through fictional narratives set in contemporary Ireland.

So far, there has not been significant critical engagement either with the films produced or with the reasoning behind their promotion – this paper is only a beginning. However, there is no shortage of ideas for new films, and if conditions improve in relation to funding, there is likely to be a greater development in Irish language cinema. From the bases of *Oscailt* and *Lasair*, independent production companies are encouraged, and unusual or lateral approaches to narrative and character are sought. This paper begins with an overview of Irish cinema in general, and then provides a brief description of the origins and aims of the Irish language television station, TG4. This finally leads into a discussion about the *Oscailt* films and their relationship to the Irish language.

Irish Cinema

Indigenous film-making in Ireland has been a small scale enterprise, even in the English language. Until the 1970s most of the material for cinema screening in the Irish language was of an educational nature (encouraging civic spirit, domestic safety, etc.), and the same film was available in an English version. The beginning of RTÉ, the first national television channel, saw some innovative productions, based mostly on theatre drama, but, as in the wider context of cinema, there was a greater emphasis on instruction than production.

Since the coming on air of TnaG, and especially since the *Oscailt* scheme was begun in 1998, the number of Irish language fiction films made has doubled. (14 *Oscailt* films had been made by 2001.) The first pre-*Oscailt* TnaG film *Draíocht* (starring Gabriel Byrne and broadcast on TnaG's opening night) was a cold look at 1960s rural Ireland, less remarkable for its subject matter than for the fact that it was in Irish.[1] However, the films made since then have explored different modes and, following the guidelines, focus on contemporary rather than past visions of the country. The *Oscailt* scheme is the first sustained effort to create a filmic

---

[1] The kitchen radio in this film reminds us of the larger context, referring to the situation in the Congo. The strength of TnaG lay in its willingness to start small, to begin with the local, and the short film. Ironically, perhaps, for the first film shown on TnaG, the script of *Draíocht* was a translation from English.

version of Irish language identity. The films are intimately linked to the image of the Irish language, and are part of the move to reclaim the language from the propaganda of the past, which associated it with school, religion and a narrow nationalism. *Lipservice* (*Oscailt* 1998), an ironic look at the Irish oral exam, was a surprise success. Winning the audience award in the Cork Festival, it drew attention to the new image of Irish as a modern language.

The notion of 'national culture' finding expression in cinematic form is made problematic by the absence of a direct tradition. As mentioned above, early indigenous film production was limited in scope, and prominence was given to foreign-made films, particularly those from America. Prior to the recent increase in Irish film production, most of the movie images of Ireland were manufactured by Hollywood or the British. The context of the present development therefore, is that of a country trying to extricate its self-image from decades of external perspectives. The short film form is perhaps the ideal cinematic format by which to attempt such an examination. Whilst participating in the wider film culture, it has more artistic room (and less financial risk) to attempt to represent a minority than is afforded by the formulaic approach of mainstream commercial cinema. The present structures for film-making in Ireland provide a degree of support for innovation and experimentation. As the American film critic Geoffrey Chesire summarises it: "As a result of the boom, Ireland became the prime creator of its own images, Ireland from an Irish perspective ... this was an epochal shift [despite] compromises in choosing to employ Hollywood film language ... and conventions. [The] growth that Irish cinema has experienced in just the last eight years...should not be underestimated. Nothing comparable has happened in any other European cinema during the same period ..." (Chesire, 2001).[2]

Darach Ó Scolaí, speaking at the *Oscailt* seminar in Galway, suggests that in the absence of a continuous tradition in cinema, film should be explored by creative artists in neighbouring disciplines (Ó Scolaí, 2001). He argues that the strong stories of the films so far are a result of the story-telling tradition, both oral and literary, that characterise Irish language culture. However, it is undeniable that a cinematic way of telling these stories has yet to be found. Whilst some *Oscailt* films attempt to uncover specifically Irish situations, they deploy the conventions of mainstream anglophone cinema to do so. This dependence on foreign input, ironically, may be the most indigenous aspect of the scheme, as English language productions in Ireland rely similarly on external models. Far from being conservative, Irish society has traditionally been a great assimilator (even if some elements have yet to be fully digested). As Fennell remarks, "A rootless, pragmatic and often frenzied grasping at the new, the imported and the trendy ... has characterised the Irish since the nineteenth century" (Fennell, 1985: 93).[3] As the age of monolithic certainty (if it ever existed) is no more, the use of heterogeneous sources is a valid approach to the portrayal of Ireland.[4] Ó Scolaí advocates casting

---

[2] Film-making in the North has been advanced by the formation of The Northern Ireland Film Commission (successor to the Northern Ireland Film Council) in April 1997. The Derry Film Initiative is currently working on an Irish version of *Hamlet*.

[3] "– Puritanism in Victorian times, consumerism in the swinging Sixties, cinema, then radio, then air travel, television, mini-skirts, pool tables and disco-dancing" (Fennell, 1985: 93).

[4] Juxtaposition is one response: TG4's international weather reports are integrated with time-lapse shots of (the usually rainy) Baile na hAbhann.

the net more widely, beyond film to other art forms. This is a first step in finding themes and stories, but the problem of film language remains.

TG4/Teilifís na Gaeilge[5]

Teilifís na Gaeilge made its first broadcast on Hallow E'en night, 1996. The opening ceremonies, a blend of traditional and modern dance, fireworks and Afro-Celt rhythms set the tone for what was to follow: a new perspective on Irish language, culture, people and society. The origins of TG4 are a mixture of community activism and a personal commitment on the part of Minister Higgins (the Minister for Arts, Culture and the Gaeltacht, 1993-7), combining civil rights and aesthetic elements. The campaign for a specifically Irish station dates back to the late 1950s, when Gael Linn made a bid to establish and operate Ireland's first television channel.[6] The 1960 Broadcasting Act reiterated the *national aims* of the country at large in setting RTÉ the task of "*restoring the Irish language and preserving and developing the national culture*"(Barbrook, 1992), a task the station signally failed to fulfil.

The original aspirations behind TnaG were to cover local and regional topics of interest, with a special emphasis on Gaeltacht[7] issues, to provide non-Dublin-based television without alienating Dubliners, to screen European films not usually found outside Ireland's (four, metropolitan) art house cinemas, and to promote the Irish language, particularly among a younger audience. The motto, *Súil eile* (another perspective), is the criterion for many of TG4's projects.[8] Funded to produce two hours of Irish programming per day, by July 1998 TnaG was showing four – and by 2000 – six hours per day. In October of that year, 60% of their broadcasting had been through Irish, and a further 20% was home-produced. TnaG/TG4 has achieved a distinct identity through inventive scheduling and an original branding strategy. Promotional advertising for the station won gold at Worldfest Flagstaff International film and television festival in Arizona in 1999. These ads sell the Irish language to the general public as something strange and unpredictable, and as something to be proud of. The new Breton television station (TV-Breizh), broadcasting since September 2000, has a similar approach, as its language director Mikaël Baudu explains: "*Pour nous, la question de la langue se pose cependant beaucoup plus en terme d'image de marque. La pluspart* (sic) *des bretons perçoivent la langue bretonne comme une partie de leur patrimoine même lorsqu'ils ne sont plus en mesure de la parler*". [For us, the question of language falls very much in the area of image and branding. Most Bretons see the Breton

---

[5] The station was called Teilifís na Gaeltachta (Gaeltacht TV) in the original plans, TnaG (Irish language TV) for its launch, and finally TG4 (Teilifís na Gaeilge 4) in order to ensure a good position on the remote control.

[6] Although primarily an Irish language organisation, *Gael Linn* also emphasised culture (music label, etc.), and this interconnection between the Irish language and Irish culture is still very strong. However, in the context of TnaG, they are sometimes regarded as being in competition with each other.

[7] There are seven *Gaeltachtaí* ['Irish-speaking areas'] in Ireland.

[8] Pádhraic Ó Ciardha (advisor to Geogheghan-Quinn and involved in setting up TnaG) invented this term

language as part of their heritage, even if they cannot speak it.]

Broadcasting in a minority language is extremely important in legitimising that language for speakers and learners alike. The use of Irish in this context means not only a development of the language itself, but also a new departure in broadcasting. The remit as expressed by the Minister was to find "*bealaí suimiúla leis an nGaeilge a shníomh isteach i gcláracha nach mbaineann le pobal na Gaeilge amháin*" – to bring Irish into a more mainstream position in Irish media. Once more, the intertwined nature of language and culture make it difficult to see which should take priority. It is not denied that the distinctiveness of TG4 is in part dependent on its language, but it is much more than a translation of RTÉ. It is not clear if the use of Irish per se results in this different outlook, or whether any other language would provide this freedom from the anglophone tradition.

TG4 caters for two audiences: Irish speakers (their primary concern), and the general public. These groups may have comparable interests, but they also have vastly differing language abilities. Confused state policies, an unimaginative education system, economic difficulty and linguistic fundamentalism have combined to produce a majority of Irish citizens who cannot speak the Irish language, but paradoxically have a strong emotional response (whether positive or negative) to the idea of its conservation. Between 11-12% of the population have a good knowledge of Irish, and together with those who are interested in Irish language programmes, represent a core audience of about 350,000.[9] Since the foundation of TnaG, broadcasting in Irish has been directed at the entire country instead of merely at the smaller specialist group, and this is its most innovative feature. For the first time, people from a non-Irish-speaking background can see something of how life may be lived in this language. It is not suggested that fiction film can adequately explore such issues, but it should be noted that the *Oscailt* scheme in connection with TG4 is providing the first real opportunity for one group to communicate with the other on an imaginative and expressive basis.

Given a reluctant welcome by most journalists at its inception, and denied parity of visibility by (of all publications) the *RTÉ Guide*, the station had to take on the almost completely negative image that was the heritage of the Irish language.[10] TG4's unusual view of things soon won approval from jaded reviewers.[11] The 1999 *Oscailt* films were greeted with a mixture of relief and amazement. James Phelan, writing for *Film West*, focuses on the quality of the filming, and especially on the policies of the station. In relation to *Lipservice*, he says "*TG4 deserve ... immense credit for ... having a sense of perspective and more importantly, a sense of humour*" (Phelan, 1999). The *Oscailt* series may be seen as a testing ground for what the station wishes to portray. What is being sought above technical expertise is *splanc* – a new story, a different perspective.

The funding bodies regard the *Oscailt* scheme from two perspectives: offering practical encouragement to new film-makers, and encouraging a new portrayal of

---

[9] Now the total reach is in the region of 600,000 (Minihan, 2000). According to the MRBI, 85% of Gaeltacht people watch TG4 regularly, and 600,000 watch every day.

[10] The whole project is seen by some as an elaborate PR exercise for a dying language, although as time passes, the cultural aspect seems to be taking priority over the linguistic.

[11] By April 2000 Paddy Murray was writing "top marks to TG4 for being different, it's what they do best".

Irish life. TG4 sees them as a step forward for native film-making, as well as a valuable means of publicity for the station and the language at international festivals (not to mention schedule-filling). *An Bord Scannán* takes the avuncular role of nurturing new talent.[12] The ideal is to effect, through these films, the *súil eile* – another perspective. Certainly, there is a case to be made for categorising the *Oscailt* shorts as a Third Eye on Irish life. The distinctiveness of Irish film as cultural if not national expression has been expressed by McLoone as an exploration of *"indigenous culture, in all its contradictions, with an outsider's eye,...* [which] *at the same time subjects this outsider's perspective to the peculiar interrogation of the local culture"*(McLoone, 2000: 128). The Magic Eye of the *Oscailt* film looks closely at particularity, at a detail, rather than simply reflecting a general 'reality'. It is a step through the mirror, affording us a glimpse of details usually invisible in mainstream cinema, where they blur together to form a backdrop for the main action.

Stuart Hall argues that in the contemporary world, it is the monoglot who is in the minority. Most people are obliged to inhabit at least two identities, to speak at least two cultural languages, to negotiate and 'translate' between them (Hall, 2000: 362.). Hall speaks here in metaphorical terms, which may well be applied to contemporary Ireland. The gulf of incomprehension and resentment between the linguistic communities (if distinct communities they are) is cultural rather than literal, and translations must bridge this divide. There are two 'Irish' cultures: one *Gaelach* and one *Éireannach* – one cultural and increasingly tourist-based, and one more dependent on anglophone world culture. As in the case of the linguistic communities, the dividing line between these cultures is by no means indelible. The divide in Ireland (*deighilt tíre*) is intensified when there is a language difference; and the perception that you are being observed instead of doing the observing is one that fuels the paranoia of an already marginalised group of people. As Ó Cofaigh has it, much Irish film, television and literature consists of *"daoine amuigh ag breathnú isteach orainn ... ní muidne ag breathnú amach"* (Ó Cofaigh, 2001). [people on the outside looking in at us ... never us looking out.] The time for cultural self-determination has arrived, and *Oscailt* should reflect this pushing to define self and other, and to rework the usual perspective of Irish short films.

OSCAILT

The film-makers vary in their approach to *Oscailt*. To a large extent, it is here that the gap between the language groups becomes apparent. The English-speakers make their *Oscailt* in order to break through into the industry in general, and disregard the language as a tool for expression. The Irish-speakers, on the other hand, tend to see *Oscailt* as a chance not only to extend their film-making career, but also to comment on the nature of contemporary society in a different way. This is in theory, though. In practice, the plots are not hugely complex. The more aesthetic ideal, held by some of the *Oscailt*-makers, is connected to the use of film language as a means of expressing not only a story, but also the art of story-telling. In films like these, visual features and music play an equal part in creating

---

[12] Chief executive Rod Stoneman says contemporary fiction in Irish is a "vital component" of the range of films the board aims to support.

atmosphere as opposed to a strictly linear sequence of discrete events. Such awareness of the possibilities of cinema is important, as using another language in film-making, whilst implying another outlook – or insight – also carries the risk of dominating other modes of cinematic communication.

Our pushmipullu relationship with Irish, or what Kiberd (2000: 604) terms the "divided mind", is also reflected in the literary tradition. Even writers who have spoken Irish since childhood face bilingual teetering when it comes to producing a script or a story. Who are you writing for? Will a translation be necessary? TG4's attitude to Irish is necessarily complex. Whilst they aspire to total fluency, practical shortcomings force them to accept translated scripts for *Oscailt*. Commissioning editor for TG4, Ní Ghráinne prefers to call this a version (not a translation), and emphasises that their policy is for authentic Irish. At least five of the fourteen shorts were originally written in English, and subsequently translated by someone other than the author.[13] Translators ranged from friends to TG4-recommended experts, and most writers professed themselves satisfied with the Irish version. The linguistic abilities of several filmmakers are such that they are forced to take a distanced standpoint.[14] The English-speakers have an ambivalent attitude to the medium, often wondering why I had chosen to study this element of Irish short film-making. They evinced a lack of confidence in the efficacy of Irish (mostly in relation to audience-accessibility), but at the same time, an almost mystical love of its "poetry", making the film-making process "an exercise in purity" (Lehane, 2001).[15] Those who could not speak any Irish were in the difficult position of directing lines they could not understand. The obvious problems here were somewhat offset by the presence of a linguistic advisor (although their counsel was not always accepted). Two directors also referred to the freedom this ignorance of the language gave them in relation to tone and pace. Some go so far as to say that the language gives the film an extra dimension and makes it "more cultural". Whilst their lack of Irish may free these directors to explore other ways of using cinema, it is not ideal that the language of the characters be completely disregarded.

The greatest difficulty in a directorial lack of language is probably the mixing of dialects within a given setting. "*Go háirithe, nuair a thagann dhá chanúint le chéile, baintear léim beag asat*" (MacEamharcaigh, 2002). [When two dialects are mixed, it gives you a bit of a jolt.] Verisimilitude is lost – although the counter-argument, that a global audience will be oblivious to this factor, presupposes a

---

[13] Zanzibar was the first non-native production team to be awarded funding for Oscailt – and it is now the most prolific. It produced three of the five translated scripts (*Cáca Milis, Iníon an Fhiaclóra, Clare sa Spéir, Deich gCoiscéim* and *Óstán na gCroíthe Briste*).

[14] Although how they can be sure is a mystery, if they cannot understand the language. In few cases is the qualitative difference between the versions referred to as an issue, which is surprising for people who deal in words. A lack of Irish did not prevent actors and directors quibbling with their language advisor on issues of accent and líofacht, however.

[15] Lehane has no compunction about writing in a language he doesn't speak, and his current project is *Nom*, about the rootlessness of an amnesiac francophone immigrant. Seán McGinley (actor in *Clare* and *Lipservice*) says it is hard to be ironic in Irish (childlike), and so easier to be more whimsical. To what extent this is a function of the speaker's ability/familiarity or ideology is another issue.

much wider audience than the *Oscailts* currently reach. Only one of the films by a native speaker (*Dillusc*) mingles the dialects in this way,[16] with no specific purpose.

As might be expected, the Irish-speakers had different attitudes. "*An rud a bheith ráite i gceart*" [saying the thing properly], including the quotidian mélange of the real world (also encouraged by the various TG4 script advisors) takes precedence over a grammatically perfect and thus unrealistic version.[17] Is the real story (the original script) being told if the language of shooting is incomprehensible to the director? Who decides on the standard of 'correctness' or indeed verisimilitudinous Irish mixed with English? What agenda is being served (is any?) To what extent does the narrative depend on the language? This line of questioning represents one approach to the phenomenon. Issues of control, mediation and authenticity arise:[18] do the new schemes risk accepting 'hothoused' Irish from people who are neither linguistically nor cinematically competent? There was an element of the defensive in the assertions of the Irish-speaking film-makers that the language is merely a medium, and that the story is the main thing. Once outside the *Gaeltacht* area, speaking Irish is perceived as a political act, or at the very least, as a conscious decision. The quality of Irish used should be the highest possible, matching the technical standards such as lighting, acting and cameras…Whilst aspiring to *le mot juste*, the TG4 policy, as mentioned earlier, is to accept the best versions they are given.

Most of the *Oscailt* series so far take the perspective of the outsider, a recurrent trope in the literature of both languages. Traditionally, the outsider or blow-in provides an external perspective on a given society, and is often the storyteller. Most films are from the point of view of the English-speaking outsider. Films made by 'insiders' (if a disaffected film-maker may ever be said to be inside a given community) focus on the self in that environment, and not with the issue of a linguistic, geographical or cultural distance. They do not dignify the 'tourists' with a representation – even in the background. This cannot be dismissed simply as a refusal to deal with the issue, as there are often more pressing matters to

---

[16] *Iníon an Fhiaclóra* provided the most linguistic challenge. Originally written by an Englishwoman (of Irish parentage), and translated twice (once by cousins, once by an approved translator), the script was sent out to the actors in both languages. The actors came from a variety of areas, and had different regional accents, their standard ranging from vague school memories to native-speaker competence. Half of the crew were English, and continual translations were necessary on set. The language advisor Diarmaid de Faoite provided the leading man with a tape of Connacht Irish to counteract the Donegal influence of the leading lady, but it was still a struggle. There was no facility for the director to see the rushes either, due budgetary constraints. However, despite all of this, the finished film is remarkably coherent. Whilst native speakers dislike the unexplained mixing of dialects within one family, the larger audience of those with little Irish do not tend to notice.

[17] *Misteach* is an obvious exception here, as the story relies on pedantry for its humour.

[18] Whilst grammatically accurate, the translated versions often lack something of the energy of the original. However, *Clare sa Spéir* at least has gained in translation, according to the writer O'Reilly, who remarks with pleasure on the improvement occasioned by a particular improvisation: the husband's nasty 'serves her right' as the tree shakes in a high wind becomes *is olc an ghaoth* – with all the added nuance the *seanfhocal* [proverb] implies (O'Reilly, 2001).

examine. *Lipservice* and *Tubberware* set out explicitly to examine this inside/outside schema in Irish life. The latter film takes a year in the life of a place in Conamara, and watches the type of people who pass through. What are they looking for? What do they bring/take? Can a community sustain this flow of observers?[19] It would be interesting to see more insider views on the outsiders in future *Oscailt* and Lasair films.

Surprisingly, there is not a significant thematic emphasis on what for most Irish viewers would be the defining characteristic of the film – the language. Three films include snatches of other languages. Lest we become too caught up in the Irish/English binary, it should be noted that other languages feature in the films as well, making cameo appearances: French is used in *Cosa Nite* and *An Leabhar* to denote a cosmopolitan European context. Ireland's involvement with European tradition is also indicated in *Aqua*, where medieval Hiberno-Latin foretells the future. Incidentally, in this film, the throwaway reference to grammar strikes at what many audience members would regard as the heart of the Irish language. The professor identifies the strange River language as twelfth century Hiberno-Latin. The prospect of the end of the world loses its sting as it is couched in ungrammatical terms.

Whilst there are interesting differences between city and country characters' use of Irish, few characters in the *Oscailt* films have a psychologically complicated relationship with the language – usually it is a question of blind acceptance. In some films this is an ideological decision (Irish as a normal and natural means of communication: *Dallacán*). In others, it is due to a reluctance to burden the short film with such a complex theme. In *Cosa Nite* and *An Leabhar*, attention is drawn to the existence of other linguistic options apart from English. These are the films made with a specifically Gaeltacht colouring. Paul Mercier, a former teacher of Irish, but not a native speaker, has the most developed argument to make in this area. He thinks that a powerful story will, as a side effect, promote the language in which it is made (Mercier, 2001).

The Future

The future of Irish film-making in general, and in film-making in Irish in particular, remains uncertain. As Higgins puts it: *"we're really... seed-planting... at the moment. We haven't yet reaped any harvest"* (Higgins, 2001). Irish film has yet to define a voice or voices that would distinguish it from other anglophone cinemas. Starting with the advantage of a literally alternative language, the *Oscailt* scheme is ideally placed to explore themes such as official pretence and local reality, questions of belonging, aside from specifically Gaeltacht or linguistic issues. However, the use of this alternative language brings its attendant

---

[19] There is by no means universal hostility between the communities: tourists and students enrich and energise the *Gaeltacht*: TG4, 2001

[20] Mercier envisages a distinctive Irish film style emerging in the future, once the twin hurdles of funding and foreign influence are vaulted. Mercier is also quoted in Hayden, 1999: "We can't afford to lose this language under any circumstances. We're losing vocabulary by the week. We're losing words. We're losing a view of life, a way of looking at life".

difficulties. As well as the burden of trying to find or express a unique Irishness in the cultural or stylistic sense, the *Oscailt* narratives are also expected to justify the use of the Irish language. In order to refute charges of gimmickry, they must use this medium to show something that could not have been done in any other way.

If there is to be a new view of this self, we must also consider the audience. To whom are we mediating these versions? And to what end? Inevitably, in a study of this kind, there will be as much a focus on the teller as on the tale. This self-reflexivity and awareness of the medium relates closely to the traditions of *Béaloideas*.

Obviously, a project of this scale cannot hope to ride to victory on the back of an under-funded television station. Nevertheless, since 1996, TG4 has been widely regarded as iconoclastic in relation to Irish language and associated culture. TG4's policies to date have been consistently innovative. They rely on the enthusiasm of independent production companies, and their very raison d'être is to be different. Most importantly of all, they do not have the burden of serving the entire nation. This frees them to experiment and to find minority interests for niche audiences. In spite of the obvious difficulties, present prospects are the brightest yet seen in Ireland. There is a new scheme for a feature in Irish (jointly funded by TG4 and An Bord Scannán). Scripts are currently being shortlisted for development funding, and it is hoped that a full-length Irish language feature will appear in the next five years. According to Cilian Fennell, director of programming at TG4, it will take at least another ten years (not only for Irish language, but Irish film in general) to evolve a distinctive Irish film style – or failing that, at least a greater confidence with the medium. This implies different approaches to the process of film-making as well as to narrative itself.

The *Oscailt* films to date are *preabadh na súl* ['blink of an eye'] – a glimpse of an aspect that may or may not deserve a deeper treatment. They are the first step into unexplored territory, to a place where others may have been, but where the *Oscailt* perspectives reveal aspects that the others have not seen.

References

Barbrook, Richard. 1992. "Broadcasting and National identity in Ireland". *Media, Culture and Society*. 14.2: 203-27

Chesire, Geoffrey. 2001. "Let's Have More Playfulness". *The Irish Times*. 16 July.

Fennell, Cilian. 2001. Personal Interview. 26 June

Fennell, Desmond. 1985. "How Not to See Ireland". *The Crane Bag*. 9.1: 92-3

Hall, Stuart. 2000. "Culture, Communication and Nationalism". *Cultural Studies* 7.3: 349-63

Hayden, Joanne. 1999. "A+". *Film West*. 34: 36-7

Higgins, Michael D. 2001. Personal Interview. 4 July

Kiberd, Declan. 2000. *Irish Classics*. London: Granta Books

Mercier, Paul. 2001. Personal Interview. 5 July

Lehane, Pearse. 2001. Personal Interview. 14 June

McLoone, Martin. 2000. *Irish Film: The Emergence of a Contemporary Cinema*. London: British Film Institute

Minihan, Mary. 2000. "TG4 Says Audience Figures up 92% in a Year". *Irish Times*. 13.9.2000

Murray, Paddy. 2000. 'Dúil sa Dúlra': Review. *The Sunday Tribune*. April 2000
Ní Ghráinne, Proinsias. 2001. Email correspondence, 12.7.2001
Ó Cofaigh, Ciarán. 2001. Personal Interview, 5.6.2001
O'Reilly, Audrey. 2001. Personal Interview, 10.7.2001
Ó Scolaí, Darach. 2001. Public Seminar, 24.8.2001
Phelan, James. 1999. in *Film West*. 35: 62-3

Personal, Political and Preternatural: Troy Kennedy Martin's *Edge of Darkness* and A.L. Kennedy's *So I Am Glad*

Kirsty A. Macdonald

> The only thing you can do if you are trapped in a reflection is to invert the image.[1]

"Apart from all the bad things in the world and all the bad things in my head, we were all right" (222), claims the narrator, Jennifer, of A.L. Kennedy's 1995 novel, *So I Am Glad.* She is referring to her relationship with the ghost of Savinien de Cyrano de Bergerac, somehow translated from seventeenth-century France into present-day urban Scotland. Savinien is an ambiguous presence, an evasive spirit who is nevertheless intimately physical to Jennifer. Similarly, in Troy Kennedy Martin's 1985 television serial, *Edge of Darkness,* central protagonist Detective Inspector Ronnie Craven maintains a relationship with his murdered daughter Emma, who guides and encourages him through his investigations into her death. The nature of this problematically supernatural relationship subverts conventional realism. During his grief-driven investigations Craven uncovers global corruption and the rotten core of the nuclear power industry, illustrating the central theme of both works: time and again, the bad things of the mind correspond to and comment upon the bad things in the world. The preternatural figures of Savinien and Emma symbolise and catalyse the exposure and potential resolution of individual pain and public sickness, as the ontogenetic is translated macrocosmically into the phylogenetic.

This interpenetration of the personal and the cultural is discussed by Freud in his seminal essay on the inexplicable in literature and in life, "The Uncanny". Freud traces how the origins of uncanniness can be located ontogenetically in the repression and due return of infantile complexes, and also phylogenetically in the case of general primitive and superstitious beliefs which have been surmounted, but which then appear to be confirmed by some impression. In literature, such impressions often take forms which could be interpreted as supernatural. Freud states, however, that:

> we must not let our predilection for smooth solutions and lucid exposition blind us to the fact that these two classes of uncanny experience are not always sharply distinguishable. When we consider that primitive beliefs are most intimately connected with infantile complexes, and are, in fact, based on them, we shall not be greatly astonished to find that the distinction is often a hazy one. (249)

Indeed, these texts confirm this lack of distinction. Individual protagonists struggle to cope with personal trauma, symbiotically reflecting and reflected by national depravity. Moreover, the manifestation of potentially supernatural forces undermines and destabilises certainties held by the educated, middle class and

---

[1] Juliet Mitchell. 1975. *Psychoanalysis and Feminism*. London: Penguin

seemingly, therefore, sophisticated protagonists, betraying them to the superstitions they should have surmounted. This preternatural eruption into the 'real' also has an artistically subversive effect. Rosemary Jackson views fantastic literature, those ambiguous texts which Freud would deem 'uncanny', as already inherently subversive.[2] She states that, "Its introduction of the 'unreal' is set against the category of the 'real' – a category which the fantastic interrogates by its difference" (4). These texts initially employ the Realist mode and often an urban setting, dominant features of twentieth-century Scottish fiction and drama, but then transgress the rules of 'reality' through the introduction of that which is blatantly unreal, even anti-real. Freud argues that this technique magnifies uncanniness, stating: "[The writer] deceives us by promising to give us the sober truth, and then after all overstepping it [...] by the time we have seen through his trick it is already too late and the author has achieved his object" (250). Here, as elsewhere, the object is subversion of Realism and the restrictions it conventionally imposes. Yet in *Edge of Darkness* and *So I Am Glad* this automatic subversion of the rules of the 'real' is further employed to energise, stimulate and foreground a deeper political critique and interrogation.

The supernatural nonetheless remains highly ambiguous in these texts, a motif in Scottish literature with a lengthy and notable history.[3] Are the ghosts supernatural or psychological? This conventional tension is radically reworked in both texts, as the 'ghosts' are placed in an almost entirely secular context, and are also in no way malevolent, proving remedial rather than diabolic. Tradition and innovation are combined to produce a textual ambivalence, simultaneously new and old. Yet regardless of their exact origins, the ghosts advance a direct influence over events. Douglas Gifford interprets Savinien thus:

> Jennifer needs both to avoid and atone; Cyrano answers both needs. He has lived with violence yet has a code of honour; is disfigured yet acceptable; and has sensitivity unavailable to modern males. He can understand distortion and articulate dilemma – and Jennifer desperately needs to understand and articulate. He is the correlative for her yearning to be free of herself. Read thus, the book is about a process of self-healing in a nasty modern world [...]. (620)

---

[2] A lack of terminological distinction in the field of fantastic literature is confusingly prevalent. Tzvetan Todorov defines the fantastic as something very similar to the Freudian uncanny, yet uses the term 'uncanny' to label something else entirely. See Tzvetan Todorov. 1975. *The Fantastic: A Structural Approach to a Literary Genre*. Trans. Richard Howard. New York: Cornell University Press. Meanwhile, Rosemary Jackson uses the terms 'the fantastic' and 'fantasy' interchangeably – an inaccuracy in my opinion. 'Fantasy', I argue, is that literature dealing entirely with tertiary worlds, and not set in or making reference to our world, similar to that which Todorov deems 'marvellous'.

[3] The juxtaposition of the supernatural with a pragmatic realism has been present in Scottish literature from the ballads onwards, and this supernatural/psychological tension has become a Scottish literary tradition since James Hogg's novel, *The Private Memoirs and Confessions of a Justified Sinner* (1824). It is evident in many other recent texts, such as Wilson Harris's *Black Marsden* (1972), Alasdair Gray's *Lanark* (1981), and Muriel Spark's *The Ballad of Peckham Rye* (1960) and *Symposium* (1990).

Intimating a wholly psychological reading, this interpretation fails to satisfy and leaves many questions unanswered. Savinien is seen by others, and forms a close fraternal bond with Jennifer's housemate Arthur. Moreover, in an appealing, magically real touch, he glows in the dark, something that Jennifer initially finds frightening. She tells us:

> The kitchen is really quite gloomy by this time and it should be difficult to see Martin, but in fact he is far more visible than he has any right to be. When he opens his mouth for any length of time there is a pale gleam which reminds me insanely of the light from a self-sealing envelope if you peel it apart in the dark. An unnatural, static blue flash. His hands and face are simply burning. (12)

If inventing an imaginary lover, why choose an alien and unnerving detail such as this? A fabrication has the potential to be perfect, whereas Savinien is attractively flawed. The ambiguity, however, is maintained to the last through the fact that Jennifer relates the entire story. She tells us herself at the beginning, "If you find what I tell you now rather difficult to believe, please treat it as fiction. I won't be offended" (12), and at the novel's conclusion that "sometimes the best beginning is a lie" (280). Savinien's origins, then, become of secondary importance. What is significant is the function he performs in the novel. As a seventeenth-century French gentleman whose favoured pastimes were writing and fighting, he is an alien in terms of time, place and social class. His incongruous perspective, as he comes up against poverty, crime, homelessness and drug addiction, allows for the defamiliarisation of our world. Savinien remarks:

> You are defenceless and your world is breaking in half. In all honesty, I believe your world has broken, it has split itself apart. There is such savagery and darkness and then such ridiculous openness. (228)

This sounds uncannily like a contemporary re-eruption of the Caledonian Anti-syzygy; that ghost which haunts Scottish writing. Through this estrangement, Kennedy's critique of our world comes to the fore. What is revealed through Savinien's untrained eyes is the horrific actuality of society, violent and malevolent, but also the kindness and love an individual is capable of within that society. Modern urban Scotland is the place where extremes meet.

Savinien can additionally be interpreted as an individual symptom or product of this warped community. Like Emma in *Edge of Darkness,* he exists in a most tangible form for his earthly counterpart, and like Craven, Jennifer has a dark and as yet unresolved past. Drawing on Freud's earlier work, the psychoanalysts Nicolas Abraham and Marie Torok theorise the presence of such spectres in their formulation of "the phantom".[4] The phantom bridges Freud's ontogenetic and phylogenetic categories of the uncanny, moving the focus of psychoanalytic inquiry from the individual to the dark secrets of the collective psychology inherited by that individual from their forefathers. As Torok states: "In general

---

[4] Abraham and Torok first posit their theory of the phantom in 1975 in the essays "Notes on the Phantom: A Complement to Freud's Metapsychology" and "Story of Fear: The Symptoms of Phobia – the Return of the Repressed or the Return of the Phantom?"

terms, the 'phantom' is a formation in the dynamic unconscious that is found there not because of the subject's own repression but on account of a *direct empathy with the unconscious or rejected psychic matter of a parental object*" (181). The afflicted individual is unwittingly compelled to repeat or perform displaced representations of the repressed family secret, such as Jennifer's repeated meditation on guilt which stems from the psychological abuse she suffered from her parents. Yet it is also a national secret, unavoidably passed down from generation to generation. She says: "I have a feeling about that – I'm guilty. Guilt is of course not an emotion in the Celtic countries, it is simply a way of life – a kind of gleefully painful social anaesthetic" (36). Savinien the phantom, then, can be viewed as the personification and outward projection of that guilt, like Emma he is a piece of an unresolved past made tangible. Later, Jennifer tells us: "I thought that my miserableness would imprint on the house, on time, and that this section of my life would remain behind me like a sad ghost" (130). The phantom's presence, with its origins in the individual psyche and the collective unconscious, is made somatic and preternatural via the weight of what it signifies. Like a sad ghost left behind and accumulating detritus, it embodies the guilt of an entire culture. As phantom, Savinien's presence in Jennifer's life obliges her to compulsively repeat and act out the repressed secret of guilt. This takes the form of re-visitation of her past, painful discussion of her family and violence, in one extreme episode in the form of a sado-masochistic sex session taken too far, echoing the perverse sexuality of her parents, and the "public sicknesses" (95) of her society. Savinien is useful to Jennifer because he is externalised and therefore safe. Yet because of what he represents, it is only when he physically and psychically leaves that resolution and coherence of identity can be achieved. As Douglas Gifford argues: "Cyrano is her means of cure; she must then paradoxically move towards losing him, since he represents her lack and need" (621). In the dramatic conclusion, Savinien returns to the otherworld, be that to the supernatural afterlife or to Jennifer's mind as the neutralised 'other', and this is when she realises: "I will be glad" (280).

In a cognate way, Emma's origins are never conclusively revealed. A psychological interpretation is attractive, given the extreme grief Craven is undergoing – he is even briefly signed in to a psychiatric hospital – and the fact that no-one else appears to witness Emma's presence. Yet there is one point in the action where she directly intervenes. During his investigation she directs him towards a list of underground stations, which actually turns out to be a map of access to the Northmoor nuclear facility, hidden in a cookery book between the pages of the recipe Craven was going to cook for Emma on the night of her death. Craven could not have known of the map's existence or location without some unexplained assistance. Through the voice-over technique Martin employs to heighten ambiguity, which allows the audience to hear Emma yet not see her, and thus still question her reality, she says to her father: "I've been trying to tell you about this for ages" (103). The either/or tension is again maintained to the last, as the high speed and rapid scene-change involved in the medium combines with the extreme ambiguity of events to elude any solid conclusion.

Yet in many ways more significant than Emma's potential preternaturalism is the suggestion of the supernatural around other characters, in particular Craven himself and his other guide, the formidable yet fun Texan CIA agent, Darius

Jedburgh. Jedburgh himself tells Craven, "I'm your magic helper" (67), a direct reference to the supernatural agents discussed by Vladimir Propp in his *Morphology of the Folktale* (43-6). Moreover, when discussing the misdeeds of Jerry Grogan, boss of the American Fusion Corporation, Jedburgh instigates the following exchange:

> JEDBURGH: He's part of the Dark Forces who would rule this planet.
> CRAVEN: You believe in all that stuff?
> JEDBURGH: Yeah, sure. Why not? Look at yourself. You think of yourself as an English provincial Detective [...] whose daughter died in tragic circumstances. Yet where she fell a well sprang, flowers grew. Now what kind of power is that? (142)

Jedburgh refuses to let Craven dwell in his personal pain and forces him to witness and play a part in the wider global implications of that which he is uncovering. What he discovers is that Emma was murdered indirectly by the representatives of a conspiracy involving certain government officials and the company running Northmoor, due to her membership of the direct action environmental group GAIA and her subsequent discovery of an illegal and dangerous 'hot cell' with nuclear reprocessing capabilities within Northmoor. Gaia, the Greek earth-goddess, also lends her name to a theory expounded by NASA scientist James Lovelock, explaining how the earth will always maintain its equilibrium regardless of humanity's actions, pollution and climate change etc.[5] Ultimately, Gaia is the phylogenetic role Emma metaphorically assumes for Craven, instructing him on how the planet will regulate itself and always in the end overcome adversity. Emma pleads with her father: "don't spend your last hours seeking revenge, Dad. The planet will do it for us...in time" (165), something which Craven ultimately accepts, telling Jedburgh that he is "on the side of the planet" (175). As the story develops into global allegory, Craven comes to represent the figure of the Green Man of nature from Celtic legend, a man yet "on the side of the planet". This was to have been affirmed in the original ending of the series, which Martin agreed to scrap after discussion with director Martin Campbell. Craven was to have been shot by a sniper under the direction of the conspiracy due to the knowledge he held, his body then metamorphosing into a tree over many years. As a literary metaphor this may well have been acceptable, but visually perhaps it would have been rather excessive. Instead, black flowers begin to grow – the black flowers Emma discusses as the representatives of the spirit of Gaia and indicators that the planet is about to shed itself of its human hindrance. With either ending, Craven's personal history and struggle become representative of that of the planet.

The bodies of Craven and Jedburgh add a further layer of meaning to this theme. During their illegal expedition into Northmoor they willingly expose themselves to radiation, Jedburgh going so far as to steal several bars of plutonium and carry them out of the facility in a plastic Harrods bag. As the final episodes progress, we witness the men's steady deterioration towards death, radiation sickness effectively corrupting them from the inside out. The outward visual

---

[5] James Lovelock. 1979. *Gaia: A New Look at Life on Earth*. Oxford: Oxford University Press

symptoms – the dark lesions that begin to disfigure and dehumanise their faces – are the last signs to appear, an impotent and ironic warning as by then death is inevitable. In a contemporary review of the series, Ruth Baumgarten brilliantly comments on the rotting bodies of Jedburgh and Craven thus:

> They resurface as contagious, deadly spectres whose one and only ally against the greedy, power-hungry plutonium lords and politicians is their own disintegration, their own physical alliance with the earth's merciful power to decompose. (36)

They willingly return to the earth and to inertia, that which according to Freud all humanity ultimately desires as a means of concluding pain and anxiety,[6] but not before their symbolic bodies have given testimony to and interrogated the concealed corruption at the heart of the nuclear industry. Signifying and prefiguring the effect large-scale nuclear accident or war would have on the planet, their physical deterioration acts as a bleak warning to humanity. Yet the visible manifestations of this individual, and potentially global the metaphor suggests, illness indicate irretrievability. This increases the poignancy and immediacy of a warning that in Thatcherite Britain during the Cold War would have already been terrifyingly current for many. The series crystallised the contemporary fears of an entire community, symbolised in the way in which the body becomes the potential national body, internally corrupt and inevitably drawn towards self-annihilation and death.

Similarly, in Kennedy's novel, the state of the nation is temporarily metaphorised in the illness-riddled body of Savinien. He returns to Jennifer after several months' absence, having experienced the urban underworld of homelessness and drug addiction. Yet this journey does not leave him untouched. Jennifer notes how: "[I]t was obvious he had lost a good deal of weight. His arms and legs were pale, marked with old and new bruises, cuts, his feet were raw, swollen" (152). His return forces his withdrawal from an addiction to 'atties', Ativan or "happy pills" (162), which involves copious vomiting, shaking, sweating and aggressive behaviour. This incident is prefigured by Jennifer's socially critical comments on the contents of a skip: "Probably there are some abandoned syringes in there, too. We have passed the time when anywhere in this city will be entirely free of used syringes, of our public sicknesses" (95). Public sickness is translated into Savinien's personal suffering, and later, when observing her friend and lover in his misery, Jennifer tells us:

> I moved close enough to notice the whole bed was shaking. The hands clutching the quilt to his throat were shuddering. I watched his mechanism breaking down and didn't know if there would be anything to replace it […]. (163)

Yet Savinien does get better, an alternative mechanism presenting itself in the form of his love for Jennifer, a different kind of dependency from which they must

---

[6] See Freud's discussion of the "death instinct" – which he believed to be the strongest of human drives – in *Beyond the Pleasure Principle*.

both later undergo a withdrawal. His process of healing optimistically implies the possible resolution and rectification of society's ills. Yet this remains a potential unfulfilled as yet, as confirmed by Jennifer's future tense concluding statement: "I will be glad" (280). The novel's exposure of these ills, like the decomposing bodies of Jedburgh and Craven, acts as a call for change. Healing is possible for the individual, but for society it remains to be seen.

The ontogenetic and the phylogenetic, therefore, dialectically co-exist and interfuse in these texts. The supernatural performs the translation from personal pain and suffering to political corruption and national malignancy, its radical departure from Realism allowing it to metaphorise and embody the macrocosmic within the microcosmic. Restricted by the domination of Realism in twentieth century Scottish fiction and drama, many late twentieth-century writers choose to 'invert the image'. Troy Kennedy Martin and A.L. Kennedy carry out this inversion in these texts by self-consciously introducing that which is overtly 'not-real', transgressing the conventions of urban and political literature. This initial subversion sanctions a further and more recondite interrogation of how things are, offering, through the call for change these critical texts represent, the optimistic possibility of the human ability to transform.

References

Abraham, Nicholas and Marie Torok. 1994. *The Shell and the Kernel*. Vol. 1. Ed. Nicholas T. Rand. Chicago: Chicago University Press

Baumgarten, Ruth. 1985. "Nukes and Spooks". *The Listener*. 31 October: 36

Freud, Sigmund. 1955. *The Standard Edition of the Complete Psychological Works of Sigmund Freud*. Vol. XVII. Trans. James Strachey. London: Hogarth Press

Gifford, Douglas. 1997. "Contemporary Fiction II: Seven Writers in Scotland". Douglas Gifford and Dorothy Macmillan. Eds. *A History of Scottish Women's Writing*. Edinburgh: Edinburgh University Press. 604-29

Jackson, Rosemary. 1981. *Fantasy: The Literature of Subversion*. London: Routledge

Kennedy, A.L. 1995. *So I Am Glad*. London: Jonathan Cape

Lovelock, James 1979. *Gaia: A New Look at Life on Earth*. Oxford: Oxford University

Martin, Troy Kennedy. 1990. *Edge of Darkness*. dir. Martin Campbell. london: Faber and Faber.

Mitchell, Juliet. 1975. *Psychoanalysis and Feminism*. london: Penguin

Propp, Vladimir. 1968. *Morphology of the Folktale*. austin: University of Texas Press

Objectifying the Body and Embodying the Object in the Poetry of Eavan Boland

Claire McEwen

Eavan Boland began to write in what she terms as "an enclosed, self-confident literary culture", a time when women were repeatedly denied access to all areas of social and cultural discourse (1996, ix). One of her key themes, made explicit in her prose writing, is the relationship between woman as object and woman as subject, and the need to address the objectification of women in Irish literature. In her prose work, *Object Lessons*, she outlines the ways in which she believes women have been written out of Irish literature and how they have been used as symbols of a nation that they are denied full active participation in. The subjugation and silencing of women in Irish literature and history is well documented and the image of Ireland as a woman, a beautiful maiden or a mother sending her sons out to die for their country, has become such a prevailing image of the nation that it has permeated all aspects of Irish women's experience. The Cathleen of Celtic Revival literature, the impossible perfection of the Virgin Mary and the prevailing figures of Erin and Mother Ireland are myths which have reinforced each other creating a powerful and enduring fiction. This concept of an iconic feminine is, as Sabina Sharkey notes, highly problematic:

> [T]his configuration of Ireland, namely one which presents a mythical eternal Goddess enshrined within a collective psyche […] avoids any sense of its constructedness, rather it presents itself as an already given. […] This process is given little explanation, it is read as the activation of an enduring consciousness. (6)

Boland's efforts to rewrite the mythic representation of women in Irish literature become limited by her topological engagement with the very myths that she seeks to undermine. She attempts to challenge the 'given' of female representation, by adopting Gerardine Meaney's proposition of a "demythologizing critique", in which the poet confronts the "myth of Mother Ireland with the reality of women's lived experience" (1998, 237). However, this approach fails to establish a critique which is sufficiently discrete from the original myth in its acceptance of it as a 'given'. As Eibhlín Evans notes, such critiques must be concerned as much with "revival" as with "resistance and revision". This 'revival' entails, according to Evans, "a reaching through history and tradition to an other space, a going beyond that tradition, political, religious and literary, whilst in dialogue with it, in an attempt to create and partake of a new one."[1] It is this lack of an alternative space or tradition that limits Boland's engagement with a nationalist discourse. She fails to recognise the existence of an alternative tradition of women's writing and perpetuates the myths of silent and objectified women without questioning them to any significant extent. Her efforts to give voice to women's silenced history are

---

[1] Eibhlín Evans, 'Making Up', *The Conference on Contemporary Poetry*, Rutgers University (24th-27th April 1997), conference paper published at http://english.rutgers.edu/making_up.htm

similarly limited by her engagement with the nation as it has been represented in the past. Edna Longley has criticised Boland for this, arguing that:

> [S]he takes the 'national tradition' for granted [...]. By not asking *why* 'as a poet I could not easily do without the idea of a nation', Boland fails to challenge an idea of Irish poetry which is narrow as well as patriarchal. She [...] regrets that 'the Irish nation as an existing construct in Irish poetry was not available to me', without considering how that construct itself, both inside and outside poetry, has marginalised and scarred many Irish women and men. (16-7)

By failing to interrogate the tradition that she claims to reject, Boland is fundamentally accepting of its authority. Her earlier work, in particular the poems "The Achill Woman" and "Mise Eire", seems to operate very much within the discourses that she attempts to redress; the women in these poems have little or no agency and appear emblematic and silent. Indeed, Clair Wills comments that "Boland herself does not so much represent female experience as trope it" (258). There is a danger that, in an effort to foreground women's lived experience in relation to the nation, Boland fails to engage with the clichés that she seeks to undermine and simply substitutes them with new ones.

However, when Boland adopts an object as emblem, her representations of womanhood, and nationhood, are significantly more successful. This strategy perhaps leans more towards Meaney's second definition of a "feminist critique of Irish culture" in which the writer "concentrates on destabilizing myth from within, through parody, revision and re-appropriation of the figures, forms and representations of women" (1998, 237). Boland has discussed the use of the object as symbol in her poetry as a means to replace the use of the 'erotic object', which she views as a specifically masculine form. In *Object Lessons* she states:

> It stands to reason that the project of the woman poet, connected as it is by dark bonds to the object she once was, cannot make a continuum with the sexualized erotic of the male poem. The true difference women poets make as authors of the poem is in sharp contrast with the part they were assigned as objects in it. As objects they were once images. As images they were eroticized and distanced. ... [they] became tropes and figures, at once celebrated and silenced. (1996, 232)

Boland asserts a definitive move away from the literary tradition here; she sees no way of establishing a continuum with the past and asserts her intention to use her power as author to undermine that tradition. The object itself perhaps becomes what Bill Brown has described as a 'thing' in which "the thing really names less an object than a particular subject-object relation" (4). This concept works in two ways in Boland's poetry. Firstly, Boland uses domestic objects that are part of her life as a woman and a mother and juxtaposes them with her role as a poet. This opposition is made explicit in her writing and serves to foreground the function of the object as emblem rather than the woman; the woman is finally the subject of the poem. Secondly, the creation of a space between the subject and the object, rather than establishing a binary, merges the two and echoes the disconnection associated with women's roles within Irish society, history, and literature. The 'space' represents the hidden history of Irish women and affords an opportunity to 'revive' their voices. Sheila C. Conboy comments that, in this aspect of Boland's work, she is:

> attempting to redefine femininity – most obviously by exploring the ways in which the realm of domestic life can be translated into poetic material, more subtly by appropriating and transfiguring classical forms of literature previously dominated by men. (65)

Thus, the relation between subject and object in Boland's work demonstrates her desire to re-write the masculine poetic tradition of woman as emblem by replacing it with object, or emblem, as representative *of* woman. In addition, the use of the domestic object also serves to legitimise and reconcile her own roles as woman and poet. Boland uses objects as a means to negotiate with the Irish literary and national traditions in an attempt to justify her own writing and role within them. Brian Dillon remarks of the poem "The Black Lace Fan My Mother Gave Me" that Boland "leaves important questions about how the fan functions as both real object and symbol suspended in uncertainty. And with that suspension the poem sings" (322). Rather than establishing binaries, as in much of her other work, the use of objects offers an alternative space for Boland to explore the intersections between myth and history, gender and nation. It is this aspect of her work that I wish to examine here by demonstrating how she attempts to create her own emblems of history and how she ultimately comes to terms with the inability of objects to represent.

"Lava Cameo", from the 1994 collection *In a Time of Violence*, uses a brooch made of volcanic rock that she found in an antiques fair as a metaphor for Boland's construction of the silent and painful history of her grandmother. In *Object Lessons*, Boland describes how the brooch came to be an emblem of her ancestor, how she "found an emblem for her even before I realized I would find it difficult to name her life. Or my own" (1996, 32). She continues:

> There was a complexity for me remembering the cameo, and the more I thought about it, the more complex it became. […] To cut a human face into what had once flowed, fiery and devouring, past farms and villages and livestock. To make a statement out of something which was already a statement of random and unsparing destruction. All these acts were very far from being simple. They were ironic and self-conscious. (1996, 33)

The lava cameo symbolises the writing-out of Boland's grandmother's life as it is described in *Object Lessons*, the lack of naming, how she "will never even be / sepia" (1995, 196). This attempt to use the violent construction of the lava cameo as an allegory for the woman's life is what David Lloyd defines as "migrant kitsch" whose "allegorical function is to gesture towards a trauma which will not and cannot be fully acknowledged" (92). Boland recognises that she is incapable of representing the unrepresentable; the trauma of history and the silencing of her grandmother. By embodying history in an object rather than a woman, Boland identifies the problems she faces in trying to write the nation and avoids the feminisation of history that has prevailed in the past.

"Lava Cameo" begins with a single line, "I like this story". Separated from the rest of the poem by space and by a dash, this line establishes the poem as a construction, particularly when it is later reinforced by the lines: "except that it is not a story,/ more a rumour or a folk memory". Boland appears to be conscious of her own collusion with mythic tropes here and of the intersection of poetry and prose, oral and written accounts. Her representation of her grandmother is entirely fictional and this is underlined throughout the poem in various ways including the use of prepositions, for example: "If I say wool and lace for her skirt" and "If I make her pace the Cork docks". Although Boland's use of the lava cameo is problematic, she appears to be very aware of that and makes this clear in the poem. She writes:

> there is a way of making free with the past,
> a pastiche of what is
> real and what is
> not, which can only be
> justified if you think of it
>
> not as sculpture but syntax:
>
> a structure extrinsic to meaning which uncovers
> the inner secret of it. (1995, 196)

Boland argues that the use of the object as a representation of a real figure is justified as a poetic tool, as "syntax", and that it is a means for her to interrogate history without implicating herself in any direct way. The play on "past" and "pastiche" emphasises the danger of falling into kitsch when conflating memory with history. The inner rhyme pulls the poem down, linking the key words such as "justified", "sculpture", "syntax", "structure", "extrinsic", to the final line here, "inner secret", which is in turn linked to the concluding line "*In*scribe catastrophe". The words that are highlighted demonstrate the problematic nature of representation, the inability of words to "inscribe catastrophe", to represent. In her awareness of this, Boland uses the lava cameo in the sense of Pierre Nora's "*lieux de memoir*" or sites of memory. According to Nora:

> History, because it is an intellectual and secular production, calls for analysis and criticism. Memory installs remembrance within the sacred ... Memory takes root in the concrete, in spaces, gestures, images, and objects; history binds itself strictly to temporal continuities, to progressions and to relations between things. (8-9)

For Nora, memory is firmly embedded in, and can only be represented by, an object or a site of memory. In "Lava Cameo", the object functions in just this way, representing a life about which Boland knows very little and constructing a version of that life which is not history but memory. As such, the object becomes an emblem of the relation between the object and the subject, rather than of the woman herself. In this way, Boland demonstrates the inherent lack in representation and avoids limiting the figure of the woman to emblematic status by making it clear in the poem that the object is a 'structure' which, in a highly personal way, "uncovers/ the inner secret" of her grandmother's history. In the final stanza of the poem, Boland appeals directly to the memory of her grandmother:

> Look at me, I want to say to her: show me
> the obduracy of an art which can
> arrest a profile in the flux of hell.
>
> Inscribe catastrophe.

Boland seeks reassurance that her means of representation is valid and appropriate, that she has the ability to write her grandmother's life into the text. However, the use of "I want" and, earlier, "Please", suggests that this desire cannot be fulfilled. In addition, the frequent use of pronouns ensures that the poet's presence is felt throughout the poem; this is a direct appeal and one which is carefully structured in three distinct sections indicated by the use of the separated lines and the dash and colons. The final line, again separated, demonstrates the poet's ultimate failure and the use of "arrest" suggests her own forced attempt to "inscribe". The lava cameo is a problematic emblem of a woman's lived experience and Boland is very aware of this. That she feels the need to justify and elaborate upon the metaphor in *Object Lessons*, a fact that Brian Henry believes "diminishes the poem's importance" (197), also suggests her discomfort with the object. She searches for an art which can represent pain and suffering without becoming a clichéd version of the masculine tradition of woman as nation. In the final line, Boland parodies the use of a decorative object as a means of female representation and, questions the right of poets to "inscribe catastrophe" in a decorative emblem.

In the collection, *The Lost Land*, Boland's distrust of emblematic representation is more clearly expressed. In "Heroic", she describes her relationship with the nationalist tradition through her experience of seeing the statues of (male) historical figures in Dublin, and writes: "I looked up. And looked at him again./ He stared past me without recognition" (1998, 50). She is distanced from this male dominated history which offers no space for her and her writing and her role is one of observer, as emphasised by the repetition of "looked". However, she seeks acceptance and inclusion from that history when she states:

> I moved my lips and wondered how the rain
> Would taste if my tongue were made of stone.
> And wished it was. And whispered so that no one
> Could hear it but him: *make me a heroine*. (1998, 50)

Boland's desire for the same sort of immortality, the same impact on history as these men have had is implicit in the final line. She is ashamed to admit to her respect and adulation for them (she whispers her request) yet she is still assured enough to desire to be a "heroine", not a hero and not silent. Here, it is the men who have been silenced, their tongues are "made of stone" whilst Boland speaks. However, the mixture of tenses in the third stanza foregrounds the men's role in the present despite their confinement to the past and existence as objects: "His lips were still speaking. The gun / he held has just killed someone." Boland recognises the power of symbolic representation here; the statue, an object, is still relevant to and has an impact on contemporary society. The opening line, "Sex and history. And skin and bone", links the statue to life, the past to the present. In particular, the pairing of "Sex" and "history" highlights the way in which history has been gendered into distinct areas: the heroic male and the passive female. The relentless rhyme and use of short sentences create a sense of affirmation, foregrounding Boland's desire and formal ability to enter into the national tradition through her writing. This poem is linked to "Unheroic" from earlier in the same collection which describes Boland, at the same age, working in a summer job in a hotel. The manager of the hotel has a "wound / from war or illness – no one seemed sure" and she creates a symbol of this wound which acts, for her, as a more appropriate emblem of the nation than the statues in Dublin. The final stanzas of the poem read:

> How do I know my country? Let me tell you
> it has been hard to do. And when I do
> go back to difficult knowledge, it is not
> to that street or those men raised
> high above the certainties they stood on –
> *Ireland hero history* – but how
>
> I went behind the linen room and up
> the stone stairs and climbed to the top.
> And stood for a moment there, concealed
> by shadows. In a hiding place.
> Waiting to see.
> Wanting to look again.
> Into the patient face of the unhealed. (1998, 23)

For Boland, the painful history of the past must be emphasised: she has written in her prose work about her use of a scar as a metaphor for trauma, a constant reminder of past violence, and this poem demonstrates her desire for a symbolic representation that can encompass that without glossing over the suffering that lies beneath. She challenges the authority of the terms "heroic" and "unheroic", ultimately replacing both with "heroine", and juxtaposes the statues with aspects of her own lived experience in order to integrate her voice in the national tradition. In these poems, Boland perceives that her efforts to give voice to women's silenced history can be achieved as part of the existing tradition rather than having to operate on a completely separate sphere, but in a different way and on her own terms.

   In "Imago", also from *The Lost Land*, Boland self-reflexively demonstrates her previously limiting use of objects as a means to represent women. The poem articulates the way in which stereotypes, as manifest in objects, have pervaded and influenced Irish writing:

> Head of a woman. Half-life of a nation.
> Coarsely-cut blackthorn walking stick.

Old Tara brooch.
And bog oak.
A harp and a wolfhound on an ashtray.

All my childhood
I took you for the truth.

I see you now for what you are.

My ruthless images. My simulacra.
Anti-art: a foul skill
traded by history
to show a colony

the way to make pain a souvenir. (1998, 18)

Boland defiantly lists the clichés of Irish cultural nationalism and acknowledges her own trade in them; they are *her* "ruthless images" and *her* "simulacra". Jean Baudrillard's concept of simulacra defines the usage as follows:

> When the real is no longer what it was, nostalgia assumes its full meaning. There is a plethora of myths of origin and signs of reality – a plethora of truth, of secondary objectivity, and authenticity. Escalation of the true, of lived experience, resurrection of the figurative where the object and substance have disappeared. (6-7)

By stating "my simulacra", Boland recognises her own role in the construction of an unrealistic representation of woman and land, of presenting Ireland as a wounded nation, and in making that a cultural commodity. The vehemence of the assertion in this poem is underlined by the lack of rhyme, ironically highlighted by the half rhyme of "what you are" and "simulacra", and the list of objects and short lines. Again, David Lloyd's notion of 'migrant kitsch' is important here for he states: "kitsch is congealed memory that expresses simultaneously the impossible desire to realize a relation to a culture only available in the form of recreation and the failure to transmit the past" (91). Rather than viewing 'migrant kitsch' as a collection of potent symbols or a form of cultural nationalism, however, Boland regards the objects as constructing a sense of history which is outdated, whose purported 'authenticity' is now recognised as a strategic construction. This is underlined by the use of compound and hyphenated words echoing the fragmented and jarring nature of their emblematic status, ultimately negating them with the juxtaposition of the infamous national emblems "harp" and "wolfhound" with the modern and everyday "ashtray". The rhyming of "history" and "colony" with the final word, "souvenir", highlights the way in which these emblems of an anti-colonial discourse no longer hold currency in a modern Ireland, how they have become "souvenirs" for both the booming tourist industry and a sentimental migrant kitsch. However, the final line also suggests that the way in which these emblems have been used has diminished their importance and sanitised their political relevance. Boland regrets her acceptance of traditional tropes and her own use of objects which are fundamentally limiting representations of the nation, yet she is aware that her use of these objects stems from her desire to be part of the Irish literary tradition. She has said of this desire, and her inability to realise it, that it was her "own need to locate myself in a powerful literary tradition in which [...] I had been an element of design rather than an agent of change" (1996, 138). She recognises that she has been highly influenced by the tradition and, although she wants to be able to engage with the past and with the nation, she does not want to indulge in the associated stereotypes of objects and emblems.

Mary Kenny states that the "dream of a 'Gaelic culture' is no candidate to define Ireland today", and it is this notion of a limiting myth, which holds no currency in a modern nation, that has inspired Irish women artists and writers to produce work which redefines and dispels them (388). "Women's lives *were* changing", continues Kenny, transformations in social, political and religious attitudes and legislation, fuelled by the Women's Movement, have dramatically changed the way in which women are both represented and regarded (295). In effect, the mythic representations of women that have, for so long, preoccupied female artists no longer hold the same currency or influence that they once did. Paula Murphy observes that:

> If the century opened with emphatic nationalistic depictions of woman as the image of Ireland, developments that have taken place in art and symbolism across the last hundred years reveal that related images of womanhood and Irishness at the close of the century are questioning rather than accepting, exploratory rather than declamatory. (100)

Boland's fundamental acceptance of ideas of 'the nation' and its relation to women makes her work reactionary rather than revisionist; she can only create new versions of established myths, emblems and landscapes rather than offering an alternative. Her early work fails to undermine the established literary tradition because she is both 'accepting' and 'declamatory'; she addresses concepts that, in their definitions, are highly problematic and set up binaries rather than subversions. In her use of objects Boland strives to create an alternative form of female representation to the traditional trope of woman as land without denying herself access to a national discourse. However, her success in this is limited by the assumptions that she makes about the relationship between gender and national identity, how, according to Gerardine Meaney, she assumes "either gender or nation to be constants for all (Irish) women across history" (1993, 145). By continually striving for a valid symbol of the nation and of woman, Boland fails to distance herself from the limiting discourses of the past, she simply creates new versions of them. In "Lava Cameo", the tensions between writing a feminine and a national poem and her own awareness of these limitations are demonstrated in the ambiguous nature of the writing and her inability to achieve any form of resolution. It is not until "Heroic" and "Imago" that Boland recognises these difficulties in her early work and succeeds in separating national and feminine objects and in resolving her own relationship to her predecessors in both literature and history.

References

Baudrillard, Jean. 1994. *Simulacra and Simulations*. Trans. Sheila Faria Glaser. Michigan: University of Michigan Press

Boland, Eavan. 1995. *Collected Poems*. Manchester: Carcanet

Boland, Eavan. 1998. *The Lost Land*. Manchester: Carcanet

Boland, Eavan. 1996. *Object Lessons*. London: Vintage

Brown, Bill. 2001. "Thing Theory". *Critical Review*. 28.1

Conboy, Sheila C. "'What You Have Seen is Beyond Speech': Female Journeys in the Poetry of Eavan Boland and Eilean Ni Chuillenain". *Canadian Journal of Irish Studies*. 26.1: 65-72

Dillon, Brian. 1999. "Attempts to Recover the 'Ordinary' in the Poetry of Eavan Boland". *Canadian Journal of Irish Studies*. 25.1-2: 309-322

Henry, Brian. 1997. "The Woman as Icon, The Woman as Poet". *Michigan Quarterly Review*. 36.1: 188-202

Kenny, Mary. 1997. *Goodbye to Catholic Ireland: A Social, Personal and Cultural History from the Fall of Parnell to the Realm of Mary Robinson*. London: Sinclair-Stevenson

Lloyd, David. 1999. *Ireland after History*. Cork: Cork University Press in association with Field Day

Longley, Edna. 1990. *From Cathleen to Anorexia: The Breakdown of Irelands*. Dublin: Attic Press

Meaney, Gerardine. 1998. "Landscapes of Desire: Woman and Ireland on Film". *Women: A Cultural Review*. 9.3: 237-51

Meaney, Gerardine. 1993. "Myth, History and the Politics of Subjectivity: Eavan Boland and Irish Women's Writing". *Women: A Cultural Review*. 4.2: 136-53

Murphy, Paula. 1998. "Madonna and Maiden, Mistress and Mother: Woman as Symbol of Ireland and Spirit of the Nation". James Christen Steward. Ed. *When Time Began to Rant and Rage: Figurative Painting from Twentieth-Century Ireland*. London: Merrell Holberton. 90-101

Nora, Pierre. 1989. "Between Memory and History: *Les Lieux de Memoire*". Trans. Marc Roudebush. *Representations*. 26: 7-25

Sharkey, Sabina. 1994. *Ireland and the Iconography of Rape: Colonisation, Constraint and Gender*. London: University of North London Press

Wills, Claire. 1991. "Contemporary Irish Women Poets: The Privatisation of Myth". Harriet Devine Jump. Ed. *Diverse Voices: Essays on Twentieth Century Women Writers in English*. Hemel Hempstead: Harvester Wheatsheaf. 248-72

Self-representation in the Poetry of W.B. Yeats and of Fernando Pessoa

Patricia Silva McNeill

The poetry of Yeats and Pessoa displays a type of self-representation that involves a rather experimental and innovative use of poetic *personae*. Their effort represents a conceptual and stylistic subversion of the convention of the poetic *persona*, which entails a differentiation between the poet and the subject of the poem. The changes enacted by the two poets upon this convention derived from an intention to achieve greater objectivity of expression, while still maintaining the subjectivity required by the lyric genre. Referring to Yeats's theory of the Mask, John Unterecker claims the following: "His problem was to discover a technique by which the personal could somehow be objectified, be given the appearance of impersonal 'truth' and yet remain the emotive force of privately felt belief" (30). His observation could equally apply to Pessoa's theory of heteronymy, which the poet envisaged as an "objectified subjectivity". On the one hand, they operated a division of the enunciating *persona* into several recurring *personae*. On the other hand, they extended the function of the *persona* outside the limitations of the poem. Conscious of the innovative practices, the poets developed a new terminology that could address the modernity of the process. The status of the poetic *personae* and the negotiation of dependency and autonomy are complex issues, undergoing various changes throughout their poetic development. In the early stages of their poetry we observe a greater interdependency between the poet and the *personae*.

The interdependency of the Yeatsian mask is particularly patent in the collection *The Wind Among the Reeds* (1899). In a first edition the *personae* Aedh (Aodh), Michael Robartes, and Hanrahan appear recurrently in the love poems (another *persona* being Mongan, though with only two occurrences in the collection). The function of these *personae* is akin to that of a pseudonym, in that they attempt to differentiate the poet from each particular *persona*. The content of the lyrics was autobiographical, concerning the poet's affective relationships with Maud Gonne and Olivia Shakespear. Therefore the personae functioned as masks, allowing the poet to express subjective emotions objectively. Unsurprisingly, the poet did not attribute much individuality to these personae, referring to them as 'principles of the mind' in his notes to the collection, in opposition to the term 'personages', which would have conferred a greater autonomy unto them (Yeats, 1996: 509). Alasdair Macrae claims that "each [of these *personae*] stood for a psychological attitude, as well as, for an occult quality" (129).

Subsequently, Yeats substituted the personal names for general types such as 'lover' or 'poet', 'hero' and 'sage', borrowed from Baudelaire. These entities possessed an archetypal quality (in Jung's sense of archetypes from the collective unconscious) that would perhaps render them more adequate, in the poet's view, for the articulation of mental, psychological and metaphysical questionings, as Ellmann identifies some of the 'types' that Yeats used in *Responsibilities* (1914) – – 'beggars', 'hermits' and 'fools', which Yeats used "to voice with safety opinions about life and afterlife that he is not prepared to guarantee" (205). His comment suggests that these imaginary figures were seen as a medium of self-revelation, of occultation. The poet resorted to this method from an early stage, and continued voicing often contradictory and disparate points through other such figures as 'shepherds', 'goatherds', 'foxhunters' and 'fishermen' throughout his work.

Yeats was beginning to systematise the 'theory of the Mask' around the time he wrote the poems in *Responsibilities*. Yeats envisaged the donning of a Mask as a transformation of the personality, claiming in *Per Amica Silentia Lunae* – "I think that all happiness depends on the energy to assume a mask of some other life; on a rebirth as something not one's self".[1] Elsewhere, he reinforces the differentiation between the poet and the Mask, arguing that poets should be "seeking an anti-self, a Mask that delineates a being in all things the opposite to their natural state" (Yeats, 1980: 247). Accordingly, the 'types' listed above embody lifestyles that are diametrically opposite to the poet's lifestyle. Much later in *A Vision*, he would establish this antinomy in the Great Wheel between the 'Daimonic' poet of phase 17 and the figures of phase 3, among which he lists 'shepherds', 'wandering lovers' and 'sages', characterised by being "almost without intellect" (Yeats, 1981: 108-9).

Another conclusion to be drawn from the use of these figures is that the initial dualism of the 'anti-self' was soon multiplied by a plurality of *personae*. The poet himself achieves this realisation – "Is it simply the doctrine of the Mask? The choosing of some one Mask? [...] Is it becoming mask after mask? [...] a continual change, a phantasmagoria" (Yeats, 1972: 138). The attempt represents conflicting impulses within himself necessarily involved the continuous creation of Masks. Jaffe summarises the diversity of Masks adopted by the poet – "Often his Masks are types, such as hero, lover, or poet. Other times they are more individual, and are given names and sometimes historical identities which have reference outside the poem" (139). She adds another set of Masks to the 'types', and to the named *personae* in the first edition of *The Wing Among the Reeds*. Yeats would often appropriate the names of actual individuals, usually directly related to his personal life, recasting them as personae in his poems. This technique is akin to the one applied in *Autobiographies*, in which "Yeats deploys other characters to depict aspects of his own personality" (Wright, 52).

Pessoa's development of the method of composition through *personae* displays several affinities with Yeats's own development. Since the age of fifteen (1903), Pessoa had been creating what he called 'literary personalities'. Under the name of these imaginary figures he wrote poetic and prose texts. In the early stages of his poetry, they had mainly English names, such as Charles Robert Anon, Alexander Search, given that the poet was living in South Africa. As with Yeats these *personae* have a similar status to that of pseudonyms, allowing the poet to convey emotional and mental states which had a serious autobiographical nature. Teresa Rita Lopes argues that "the barrier that existed between him and his 'personalities was tenuous", adding that "through all his 'literary personalities' [Pessoa] rendered his diary in the form of a continuous monologue, changing masks now and then, but without loosing the support of a body which was always the same" (Lopes, 22).

This initial stage was followed by the creation of the heteronyms and the theorisation of his method of composition. Heteronymy was as fundamental for

---

[1] Yeats, 1982: 334. Though the essay mentioned was published in 1917, Yeats was quoting in this passage from diaries dating back from the early 1900s.

his development as a poet as Yeats's 'theory of the Mask'. The process developed over two years. In 1912, Pessoa started sketching some poems with diverse themes and form from what he had produced thus far. By 1914, he had created the first heteronym, Alberto Caeiro, who can be compared to Yeats's anti-self. By creating Caeiro, Pessoa was adopting, in Jacinto do Prado Coelho's words, "a position diametrically opposite to his own". Accordingly, Caeiro calls himself a 'shepherd', embodying opposite elements to Pessoa's highly intellectualised mind: "Imprisoned in futile meditation and dream, he would become, through imagination, the instinctive and happy man, freed from the subjective" (185).

As with Yeats, the phenomenon did not stop here. He soon created other *personae*, namely Ricardo Reis and Álvaro de Campos, who also embodied different existential postures from Pessoa, his first heteronym. Thus, the initial dual division, gave way to a multiple array of *personae* that "give expression to possible feelings, thoughts, and emotions which could only be reconciled with difficulty" (Jaffe, 128). Pessoa called these imaginary entities 'heteronyms', in semantic opposition to the term 'orthonym', which he adopted to designate the poetry signed by Pessoa himself. Yet, it is problematic to attribute the role of creator to this orthonym, rather than to consider him as part of the process of heteronymy. This view has been defended by several major exegetes of Pessoa's work, among which Jorge de Sena, José Augusto Seabra, and Eduardo Lourenço, who consider Pessoa-orthonym a fourth heteronym. Pessoa attributed significantly greater autonomy to these *personae* than Yeats did to his, writing complete biographies for his three major *personae*. Apart from the biographies, he endowed each of these entities with a particular conception of reality, particular traits of character, as well as particular styles, and "made of this personality an author, with a book or books" (Pessoa, 1985: 24).

Dramatic and Fictional Aspects of the technique of *personae*

Yeats wrote and produced a substantial number of plays for the Abbey Theatre, which led to further alterations to the concept of poetic *persona*. His account of the process of writing through *personae* in *Memoirs* betrays an accentuated influx of dramatic principles:

> Every now and then, when something has stirred my imagination, I begin talking to myself. I speak in my own person and dramatize myself [...]. Occasionally, I write out what I have said in verse [...]. I do not think of my soliloquies as having different literary qualities. They stir my interest, by their appropriateness to the men I imagine myself to be, or by their accurate description of some emotional circumstance, more than by any aesthetic value. When I begin to write I have no object but to find for them some natural speech, rhythm and syntax... (Yeats, 1972: 532)

This statement is a good example of the hybrid quality that the *personae* possessed in his poetry. The words 'dramatise' and 'soliloquies' assert the dramatic quality of the poetry. Moreover, the references to imagined emotions and to the need for adequacy to the 'character' or mood that is being conveyed undeniably point to theatrical conventions.

Pessoa's description of his method of poetic composition is strikingly similar to Yeats's. In a letter to his fellow poet A. Casais Monteiro from 1935, Pessoa describes it in retrospect in the following manner:

> A witty remark which had been burgeoning within me, would occur to me, completely alien, for one reason or another, to that which I am, or to that which I suppose I am. I would say it immediately, spontaneously, as if it had come from a certain friend of mine whose name I would invent, on whose life story I would expand and whose physical appearance – face, stature, dress and mien – I would immediately see before me. (Pessoa, 1985: 18)

Like Yeats, Pessoa identifies the technique as a mental process conveyed in a linguistic form, initially verbal but subsequently transposed into written verse, alongside which is erected a plausible fictional entity capable of assuming the role of subject. In this excerpt he is describing an essentially poetic process to which dramatic and fictional elements, such as names and characterisation, are added to heighten its verisimilitude.

Additionally, their poetry displays several other dramatic elements. Jaffe observes that "Yeats employs various types of dramatic presentation, from the dramatic speech of a *persona*, to dramatic monologue in which the auditor is explicit, to dramatic dialogue between two or more characters" (158). The latter type of poem was particularly important as a medium for the confrontation of antithetical perspectives in Yeats's renowned dialectical method. Indeed, it can be argued that its use extended beyond the boundaries of the poem, occurring also between individual poems or sets of poems within different collections, as is the case with the sets entitled "A Woman Young and Old" and "A Man Young and Old". Pessoa also resorted to the dramatic lyric, though less often than Yeats did in the case of the dramatic dialogue. Nonetheless, one can find some examples of the latter in the poetic corpus of the heteronyms and the orthonym – Caeiro's poem "Olá, Guardador de Rebanhos" ("Hello, Keeper of Sheep") displays the same dialectical function as the dramatic dialogue displayed in Yeats's poetry. Regarding the dramatic monologue, the poems written by the heteronyms can be considered as such (Lopes, 38). However, there are more conventional monologues in his works, such as the poem entitled "O Ultimo Sortilégio" ("The Last Enchantment"), wherein the speaker is a witch.

The introduction of dramatic and fictional elements into their poetry by Yeats and Pessoa brought about changes in the concept of *persona*. Thus, the poetic *persona* was endowed with a degree of autonomy close to the concept of *dramatis persona*, closer in status to that of a fictional character. Both poets attributed physical and psychological characteristics to some of their main *personae* in a number of explanatory 'narratives' which must be considered fiction. In Yeats's case, this was restricted to the *personae* of Robartes and Aherne and the prefatory material of *A Vision*, whereas the creation of fictional biographies, bibliographies and critical texts constituted an important facet of Pessoa's heteronymy throughout.

Function of *Personae*

At a personal and perhaps even subconscious level, the creation of *personae* possessed a therapeutic function, providing a sophisticated, if not entirely successful, solution to psychological conflicts within the poets' personalities. Still at a personal level, the *personae* also represented solutions to the poets' existential angst. Both poets displayed a marked existentialism, questioning themselves about moral and philosophical issues, such as the nature of existence and of truth, the reality of life and death, and the forces of will and fate. Sidnell posits that "In Yeats, vision and belief, more than informing the 'content' of the poetry, determine its structural conventions, by which I mean the use of *personae* in narrative, dialogue, or dramatic forms…" (225). Likewise, Pessoa's 'drama-in-people' "[did] not consist only in seeing oneself divided or diverse, but in the fact that the heteronyms are attempts to produce a 'practical', though 'imaginary', response to the serious problem of existing" (Coelho, 166). This disquiet was as much existential as aesthetic, for the two aspects were often associated in the case of both poets. Northrop Frye refers to a historical phenomenon in late nineteenth-century literature, which led writers "to turn to the symbolic systems available in their time to develop a poetic language" (220). These symbolic systems included 'Roman Catholicism', 'pagan mythology', 'national folklore', and 'occultism' (Adams, 162).

The reflection of the phenomenon in Yeats and Pessoa's techniques of poetic composition under examination in this paper is twofold. On the one hand, they undertook a simultaneous exploration of some of the belief systems poets were adhering to, though only on a literary level. Thus, the *personae* function as dramatised solutions to the problem of a non-existent poetic language. Robartes and Aherne embodied different contemporary theological postures, the former being a fervent adept of the occult and founder of the mystical Order of the Alchemical Rose, whereas the latter was described by the poet as 'a pious Catholic'. By projecting these positions into his *personae* in the late 1890s Yeats was spared a choice between the two belief systems, which would have limited him to one source of imagery only, as well as to a limited and orthodox worldview. To these one might add the poems on occultism and Irish-mythology written by the *persona* of Yeats. Likewise, the appearance of the heteronyms stemmed from Pessoa's intention of representing in his poetry different literary and philosophical tendencies of his historical moment.[2] Eduardo Lourenço has observed that Reis and Caeiro provide an "answer to religious anxieties" felt by the poet, or perhaps more precisely, metaphysical ones (87). Hence, all three heteronyms enact alternative systems of belief to Catholicism in their varying forms of 'Paganism', whereas the orthonym embraces occultism and folklore.

On the other hand, though reflecting external tendencies, the fictional sets of *personae* in their poetry qualify as original personal mythologies, which constituted another solution adopted by artists to the question discussed above. The fictional apparatus invented by Yeats and Pessoa sought to erect a mythopoeia. In a chapter entitled "The Self as God", Langbaum emphasises the quasi-divine quality of Yeats's artistic achievement, "by assuming a mythical identity and walking through the paces of his myth or phantasmagoria…" (246).

---

[2] See Lind, 13-232.

In part III of "The Tower" Yeats raises his work to a mythical level: "I have prepared my peace / With [...] All those things whereof / Man makes a superhuman / Mirror-resembling dream" (1996: 306). This strategy is resumed in other poems that are central to his poetic production, such as "Under Ben Bulben", or the first two parts of "The Circus Animals' Desertion". Regarding Pessoa, Eduardo Lourenço has described his heteronymy as a "mythical narrative" (32). Similarly, José Augusto Seabra refers to Pessoa as a 'creator of myths', calling the biographies of his *personae* 'mythographies' (37-51). The poet regarded the creation of the heteronyms as a demiurgic act as can be seen in the following poem attributed to Álvaro de Campos: "The more I feel, the more I feel as various persons, [...] / The more I shall possess the total existence of the universe, [...] / The more analogous I will be to God, whoever he is..." (Pessoa, n.d.: 104 – my translation). Whilst still reinforcing his self-division, the poet increases the magnitude of his 'creation' by comparing it and himself to the Christian God and His Creation.

Effects of the use of *personae* on their poetry

According to Sidnell, "After *Michael Robartes and the Dancer*, discoveries made through the intercourse with the phantasmagoria endow the poetry with certitude and power" (241). The use of *personae*, in particular the more developed Michael Robartes and Owen Aherne, improved Yeats's poetry. By allowing him to experience the world from different existential viewpoints, this technique endowed his poetry with a varied emotional, intellectual and thematic content. The poet's effort of self-othering was perhaps most radical in the 'Crazy Jane' cycle of *Words for Music Perhaps*, as well as in the poems of *A Woman Young and Old*, first published as a separate collection. In these groups of poems, Yeats was able to express the emotions and thoughts of a member of the opposite gender, introducing thematic variations that differ from its remaining production. of the poet. On the other hand, the necessity to devise appropriate forms of expression for the *personae* led to stylistic changes in his poetry. These changes did not differ greatly from his own poetic style, though in some cases they led to the introduction of new poetic forms. An instance of the latter can be found in the use Yeats makes of the ballad form in certain poems attributed to a specific category of *personae*.

The use of *personae* had similar repercussions in Pessoa's poetry. Yeats's thematic variation was somewhat scattered, only achieving a certain amount of consistency in the more individualised *personae* Robartes, Aherne and Crazy Jane, or in the more uniform thematic sets mentioned above. The thematic variation provided by the heteronyms was more consistent than Yeats's manifold Masks, for each heteronym focused on a limited set of themes in his poetic *corpus*. Thematic diversity was not consigned to the poetry of the heteronyms, but thrived in the poetry of the orthonym as well. Referring solely to the poetry in Portuguese, Zenith claims that "Pessoa is subdivided thematically", proposing the following subdivisions: "Fernando Pessoa the existentialist, Fernando Pessoa the patriot, Fernando Pessoa the occultist, Fernando Pessoa the rhymester" of 'traditional folk quatrains' (Zenith, 1998: 216). To these one should add Fernando Pessoa the modernist, which appears in his initial poetic compositions. Zenith's observation unearths yet another level of multiplication in the poet's work, which was concomitant to the heteronymic production and developed similarly throughout the poet's life. The poems of these 'various orthonyms' (in Zenith's words) were not for the most part organised into separate collections, with the exception of *Mensagem* (1935), a collection of nationalist poems, and short collections of modernist poems. The orthonymic *corpus* in English introduces the theme of love, approached from different perspectives in the collections *35 Sonnets* (1918), *Antinous* (1918), and *Epithalamium* (1921). Undoubtedly, though, the most impressive effect of heteronymy on Pessoa's poetry, consisted in the adoption of diametrically different styles for each heteronym, ranging from the long free verse poems of Caeiro and Campos to the conventional prosody of Reis's odes. Their styles did not only differ from one another, but also from the style adopted by Pessoa in the poetry signed under his name, appearing in distinct collections of poems attributed to each heteronym written over several years. Stylistic heterogeneity is considered the most innovative aspect of Pessoa's aesthetics, developing the concept of objectivity of expression a step further in the direction of poetic dramatisation.

Notwithstanding the importance of this method of composition for the poetry of Yeats and of Pessoa, the use of *personae* constituted a stage in their poetry, eventually dying out as the poets' interests shifted. Feeling somewhat anxious about the growing autonomy of his *personae*, Yeats sought to reset himself at the centre of his poetic universe. Following *Michael Robartes and the Dancer* he published *The Tower* (1928), a collection which was marked by personal utterance. Indeed, the title poem of the collection is considered one of the most openly autobiographical poems of Yeats's oeuvre. Sidnell also argues that "The Gift of Harun Al-Rashid" "tends to short-circuit both the system and the Robartes fiction to bring us back [...] into the realm of the facts and occasions of Yeats's own life" (249). Hence, empowered by the demiurgic nature of his act, the subject has regained his poetic self-confidence and is once again able to 'walk naked'. Yet, this new version of the autobiographical poem incorporated the preceding fiction, which had now become a significant part of the poet's life. In part II of "The Tower", Hanrahan, a fictional character from his early stories and a poetic *persona* in *The Wind Among the Reeds*, is recalled as vividly as the real figures from his life mentioned or appearing in other poems in the collection. According to Langbaum, "The Tower is the symbol of his [Yeats's] transformed personality and as he paces its battlements he looks out on the surrounding landscape and assembles [...] the elements out of which he has made his soul..." (222).

This pattern, whereby the *persona* of the poet appears alongside imaginary *personae*, either in different poems or within the space of the same poem, would prevail in his subsequent collections. Yet, the latter are no longer given the same autonomy they enjoyed before, possessing a quality of memorabilia in the poet's retrospective recapitulation, as the last stanza of "The Circus Animal's Desertion" (1939) shows:

> Those masterful images because complete
> Grew in pure mind, but out of what began?
> A mound of refuse or the sweepings of a street,
> Old kettles, old bottles, and a broken can,

> Old iron, old bones, old rags, that raving slut
> Who keeps the till. Now that my ladder's gone,
> I must lie down where all the ladders start,
> In the foul rag-and-bone shop of the heart. (Yeats, 1996: 472)

There is a certain ambiguity in the title regarding the deserting party, which remained unresolved throughout the poem until this last stanza, wherein we realise it is the poet who is abandoning his 'animals'. The creative energy that resulted from the use of personae regenerated the poet, as seen in the following lines at the start of "The Tower": "Never had I more / Excited, passionate, fantastical / Imagination, nor an ear and eye / That more expected the impossible". (1996: 302) His poetic vitality prevailed as late as the collection *Last Poems*, displayed both in the themes, the style and colloquialism of the language.

The production of the heteronyms also shifted with time in the case of Pessoa's heteronymy, seeing the gradual appearance of inconsistencies in the positioning of each heteronym, and the consequent disassembling of the fiction by the creator. In contrast with the heteronyms Pessoa's poetry, in turn gained an increased vitality, becoming 'sharp', 'humourous', and 'cool' (Josipovici, 41). Indeed, Josipovici claims that Pessoa's "final poems, written in his own name, are very close in spirit to Yeats's "Circus Animal's Desertion" [...] we have the same feeling as with late Yeats, that at last, after so much posturing, we are coming close to the centre, to the secret source of all the masks" (42). The similarities are particularly evident in the following prose passage from *The Book of Disquietude*:

With what energy of my lone soul I produced page after solitary page, living syllable by syllable the false magic, not of what I wrote, but of what I thought I was writing! Under some ironic sorcerer's spell I imagined myself the poet of my prose, in the winged moment when it rose up in me – more swiftly than the movements of my pen – like a fallacious vengeance against the insults of life! And finally, as I spend today rereading, I see my dolls falling apart, straw coming out of their torn seams, emptying themselves without ever having been... (Pessoa, 1996: 102)

References

Coelho, Jacinto do Prado. 1982. *Diversidade e Unidade em Fernando Pessoa*. Lisboa: Editorial Verbo

Ellmann, Richard. 1978. *The Man and the Masks*. New York: Norton and Co.

Frye, Northrop. 1963. *Fables of Identity:Studies in Poetic Mythology*. New York: Harcourt, Brace and World

Jaffe, Catherine Marie. 1986. "The Reader in the Modern Lyric Poem: the Role of the Reader in the Poetry of Juan Ramon Jimenez, Fernando Pessoa, and W.B. Yeats". Diss. University of Chicago

Josipovici, Gabriel. 1977. *The Lessons of Modernism and Other Essays*. Basingstoke: Macmillan

Langbaum, Robert. 1977. *The Mysteries of Identity*. New York: Oxford University Press

Lind, Rudolf. 1981. "Teoria Poetica de Fernando Pessoa". *Estudos Sobre Ferna ndo Pessoa*. Lisboa: Imprensa Nacional Casa da Moeda. 13-232.

Lopes, Teresa Rita, ed. 1993. "Introduction". *Pessoa Inédito*. Lisboa: Livros Horizonte

Lourenco, Eduardo. 1981. *Fernando Pessoa Revisitado: Leitura Estruturante do Drama em Gente*. Lisboa: Moraes Editores

Macrae, Alasdair. 1995. *W.B. Yeats: A Literary Life*. New York: St. Martin's Press

Pessoa, Fernando. N.d. *Poesias de Álvaro Campos*. Lisboa: Atica

Pessoa, Fernando. 1985. *Fernando Pessoa: A Galaxy of Poets*. London: Borough of Camden and Portuguese Ministry of Foreign Affairs and Culture

Pessoa, Fernando. 1996. *The Book of Disquietude*. Ed. and trans. Richard Zenith. 2nd ed. Manchester: Carcanet & Calouste Gulbenkian Foundation

Pessoa, Fernando. 1998. *Fernando Pessoa & Co.: Selected Poems*. Ed. and trans. Richard Zenith. New York: Grove Press.

Seabra, José Augusto. 1999. "Mitografias e biografias Pessoanas". *Pessoa*. Ed. António Carlos Carvalho. Lisboa: Pergaminho. 37-51.

Sidnell, Michael. 1976. "Mr. Yeats, Michael Robartes and Their Circle". *Yeats and the Occult*. Ed. George Mills Harper. London: Macmillan

Unterecker, John. 1963. "Faces and False Faces: The Doctrine of the Mask". *Yeats: a Collection of Critical Essays*. Ed. Unterecker. New Jersey: Prentice-Hall

Wright, David Wright. 1987. *Yeats's Myth of Self: the Autobiographical Prose* Dublin: Gill and Macmillan

Yeats, W. B. 1972. *Memoirs: Autobiography – First Draft; Journal*. Ed. Denis Donoghue. Dublin: Gill and Macmillan, 1972

Yeats, W. B. 1980. *Autobiographies*. 2nd ed. London: Papermac-Macmillan

Yeats, W. B. 1981. *A Vision*. 2nd ed. London: Papermac-Macmillan

Yeats, W. B. 1982. *Mythologies*. 3rd ed. London: Papermac-Macmillan

Yeats, W. B. 1996. *Yeats's Poems*. Ed. Norman Jeffares. 3rd ed. London: Macmillan

"Hoy ... This is Jommy Robbitte": Nonstandard English and Narrative Technique in Roddy Doyle's *The Snapper*

Katherine Meffen

Roddy Doyle states that he sees "life in terms of dialogue" and "that people *are* their talk' (Paschel, 127). He acknowledges some kinship with writers also "writing in their English instead of conforming to the rules of formal English" (Paschel, 157). In his novels, this perception is translated into the narrative structure, which relies heavily on the dialogue of its characters, whether as first person narrative or reported speech. Rüdiger Imhof has identified the technique as a technical failure, arguing that rather than serving any artistic purpose, Doyle's reliance on dialogue is explained by "evidence [...] that the author favoured the scenic method because he could not have been good at description even if someone had held a gun at his head" (238). This paper hopes to show that the narrative structure Imhof perceives as "a cardinal shortcoming" of Doyle's writing is in fact part of a larger harmony of theme and form exemplified in *The Snapper*, the second novel in Roddy Doyle's Barrytown trilogy. The plot of the text is simple, portraying the Rabbitte family as they cope (and fail to cope) with the teenage pregnancy of Sharon, daughter of Veronica and Jimmy Rabbitte (usually referred to as Jimmy Sr).

Roddy Doyle's work presents something of an anomaly for the critics, part of the first wave of a reimagining of the city of Dublin that started in the 1980s but definitely distinct from the author he is most often grouped with. Like Doyle, Dermot Bolger takes as his subject the new suburbs of Dublin, which were constructed in the second half of the twentieth century to house the population moved en masse from the grim conditions of the old city-centre tenements. These areas had not been written about before, not, at least, by the people who lived there. The clear difference between the work of Doyle and Bolger, both writers who portray the working-class suburbs of Dublin, is the presence in Bolger's work of the traditional tropes of Irish nationalism. The Irish literary and critical tradition has for decades concentrated on issues of national identity and territory, a legacy of the long interaction with England and the UK. Without a hint of the wider nation or the national past, and set in a part of modern Dublin utterly new and without a literary past, *The Snapper* simply does not engage with many of the themes of twentieth-century Irish fiction, whether to celebrate or critique. Instead, Doyle focuses on the relatively anonymous suburbs north of Dublin's city centre and more importantly, the working-class community that live there. The speech of his characters is almost the only aspect of the characters that distinguishes them from the urban working class in any post-industrial city.

Linguistic studies of Irish English often exclusively follow the geographical model of language variation, looking at regional difference rather than social stratification. Mark Filppula identifies four basic types of Irish English, all rural except for the final one, "the urban speech of urban Dublin" (37), which is by virtue of its metropolitan nature, "more open to outside influences" (32-3), and perhaps less influenced by the Irish language than the others (69). Other linguists have separated Irish English into varying numbers of categories, but agree that attitudes to the language follow the general hierarchical patterns described by linguists, with urban forms having the least prestige (Edwards, 491). The geographically defined dialects offered by Filppula may seem to implicitly reject any model built on social stratification within a geographic area, but Harris is explicit in his rejection of class stratification. He argues that in Ireland there has been no national standard developed, resulting in a "written model … more or less indistinguishable from that of standard British English" (39), and chides other linguists for "assuming" the existence of a class accent comparable to RP in Britain. Delahunty, however, refers to just such an accent, "the one which is referred to as not being an accent at all … used by people from widely separated parts of the country who share many features of education, life-style and assumptions" (133). Edwards also notes the existence of this "supra-regional variety", and expressly likens it to RP. Sharon teasing her brother with "How Now, Brown Cow", the rhyme used to demonstrate that epitome of class-based language, English RP, certainly implies that Doyle agrees that there is.

Siegfried Bertz offers a description of Dublin English that does allow the existence of social stratification within the city. He defines three types of Dublin English, which he argues are spoken generally by distinct social groups: Popular Dublin English, PDE; General Dublin English, GDE; and Educated Dublin English, EDE. His "impressionistic" definition is problematic (Harris, 42), since it equates social class and education, an assumption that in post-1960s Ireland is a less than accurate generalisation. He does allow for code-switching, though, noting that in more formal situations, speakers can and do change the more stigmatised aspects of their language. In his model, PDE is the least formal, and has the lowest prestige. Exclusive speakers of this type are characterised as people with primary education and "corresponding occupation" (Bertz, 38). Cheshire's observation that "speakers from the lower end of the socioeconomic scale … use the higher proportion of nonstandardisms" (193) offers an alternative model of language as a spectrum from standard to nonstandard rather than discrete social languages, but Bertz's PDE closely resembles the language of *The Snapper* and also has the highest level of nonstandardisms of the three, so the two models combine well. John Kirk identifies the language of Doyle's novels as nonstandard English, a term that denotes a form that "departs from the norms" of standard English, but which does not "qualify" as "traditional dialect". The status of this type of English is hinted at when he describes the "slang, foul language, and other conspicuously colloquial vocabulary", and identifies it with "particular social and usually stigmatised accents or styles of speaking" (193). Rüdiger Imhof comes perilously close to demonstrating this argument when he argues that Doyle "relies too heavily on dialogue couched in the idiom of the Dublin working-class and prodigiously peppered with scatological expressions" (241). The problem with the Barrytown novels is apparently not just the reliance on dialogue, but on one particular kind of dialogue.

Doyle, perhaps sensibly, gives little more than an orthographic indication of accent, refraining from a more thorough "phonetic" rendering. Since the screen success of *The Commitments*, by many readers the words are "heard" in a Dublin accent anyway, but there is relatively little to distinguish it. Textually, in a select few words vowels and, less frequently, consonants are altered to indicate a nonstandard pronunciation: 'jaysis', 'buke', 'yeh', and a variety of dropped final consonants (Paschel, 103). This uses the reader's knowledge of StE orthography to indicate sound, but since orthographical conventions in English are not phonetic in the first place, this alone cannot offer much guidance to the reader unfamiliar with Dublin accents. Its major effect is to alert the reader to the different, nonstandard presentation. *The Snapper*'s dialogue exhibits many of the grammatical aspects of nonstandard English; one of which Bertz rates "[a]mong the most striking morphological features of PDE [...] preterite forms with participial functions" (46). This is a variation common to many parts of the English-speaking world and more easily identifiable as nonstandard than specifically regional. So too is the use of the second person plural pronoun "yous", and of "them" where standard speakers would use only "these" or "those" (Bertz, 48). Most of his list of "word-modifiers [...] typical for casual Dublin English" are again widespread as nonstandard, with examples like "bloody" and "fuckin", although "feckin" is immediately recognisable as geographically specific. Paschel notes the "placing of adverbials of consequence and conjunctions at the end of the sentence" (104) as typical of several nonstandard forms, and although "but" in such a position is also common to Glaswegian English, "so" is not widely used this way outwith Irish English.

While some of the examples above are geographically specific rather than class-based, the "foul language" and "heavy use of expletives and four-letter words" (if these are indeed distinct categories) that Kirk identifies in Doyle's novels as "extreme colloquialisms" (202) are clear evidence, if more were needed, that Doyle's language can more accurately be described as nonstandard than regional dialect. The nonstandard language spoken by the protagonists is also seen as an object of contempt, or at least a good reason for shame, by parts of society. Jimmy Jr is apparently aware that the way he speaks is not appropriate for public speaking, taking elocution lessons for his projected radio career. The assumption must be that his new accent represents a move away from what he perceives to be a stigmatised speech, although after the initial greeting: "Hoy... this is Jommy Robbitte" it's hard to tell (316). Unlike the later novel, *The Van*, where "the teenagers with accents like newsreaders" (254) add to Bimbo and Jimmy Sr's unease in a Dublin they no longer feel part of, Jimmy Jr's attempts are seen as an object of fun and derision by his family (Paschal, 95). Sharon tells her brother "it makes you sound like a fuckin' eejit", and Jimmy Sr is equally dismissive:

> Jimmy Jr sat down, on the other side of Sharon.
> -What's thot? he said.
> -A hudgehog, said Jimmy Sr. (314)

Such mockery establishes that Jimmy Sr's attitude to his own language is free of discontent. That theirs is a working class speech is demonstrated by Doyle's linguistic differentiation of the comparatively middle class representatives of the state, the schoolteacher and the doctor. The twins gleefully inform their father that their teacher "said yeh should be ashamed of yourself" (177) in reaction to the twins' report of their father's morning greeting, "It looks like another fuck of a day" (178). The comedy of the scene, exaggerated by the slow build up to the phrase in question, makes clear that this event should amuse rather than horrify: Veronica is alone in her appalled reaction as the rest of her family laugh.

As illustrated by their polarised reaction to the twins reporting of Jimmy Sr's swearing, Veronica and Jimmy Sr have quite different views on what is and is not acceptable language. Veronica rarely swears, although this has the paradoxical result that her one use of the word "fuck" has far more effect than when it is used by Jimmy Sr in every other sentence (295). Jimmy Sr, however, pays more attention to the message conveyed than the specific vocabulary, apologising to Sharon for using the word "bollix" in a conversation that is bursting with other swear words. The difference is that while the word "fuckin" is used frequently by Jimmy Sr, it has nothing to do with the actual activity. "Bollix", in this particular conversation, actually referred to testicles and was therefore inappropriate to a conversation with his daughter. Jimmy swears so often and so often cheerfully that it is impossible to recognise the "strong disgust or anger" that the dictionary definition suggests as an alternative to its use as a verb. The fact that an appropriately neutral definition is not recorded strongly suggests that this is a predominantly nonstandard usage. Veronica's speech is also frequently textually distinct from her husband's. Her pronunciation is represented in the text with standard spelling, which according to the logic of the novel represents more standard pronunciation. A distinction both textual and thematic is made between Veronica and Jimmy Sr in the following exchange:

-What's the buke abou'?
-Pregnancy.
-Jaysis, d'yeh need a buke to be pregnant these days?
-I didn't have a book, said Veronica. (158)

The juxtaposition of "buke" and "book" is intentional. Not all words are rendered "phonetically", and those that are, are not consistently so. Veronica's refusal to speak the same way as the other characters highlights her discontent with her place within it. Theirs is clearly a marriage in trouble even though Jimmy Sr apparently does not notice, with Veronica left completely unsupported as her husband and daughter sulk and fight. Her desire for change in her situation is shown through her attempt to change her language. Outsider status is also demonstrated in the speech of Jimmy Sr's slightly criminal acquaintance Bertie, who is always immediately identifiable in conversation. An apparently small-time criminal, he regards himself as an outlaw, and speaks in a Hollywood caricature of the accent of a Mexican bandit. His first appearance in *The Snapper* is marked by his greeting: 'Buenas noches, compadres' (198), and although he frequently lapses into simple Dublin English, his speech is peppered with Spanish words, and with Spanish pronunciation of English words, such as "steenking" (201). Bertie's connections and his relationship with the police become more apparent in *The Van*, but his speech and access to goods falling from passing vehicles provide a major clue to his outlaw identity.

Paschel notes almost in passing that Doyle's characters regard "conversation as a means of sustaining the community", and although the concept is a useful one in analysis of the author's view of dialogue, it is perhaps less accurate to impute the view to the characters themselves (101). The author may use his characters to *show* this, but not one articulates an awareness of it. White also demonstrates her awareness of the relationship between speech and community in the Barrytown novels, but she does not emphasise the extent to which this community is constituted by speech as well as enacted through it (10). The linguistic community is represented both thematically and orthographically. Sharon's troubled interaction with the wider community is entirely based on the dialogues, real or imagined, that she has with its members. When she thinks about telling her friends about her pregnancy, their inevitable curiosity about the father is imagined in terms of the ensuing conversation:

> -Was it him, Sharon, was it? And if Sharon said, No it wasn't him, they'd say, -how d'yeh know if yeh can't remember? It must've been him then.
> She'd just have to tell them that she wasn't going to tell them.
> But they'd still try and find out.
> She didn't blame them. She'd have been the same. It was going to be terrible though. She wouldn't be able to really relax with them any more.
> -There's Keith Farrelly.
> -Yeah.
> -He's a ride, isn't he?
> -He's alrigh'.
> -D'yeh not like him?
> -He's alrigh'.
> -I thought that yeh liked him.
> -Fuck off, will yeh. It wasn't him. (182)

The same preoccupation can be seen when she considers the reaction of the community as a whole: Sharon thinks to herself that "[s]oon everybody would know. Good. She could nearly hear them", before another imagined chorus of judgements about her (206). Sharon's exclusion from the community is both caused by and expressed through speech, or the lack of it. The pregnancy itself, as White observes, is accepted by her family and friends with "relative equanimity" (63): only when Sharon's refusal to identify the father becomes widely known and speculated upon does her predicament threaten her place in the community. Jimmy Sr and Yvonne express their displeasure through "silent treatment" (White, 63), but the opinion of the community as a whole is vocalised and can be heard in the gossip about her, and in the taunts of the youngster (Doyle, 258-9). The strife in the Rabbitte household is stirred up by this body of opinion, for, despite his earlier protestations to the contrary, Jimmy Sr cares deeply about Barrytown's view of the family. He gets in a fight, provoked by the fact that other drinkers were "saying things about yeh, Sharon" (277), and ends up avoiding the pub altogether for a short while, although not as long as he lets Sharon believe. That the entire family responds with violence of some sort or another to such verbal accusations and taunts simply shows the effectiveness of such pressure upon them. Tracy and Linda exact revenge by vandalising the homework and scraping the face of one of their classmates (265), and Veronica actually punches Mrs Burgess in the face (252). Jimmy Sr's unhappiness at such attention is perhaps the most pronounced, and there are other hints that he is deeply affected by community opinion. When Jimmy Sr decides to cut the grass outside the house, the narrator explains this uncharacteristic burst of activity:

> Last night Bimbo had called Jimmy Sr's house Vietnam because of the
> state of the front garden. Jimmy Sr had laughed. But when Bimbo told
> him that everyone called it that Jimmy Sr'd said, Enough; fuck it, he'd
> cut the grass tomorrow, the cunts. (319)

That the label is apt and recognised to be so is shown by his initial laughter.
Uttered by Bimbo, Jimmy simply finds it amusing; it is only when he learns that
"everyone" uses it that he is spurred to action.

Sharon's situation is similar. It is not the reality of her situation that gets her
down, nor ultimately others' knowledge of the truth, just the verbal abuse and
gossip. She begins to feel better after she suppresses the talk about her, a process
which starts with George Burgess, the baby's father. Having ensured his silence,
she turns to the boys on the street, whose taunting previously sent her skulking
home. She uses violence to back up her warning; "If you ever call me annythin'
again I'll fuckin' kill yeh, d'yeh hear me?" (262), but it is the verbal, not the
physical that bothers her. Sharon is perhaps unfair to her father when he gets in a
fight in the pub for the same reason: his crime and defence is the same as hers, but
she refuses to accept this as mitigation. She cannot rectify her situation as easily
as her father, though. To admit the truth about the baby's father is impossible, and
her silence is unacceptable. The strategy she hits upon to regain her threatened
place in the community if the identity of the father is deduced is also primarily
verbal. Initially, this goes no further than passive reaction: "She'd deny it, that was
what she'd do" (253), but she realises it will take more. Veronica understands and
approves the approach Sharon takes in inventing a "story" to account for her
pregnancy, subtly suggesting to Jimmy Sr that "[i]f she says he was a Spanish
sailor why not let her say it?" (264). Just as she immediately realises the social
consequences of Sharon's pregnancy with the cry "the neighbours [...] what'll
they say?" (150), Veronica also accurately perceives the successful outcome of the
strategy. That the story of the Spanish sailor is no more than a gesture is made
clear by the author. Crucially, in the reconciliation between father and daughter,
Doyle makes it clear that both know who the real father is and appreciate the
other's knowledge and silence:

> -What if it's a girl an' she looks like Mister Burgess?
> -Ah well, fuck it; we'll just have to smother it an' leave it on his
> step.
> -Ah Daddy!
> -I'm only messin'. I suppose I'll still have to love her. Even if she
> does
> have a head on her like Georgie Bur-
> He couldn't finish. He had an almighty fit of the giggles.
> -She'll be lovely, said Sharon.
> -She'd fuckin' better be. We're a good lookin' family. 'Cept for
> Jimmy,
> wha'. An', come here, an' anyway; it won't look like Burgess cos he
> isn't the da.ææIsn't tha' righ'?
> -Yeah.
> -Unless your Spanish sailor looked a bit like him, did he?

-Just a little bit.
-Ah well, said Jimmy Sr after a small while. (293)

They have hit on a verbal formula that can allow the functioning of the family to continue unhindered despite the unpalatable truth. The important part seems to be that by inventing a story to account for the baby, Sharon is re-negotiating her place in the community. Her initial outright refusal to even discuss the identity of the father is a confrontational strategy, which apparently denies the family and Barrytown the *right* to know, and asserts her own indifference to their reaction. Her recognition that she needs to tell them something about the father, even if that something is widely disbelieved, precipitates and allows her return to the community because it shows that she has accepted her place within it.

Some criticisms can be made of the choices Doyle made in determining the novel's narrative structure. His commitment to portraying Barrytown rather than Dublin proper creates a consistent concentration on domestic spaces where the use of such socially stigmatised language is relatively unproblematic, as the setting means there are no outsiders to judge or impress. The representation of their direct speech is unbound by inverted commas, achieving, according to one critic, a mingling of dialogue and exegesis where "[t]he distinction between talk and action becomes blurred" (Paschel, 101). However, while Doyle leaves some amount of ambiguity as to who exactly has spoken in the group dialogues, the characters' speech is marked out as distinct from the narrative by use of a dash:

> He looked at Veronica. She looked tired. He looked at Sharon again.
> -That's shockin', he said.
> Sharon said nothing.
> -Are yeh sure? said Jimmy Sr.
> -Yeah. Sort of.
> -Wha?
> -Yeah. (145)

This technique, although unorthodox, is possibly just as effective a way of marking direct speech as the conventional inverted commas. While Paschel applauds his "authentic dialogue" (69), the exclusive use of Standard English for the narrative voice carries implications of insufficiency for the nonstandard form used in dialogue. The change to first person narratives in the later novels neatly avoids the tensions created by this possible contradiction, and the change in style has perhaps been encouraged by an awareness of the problem of narrative hierarchies. Imhof's criticism that the narrative structure and (clearly annoying) working class speech that replaces exegesis are ultimately without effect or even purpose has clearly been shown to be misplaced. In this fictional portrayal of a working class community the community's voice is heard throughout the book. Instead of a stigmatised form, in *The Snapper* nonstandard language is shown more often as a positive affirmation of community and identity, through a consistent and effective co-ordination of the thematic, orthographic and structural treatment of language.

References

Bertz, Siegfried. 1987. "Variation in Dublin English". *TEANGA: Journal of the Irish Association for Applied Linguistics*. 7 (1987): 35-53

Cheshire, Jenny. 1984. "Indigenous Nonstandard English Varieties and Education". Language in the British Isles. Ed. Peter Trudgill. Cambridge: Cambridge University Press. 546-58

Delahunty, Gerald P. 1984. "Dialect and Local Accent". *Language in the British Isles*. Ed. Peter Trudgill. Cambridge: Cambridge University Press

Doyle, Roddy. 1998. *The Barrytown Trilogy*. London: Vintage

Edwards, John. 1984. "Irish and English in Ireland". *Language in the British Isles*. Ed. Peter Trudgill. Cambridge: Cambridge University Press. 480-99

Filppula, Mark. 1999. *The Grammar of Irish English – Language in Hibernian Style*. London: Routledge

Harris, John. 1991. "Ireland". *English Around the World: Sociolinguistic Perspectives*. Ed. Jenny Cheshire. Cambridge: Cambridge University Press. 37-50

Imhof, Rüdiger. 2002. *The Modern Irish Novel: Irish Novelists after 1945*. Dublin: Wolfhound Press

Kirk, John M. 1997. "Irish English And Contemporary Literary Writing". *Focus On Ireland*. Ed. Jeffrey Kallan. Amsterdam: John Benjamins. 189-206

Paschel, Ulrike. 1998. *No Mean City? Images of Dublin in the Novels of Dermot Bolger, Roddy Doyle and Val Mulkerns*. Bern: Peter Lang

White, Carmine. 2001. *Reading Roddy Doyle*. Syracuse: Syracuse Press

Being Sir Rogered: George Bernard Shaw and the Irish Rebel

James Moran

In recent years Roger Casement has achieved iconic status. Since the start of 2002 he has been the subject of books by Jeff Dudgeon and Colm Tóibín; his picture has been hung alongside Churchill, Lloyd George, and George V in London's National Portrait Gallery; and he has even featured in a marketing campaign for a new television channel, BBC Four. But Casement was not always such a celebrated insurrectionist. When Universal Studios decided to film a version of Casement's story in 1934 the officials of Hollywood encountered opposition from both British and Irish authorities; and G.B. Shaw, although usually famed for speaking out against censorship, played an active part in suppressing Universal's project. In this essay I will examine Hollywood's long-overlooked film proposal, and explore what its censorship reveals about Shaw's own work.

Roger Casement was a Dubliner, born in Kingstown to an Ulster Protestant family. As a young man he worked for the British government in Portuguese East Africa, Angola, the Congo Free State, and Brazil; during the course of which he revealed the atrocious cruelty being inflicted by white officials to the native Peruvians and Congolese. This work yielded Casement a knighthood, yet Sir Roger's true sympathies lay with Irish nationalism, and on returning to Ireland in 1912 he helped form the Irish National Volunteers. In 1914 he went to Germany in an attempt to recruit Irish P.O.W.s, obtain arms, and borrow the Kaiser's army officers in support of an insurrection in Ireland. But Casement failed to secure German support, and so finally sailed back to Ireland in an attempt to prevent the 1916 Rising. He was captured near Tralee and taken to London, where he was convicted of treason and sentenced to death. At the time of his trial and hanging, diaries containing detailed descriptions of homosexual practices, written by Casement, were circulated privately among British officials, and became that summer's main topic of gossip. Ever since, people have debated whether these 'Black Diaries' were British forgeries, or whether they were indeed written by Casement.

In 1934 Julius Klein, who worked as special assistant to the head of Universal Studios, decided to produce a film version of Roger Casement's story. Klein was a Jewish American whose varied career echoed Casement's life. Like Casement, Klein had worked as a spy during the First World War in Germany, and once the war was over he continued to be concerned with Germany, feeling so affectionately for the language that he initiated the first German language broadcasts in the United States. Klein also continued to be interested in military affairs, and he launched the South Pacific edition of the *Stars and Stripes* military newspaper. He maintained a dual interest in politics and criminality in the inter-war years, working as a crime reporter for Chicago's State Herald newspaper in the 1920s and running for Congressman in 1932. Later, in the Second World War, Klein became a hero by saving many lives during an explosion in the South Pacific, and drew on his knowledge of the 'Black Diaries' to formulate a military plan called 'Combat Public Relations' which covered such topics as psychological warfare and propaganda.[1]

Between 1934 and 1939 Klein worked in Hollywood, and as soon as he arrived he felt compelled to pursue a Casement project. Klein had covered the case as a newspaper reporter many years earlier and the story now seemed an ideal one for Universal to work on, containing many of the elements that would make a successful blockbuster: spying and secrecy, heroism in the face of seemingly insurmountable odds, and a wartime setting replete with British and German armies.

Censorship

The announcement of Klein's film was made in the *Irish Press* in July 1934 and greeted with dismay by Casement's cousin, Gertrude Parry. Parry was concerned that, although as Casement's sole heir she had control over the reproduction of copyright documents, she had no influence over a *creative* interpretation of Casement's life. She declared that a sensational Hollywood film would be "simply revolting" because:

> Roger is a national hero […]. One does not want a garbled account of his life + actions to go forth to the world − + Even from the commercial side of the venture, the producers would make a much better picture if it were true + showed Roger in the light of an Irish patriot.[2]

Parry's concerns were passed on to Eamon de Valera. He encouraged the Irish Free State's consular offices in Chicago and San Francisco to put pressure on Universal, and was particularly anxious that any indication of Casement's sexuality should be suppressed. The Irish consular officials were instructed:

> To ensure that film will be dignified and in all respects worthy of its subject. Every effort should be made to prevent introduction of any unfitting incidents such as a love story which would be much resented in United States.[3]

Julius Klein had in fact already been to the Chicago consulate and had been told to proceed with care. After the cable from de Valera the consular officials contacted a sympathetic production manager at Universal Studios who promised to follow their wishes, and who also told them that in any case the project had been temporarily delayed. The concerns of the Irish government were clearly something that worried Julius Klein. He did not want to alienate his potential Irish-American audience, and in September 1934 he contacted de Valera directly to say:

---

[1] See National Library of Ireland (NLI). MS 31732; and "Major General Julius Klein: His Life and His Work". *National Museum of American Jewish Military History* <http://www.nmajmh.org/exhibition/permanent.html>
[2] National Archive of Ireland (NAI). S7804A..
[3] NAI. S7804A.

While the screen scenario naturally must be written with fiction to be
an attraction for the movie audience, I will do all I can to do justice, not
only to a great character, but also to history. As soon as the final script
is finished, I will present it to the various governments for their
consideration.[4]

De Valera, however, was unimpressed. When he reconsidered the significance of
the Casement project his initial objections hardened. Fianna Fáil had been in
power for two years and had set about steering Irish nationalism on the
conservative course they desired. There was little room here for the radicalism of
those feminists or homosexuals who had invigorated Ireland in its revolutionary
days. De Valera struggled to escape the colonial paradigm of the feminised Celt,
by asserting, as David Norris notes, the "assumption that to be Irish is to be white,
heterosexual and Roman Catholic" (31). If de Valera reminded people of the
brilliant nationalist minds of the now dead generation of 1916 – of Casement,
Connolly, Francis Sheehy-Skeffington, or Countess Markievicz – the President
could provoke deeply subversive questions about his possession of the 1916 legacy
and his creation of a state that was a celebration of all that was rural, Catholic, and
petit bourgeois. Julius Klein received a letter to tell him that:

> The President is of the opinion that no writer outside Ireland, however
> competent, who had not the closest contact with events in this
> country during the years preceding and following the Rising of 1916
> could hope to do justice to the character and achievements of this
> great man [Casement]. The President [...] hopes that no attempt will
> be made to commercialize [*sic*] this great sacrifice either in a popular
> life or through a film in which fiction will play any part.[5]

De Valera had initially concurred with Parry's sentiments, that a film could be
made as long as it treated Casement with considerable dignity, but the President
had since changed his mind and decided that the subject itself was a problem. If
Casement was to be brought to prominence it must be done in a way that signalled
his posthumous approval for Fianna Fáil and de Valera's leadership. But if de
Valera let Hollywood control the representational agenda he could not be certain
what taboos might be broken, and so he urged Klein to abandon writing about
Casement altogether.

    Meanwhile Klein was facing further objections. As well as contacting de
Valera, Klein decided to check whether the British would object to the film. One
of Universal Studios' largest markets was England and the British colonies, and
Klein did not want to produce a film that would cause a cinematic brouhaha to
harm the distribution of both this film and future Universal productions. He had
already informally sounded out the secretary of the British Board of Film Censors,
who had advised him that the Board would be unlikely to allow such a film to be
shown in Britain. Klein then decided to make a more formal approach to the

---

[4] NAI. S7804A.
[5] NAI. S7804A.

British censors and sent them a copy of the film's synopsis, which they read with consternation at the end of October 1934.

The British chief censor between 1930 and 1946 was Colonel J.C. Hanna, who had been stationed in Ireland from 1918 to 1922. His personal feelings towards Casement were somewhat less than adulatory. Hanna believed Casement to be an insignificant "traitor" who had been justly punished (McIlroy, 31). In addition, the colonel realised that it would hardly be appropriate, when the British government was dedicated to spending £1.2 billion on arms between 1933 and 1938, to allow British taxpayers to watch a war film in which their own soldiers were scoundrels, and in which the upper echelons of the Imperial civil service were mired in deviousness and scandal (Moynahan, 164). Hanna told Klein, "my Board considers a film based on the life of this individual extremely undesirable. It would be quite impossible for us to issue our certificate for any such film".[6] News of this decision was made known to the British and Irish press. Not knowing that de Valera was working on the same side as that of the British censor in attempting to suppress the film, some Fianna Fáil members wrote to their leader to "protest against the showing of all films from British studious [*sic*] in the Irish Free State and we call on all nationals to boycott same as a protest on account of the boycott on the Casement Film by the British authorities".[7]

Shaw Joins the Debate

Faced with the intractable opposition of both the British and Irish officials, Klein wrote to G.B. Shaw to ask for his support over the Casement project. After all, Shaw had long signalled his opposition to the Lord Chamberlain's office, wrote more than fifty articles against the suppression of artistic work, and claimed that censorship was damned by the pernicious trash it allowed and by the good work that it did not (Holroyd, 377). Indeed, only a few months after being contacted by Klein, Shaw used a BBC radio talk to condemn the censorship of films, particularly those with a troublesome sexual content (Dukore 1997, 90). But Klein had not realised that Shaw had been a friend of Gertrude Parry since 1916. In addition, Klein seems unaware of Shaw's disdain for the egos of Hollywood, which the playwright had recently shown on a trip to MGM studios, when he refused to sign an autograph for the star John Barrymore and reduced the leading actress Ann Harding to tears (Dukore 1985, 272). On receiving Klein's letter, Shaw replied:

> I cannot encourage you in the matter of the film. America may be pro-Irish and to that extent pro-Casement; but America is not pro-German; and Casement's German adventure will not be popular. In England the film will probably be forbidden. Film Corporations are often very foolish, especially when politics (which they don't understand) are in question; but I doubt if any well advised firm will back Casement as a winner. Casement's relatives view the threat of a film with consternation.[8]

---

[6] NLI. MS 31732.

[7] NAI. S7804A.

[8] NLI. MS 31732.

Yet after sending Klein this letter Shaw wrote a second letter that conveyed a far more optimistic message. Klein had responded to Shaw's first letter by declaring that instead of producing a film he would write a book about Casement, and in reply Shaw sent him an interminable piece of writing explaining what Casement had set out to achieve.[9] By sending an extended statement Shaw was trying not to discourage Klein's interest in Casement. Although opposed to the idea of a film, Shaw was providing a marketable part of a prospective book, a request that Shaw would not ordinarily grant and which Klein was unsuccessful in trying to wrest from de Valera.[10] Unlike the President, Shaw wanted Klein to maintain an interest in Casement. It was only the filmic representation that Shaw opposed, and in order to understand this reaction it is necessary to examine the way that Casement affected Shaw's own work.

Scholars have overlooked Casement's influence on Shaw for many years. Even Bernard Dukore, that giant of Shaw criticism, does not include the Klein correspondence or any mention of the Casement film in his book charting Shaw's interactions with the movies, *Bernard Shaw on Cinema*. Casement's name is consistently missing from the *Shaw* journal, as it is from seminal critical books on the playwright. Michael Holroyd writes of the Casement affair, but indicates that it was an anomaly in Shaw's life by calling it Shaw's "most quixotic intervention into Anglo-Irish politics" (470). Incredibly, Casement's name does not even warrant a footnote in Sally Peters' *Bernard Shaw: The Ascent of the Superman*, a biographical study that places Shaw's acceptance of "the genius and homosexuality that he believed to be his twin inheritance" (259) at the heart of its narrative. Yet, like Klein, Shaw personally knew the difficulty of directly representing Casement in performance. Shaw was, in fact, the first person to produce a script about the rebel, which he wrote whilst Casement was still alive. In addition, Shaw was the first person to see his Casement script fail to be performed.

Casement was a great admirer of Shaw. He owned a copy of *John Bull's Other Island*, which he annotated heavily, and recommended that Shaw's journalism about the Easter Rising "ought to go to all European countries, and would have good effect".[11] After his arrest it did not take long for Casement's thoughts to turn to Shaw, and he considered that the playwright might be able to intercede on behalf of Max Daulhendy, a German detained in Java. Casement's own friends believed that Shaw might be able to help Casement himself, and in June and July Gertrude Parry (then Gertrude Bannister) and Casement's lawyer Michael Doyle were both eager to contact Shaw.

After the Easter Rising Shaw received several written appeals from those connected with the rebels, urging him to use his intellect and influence to help his jailed countrymen. He and his wife were uncommonly impressed when visited by Gertrude Bannister. After seeing Bannister, Shaw held meetings about helping Casement with a group of friends, but Casement's pro-Germanism was repugnant to most Londoners during the war and Shaw's pressure group disbanded after

---

[9] British Library (BL). Shaw papers. Add. 50520. fol. 257. BL. Add. 50678. fols 278-81.
[10] Shaw forbade Klein from using the statement as an actual preface, but gave him permission to quote from it. BL. Add. 50520. fol. 257.
[11] BL. Add. 56491. fol. 230; BL. Add. 50517. fol. 418.

hearing rumours of the 'Black Diaries'. Shaw was then visited by Alice Green and decided to help Casement by writing a defence for him. What Green actually wanted was money, as she was trying to raise enough funds for an excellent defence lawyer, but Shaw felt that this was pointless as the facts of the case could not be contested. Instead Shaw decided to produce a script in which Casement would argue for the status of a prisoner of war who could not be found guilty of treason. In language reminiscent of the Easter Rising itself, Shaw declared that this would be a "daring frontal attack on the position of the Crown" (Holroyd, 470). Beatrice Webb was dismayed by Shaw's plan, writing, "the Shaws don't care enough about it to spend money; and Shaw wants to compel Casement and Casement's friends to 'produce' the defence as a national dramatic event" (62-3). However, Casement himself was grateful for Shaw's approach. "I shall be so grateful if you will convey to Bernard Shaw my warmest thanks", he told his solicitor Gavan Duffy after Shaw's script was sent to him; "his view is mine, with this exception – that I should never suggest to an English court or jury that they should let me off as a prisoner of war, but tell them, "You may hang me, and be damned to you"" (Holroyd, 470).

Although grateful, Casement decided not to use Shaw's speech as part of his defence. Casement declared that the script was "excellent in very many respects – but it does not cover the ground sufficiently – unless it be that all the facts I want brought out are previously brought out by my counsel in cross examination".[12] Yet after the trial Casement expressed his regret at not using "the only defence possible, viz. my own plan and that of G.B.S." (Holroyd, 470-1). Casement did use a portion of what Shaw had written for him when he rose to address the court after the sentence had been pronounced, but of course by this time it was too late, his fate was already sealed. The failure of Shaw's attempt to represent Casement in performance had crushing consequences. Shaw felt quite sure that if his work had been performed then Casement would have been saved. Turning away from scriptwriting Shaw desperately changed strategy and wrote a flurry of articles and a petition in a last ditch attempt to save Casement. But the government, armed with the 'Black Diaries', was unflinching. Shaw might as well have saved his ink.

Shaw's Irish Play

Having seen his own script fail to save Casement, Shaw perceived that the production of any further script had the potential to be at best trivial and at worst highly offensive. However, Shaw's response to Klein was paradoxical: Shaw attempted to encourage Klein's interest in Casement whilst discouraging a filmic representation; and it is this approach that characterises Shaw's own writing between 1916 and 1935. On the face of it, after 1916 Casement had no more than a very minor impact upon Shaw's work, warranting only the occasional mention in letters and newspaper articles. Scholars usually assume that Shaw wrote no other dramatic work about Casement after the man was executed. And although Shaw never again attempted to write a dramatic script that would directly represent Casement, the executed rebel influenced one of the playwright's famous works in a profound if allusive way.

---

[12] BL. Add. 50678. fol. 254.

When Shaw sat down to write *Saint Joan* in 1923 he had been considering his subject for ten years (Holroyd, 520). After visiting Orléans in 1913 he mulled over the saint's life, pondering the potential dramatisation whilst war raged in mainland Europe and in Ireland, and whilst Casement was arrested, vilified, and executed. When *Saint Joan* was first staged in December 1923 the gunfire in Ireland's Civil War had only recently ceased, and so it was inevitable that Shaw's play, in which Joan rids France of English control, would evoke the Irish situation. In addition, Shaw saw *Saint Joan* as having a very Irish setting: he attempted to set up an Irish film industry to which he offered to donate the play, being "desirous that his plays shall employ and develop the dramatic genius of his fellow-countrymen and make Ireland's scenic beauties known in all lands" (Holroyd, 468). Shaw wrote most of *Saint Joan* in the summer of 1923 whilst in Glengariff and Parknasilla, County Kerry, and tested out his trial scene by reading it to two Irish Catholic priests (Tyson, 6-8). Declan Kiberd contends:

Writing in the heart of republican Kerry, the backdrop of so many recent battles, Shaw must have sensed many local resonances in the theme of a nation fighting free of the shackles of foreign ownership. Like many of the Irish rebels, Joan was not a landless peasant but the offspring of strong farmer stock. (438)

Kiberd is entirely correct, but he might have mentioned that, in addition, Kerry was the county in which Casement had been apprehended after vainly attempting to land from a German submarine, and that writing and reading out Joan's trial scene in this area must have had a curious resonance with the trial scene Shaw had scripted earlier for that county's most famous prisoner.

When writing the play, Shaw had certainly equated the Catholic saint with the Irish patriot. In the play's preface Shaw names Casement twice, in order to show that both Joan and Casement were tried by politically partisan assessors and that, despite the different political implications of their trials, they both suffered the same kind of persecution (Shaw, 45). Consequently, in *Saint Joan* the siege of Orléans recalls Dublin's Easter Rising, a springtime revolt that enables a country to rid itself of its English neighbour. Joan's battle occurs on the north side of the river Loire just as the seizure of the G.P.O. took place on the north side of the Liffey, and the French fighting begins on 29 April, the date on which the Irish rebels had actually surrendered in 1916. Prior to this, in March and in the spring, Joan persuades people to join her campaign and seeks armed support, echoing Casement's thirteen-month mission to raise an Irish brigade in Germany, which came to its largely futile conclusion at this time. Unlike Casement, Joan enjoys military success, yet her initial appeal for one horse and three soldiers seems as unlikely to shift the occupying power as Casement's ragged group of prisoners of war.

Moreover, Joan and Casement share a problematic sexual identity. When Casement sought a reprieve from the sentence of death the British government allowed the 'Black Diaries' to be circulated, and at Joan's trial her cross-dressing and masculine behaviour are important indictments. Her sexual behaviour is considered outrageous even amongst the French court where the Dauphin's paternity is questioned, where Dunois is known as 'Bastard' and where Le Hire's manners are '*camp*' (99). At Joan's trial the prosecutor cites the sexual scandal she has caused alongside her heretical behaviour:

> I must emphasize the gravity of two very horrible and blasphemous crimes which she does not deny. First, she has intercourse with evil spirits, and is therefore a sorceress. Second, she wears men's clothes, which is indecent, unnatural, and abominable (176).

Joan refuses to "stay at home" to do "women's work" (173) and so becomes problematic for both the English and the French for whom she fights. She is finally deserted by the French king, and after her death Charles declares that even if she were resurrected those who posthumously adore her would burn her again within half a year. It is not difficult to imagine that this might be Shaw's comment on the way that the similarly sexually-subversive Casement proved awkward for a hyper-masculine nationalism, and how Irish politicians like de Valera mouthed empty words of praise to Casement without engaging with the reality of his life and beliefs.

It is in Shaw's trial scenes that the narratives of Joan and Casement reach their closest point of conjuncture. Indeed, it appears that, having failed to see the Casement script performed in 1916, Shaw used it as a template for his 1923 play. Shaw wanted both characters to rely on the same basic legal argument, to claim that the courts did not have the jurisdiction to condemn them, and therefore that they did not have the right to pronounce death sentences. Joan argues that the court she faces is invalid. She states that the higher court of God, revealed internally to her by celestial voices, must be obeyed ahead of the earthly apparatus of Pope and bishops. It is by her own conscience that she must be judged, not the motley crew of the Inquisition. Shaw felt that Casement should claim that the English court had no right to try him either. Casement was to point out that Ireland was not the same nation as England and that therefore he was a prisoner of war. Only a trial in Ireland could decide whether Casement was a traitor to his own country or whether he was not.

In Shaw's scripts both Joan and Casement were to accept the allegations against them, but also to deny that they had done anything criminal or to be regretted. At no point do Shaw's Casement or Joan attempt to refute the facts with which the prosecution confront them. Joan, for example, responds to the question "You tried to escape?" with the answer "Of course I did; and not for the first time either" (170), whereas Casement was to explain that:

> His plea of Not Guilty must not be taken as implying any denial of the essential facts relied on by the Crown, but simply a denial that any guilt attaches to them [...]. As far as the facts are concerned, he embraces the Crown case, instead of repudiating it. (Shaw 2001, 131)

Casement was also to tell those judging him that, even if they were to hang him, he would not feel any ill-will toward them, whilst at the end of the trial Joan positively relishes her death because it will bring her closer to God. Execution guarantees both militants a position of permanent power. The Church would beatify Joan, and Casement would be sent to the Irish altar, to be canonised by Irish nationalism.

However, the real-life Roger Casement did not necessarily want to speak with the same voice as Saint Joan. Shaw wisely instructed Casement to distance himself from German militarism and to deny having any political quarrel with England. But in his response to Shaw's script Casement asserted, "I did want a German army in Ireland".[13] Shaw sympathised with Casement's anti-Imperialism but not his German affinities, and the playwright was exasperated by Casement's attitude. Casement refused to act his role in Shaw's carefully-planned performance and, by doing so, condemned himself to the hangman's noose. Shaw's attempt at producing Casement's life as a dramatic event had failed, and when the playwright returned to dramatise the patriot he used a more allusive approach instead.

After the debacle of the 1916 courtroom performance Shaw remained concerned with Casement but avoided any direct representation, and in responding to the proposed film of 1934-5 the playwright tried to steer Klein into following his example. By the start of 1935 Universal Studios came to realise that Shaw had been correct all along, and that the objections of the British censor and the Irish government would make the Casement project financially unworkable. Universal decided that their delayed Irish film would have to be abandoned completely, and Julius Klein never completed his script. Klein continued his Casement study and research, hoping to publish a book instead, but the outbreak of World War II and his entry into active service again frustrated him. In the years since 1935 an ever-proliferating number of film scripts about Casement's life have been written. Yet such projects have always been jinxed. Since 1935 no Hollywood film about the rebel has ever been made, and although the ghost of Roger Casement is beating at the door, cinema producers are still unwilling to let him in.

References

Dudgeon, Jeff. 2002. *Roger Casement: The Black Diaries: With a Study of His Background, Sexuality and Irish Political Life*. Belfast: Belfast Press

Dukore, Bernard. 1997. *Bernard Shaw on Cinema*. Carbondale: Southern Illinois University Press

Dukore, Bernard. 1985. "GBS, MGM, RKO: Shaw in Hollywood". *Shaw*. 5: 271-8

Holroyd, Michael. 1998. *Bernard Shaw: The One-Volume Definitive Edition*. London: Vintage

Kiberd, Declan. 1996. *Inventing Ireland: The Literature of the Modern Nation*. London: Vintage

McIlroy, Brian. 1989. *World Cinema 4: Ireland*. Trowbridge: Flick Books

Moynahan, Brian. 1997. *The British Century: A Photographic History of the Last Hundred Years*. London: Wiedenfield and Nicolson

Norris, David. 1981. "Homosexual People and the Christian Churches in Ireland – A Minority and its Oppressors". *Crane Bag*. 5.2: 31-7

Shaw, George Bernard. 1973. *The Bodley Head Bernard Shaw: Collected Plays with their Prefaces*. Vol. 6. Ed. Dan. H. Laurence. London: Bodley Head

Shaw, George Bernard. *The Matter With Ireland*. Ed. Dan H Laurence and David H. Greene. Florida: University of Florida Press

---

[13] BL. Add. 50678. fol. 254.

'… and these are the opening titles': Supplementing the Truth in *Bloody Sunday*

Daniel Smith

When Paul Greengrass announces his presence on the director's commentary of the *Bloody Sunday* DVD, he follows it with a tacit acknowledgement of the exercise's potential for redundancy. In *Bloody Sunday,* he has consciously attempted to produce an account of historical events in a way that reinforces this account's claim to truth both overtly and, crucially, formally. The drama-documentary format is intended to present actual historical events within the framework of a dramatic narrative, and this requires some interesting slight of hand in order to keep the join between these two forms – documentary and drama – from becoming too obvious. Yet, having gone to all this trouble, the director is asked, for the DVD release, to disrupt all this by talking over his film – in fact, drawing attention to the artifice involved in the entire project. He does this with some recognition of the potential for absurdity that this has by stating the blindingly obvious: "these are the opening titles".[1] Yet this good humour cannot dispel the anxiety the exercise creates. How are we supposed to react to a director telling us exactly how he deliberately created an "edge of authenticity"? Can you create authenticity, or is Greengrass saying that authenticity is an affectation, a shell constructed to make the truth more believable? How does his claim that he wanted to "create a credible account" of Bloody Sunday affect our viewing of a film that is heavily dependent on its appearance as unmediated reportage? This is a paradox that threatens not just to undermine the illusion of actuality that the film constructs, but one that reveals the lack at the heart of our assumptions about actuality, truth, and the ability of film to present either.

Jacques Derrida first articulated the concept of the supplement with regard to the work of Rousseau, and later Levi-Strauss, observing how their own ideas often contained, in apparent marginalia, a destructive critique of their own theories. Both writers used the word 'supplement' in an unproblematic way to denote an expansion or verification, yet Derrida worked through the implications of what could be seen as a minor linguistic quibble to show that the introduction of a supplement fatally threatened the unity and integrity of their central theories. The supplement makes visible the lack that was already present in the thing itself. The extra material on the *Bloody Sunday* DVD operates as just such a supplement. By drawing attention to the artifice involved in its construction, it highlights the unspoken assumptions and gaps that were already present in the way in which we accept or reject the presentation of truth and actuality. Though the commentary by Greengrass and James Nesbitt, and the separate track provided by Don Mullan, are intended to reinforce the film's claim to the truth, every time they draw attention to that authenticity, they reveal it to be a construction. In order to fully explore the implications of this paradox, it is necessary first to look at the way in which the film *Bloody Sunday* establishes its claim to present actuality, which is not a simple

---

[1] Unless otherwise noted, all quotations from Paul Greengrass are taken from the director's commentary audio track on the DVD edition of *Bloody Sunday,* 2002.

matter even before the introduction of this supplement.

The real city of Derry did not prove satisfactory for the purposes of the Saville Inquiry into the events of Bloody Sunday. The city itself is thirty years too old, and natural wear and tear have reduced its quality as evidence. The Rossville flats, for example, no longer exist, shops have changed their names, and its residents of the 1970s have scattered to foreign countries. Even representations of the contemporary Derry are of limited use; photographs show crucial areas in impenetrable shadow, while the area of the city that is in question lies at the corner of four separate Ordinance Survey maps, each updated at different times, when important structures had either disappeared or had not yet been built.[2] Ciaran Carson may have been speaking of Belfast when he wrote that:

"There is a map of the city which shows the bridge that was never built.
A map which shows the bridge that collapsed; the streets that never existed." (from "Turn Again", in *Belfast Confetti*)

but it is an observation that can be equally well applied to the Derry of the Bloody Sunday Inquiry. Since the actual Derry was so inadequate, the Saville inquiry has constructed an elaborate computer model of the city, a four-dimensional virtual Derry that is so realistic that some witnesses have been almost overcome with the rush of memories brought back by the sight of familiar, yet long-vanished sights. Jean Baudrillard would be proud of this model, more real than the real itself, and certainly more adequate than the cardboard model constructed for Widgery, the one he is seen presiding over like a colossus in Jimmy McGovern's film *Sunday*.[3]

For similar reasons, the real Derry was inadequate for the purposes of Greengrass' film. The authenticity that needed to be constructed extended to period clothes, vehicles and haircuts, all necessary to maintain the documentary illusion. Unfortunately, just as those youths who had thrown stones in 1972 were now middle-aged pillars of the community, the Creggan and the Bogside were now far too prosperous to stand in for their battle-scarred younger selves. In a twist of historical irony, the filmmakers had to turn south, to the Ballymun area of Dublin,

---

[2] "Unfortunately, the area with which the Tribunal is most concerned is one which lies at the intersection of four Ordnance Survey maps not all of which were compiled or revised at the same time. It is possible to match up those four maps either by physically placing the relevant squares next to each other or by performing the equivalent exercise on computer. The former exercise was performed in 1972 and the statements given by the solders to the Military Police have in most cases annexed to them the resulting plan. This is not wholly satisfactory since the four different plans that formed the composite both include buildings that were not and exclude buildings that were there in 1972". Christopher Clarke QC, speaking at the 1st preliminary hearing, 20th July 1999.

[3] McGovern's film is full of touches like this, in which he presents more or less reliable facts, but in such a didactic way as to leave the viewer in no doubt as to the conclusions one is supposed to draw. McGovern's production team would have had to reconstruct this model themselves – a reconstruction of a reconstruction – since the original has long since been lost and/or destroyed.

to find an area with the necessary air of barricaded despair. This ghetto is economic, rather than political or racial, but with the correct street names attached to the walls and with rubble barricades in the roads, it was evidently an adequate replacement for the streets of Derry in 1972. These streets had to be populated, and many of the parts in *Bloody Sunday* were taken by Derry residents and soldiers, who were held by all to bring the requisite authenticity to their portrayals of a former generation. The exact source of this authenticity is difficult to locate. In the case of the soldiers or ex-soldiers, it was or can be inferred largely from their deportment. Don Mullan, on a second commentary track, notes that he was shocked by the way they carried themselves like soldiers, and that he was unaware, at first, that that is exactly what they were. Greengrass comments that "they look like soldiers, don't they? They don't look like actors". They certainly sound like soldiers, and McGovern's Paras seem stilted and actorly by comparison. However, with certain other tokens, the thinking behind this assignment of authenticity becomes less clear. For example, the part of Gerard Donaghy is played by Declan Duddy, the nephew of Jack Duddy, the first person to be killed on Bloody Sunday. Since Duddy never knew his uncle and was not even born at the time of Bloody Sunday, it is difficult to see why this brought such realism to the role. Certainly, as an authentic Derry resident and an authentic teenager, Duddy has the accent and the mannerisms, and plays the role with considerable skill, but as with the soldiers, any authenticity must be perceived, projected from outside, not some inherent quality.

Bloody Sunday also uses a variety of filmic devices to enforce its claim to faithful representation of the truth. The most obvious is in the use of handheld cameras to produce the effect of contemporary news footage. We are made aware of the camera through this technique, since it differs from the more common use of the Steadicam in film and because its motion suggests the presence of a real operator, subject to the dangers he is filming. Yet at the same time we are invited, as in classical Hollywood film, to forget the camera, to ignore it as being a neutral, disinterested observer of events. Because this is 'raw' footage, with what are ostensibly the only cuts overtly marked by fades to black, it is implied (or perhaps we are intended to infer) that this is otherwise unedited reportage, and thus closer to the immediate truth. The assertion that immediacy produces a greater measure of truth is problematic at the best of times – in fact, one of the many reasons for the vilification of the initial investigation into Bloody Sunday was that Lord Chief Justice Widgery deliberately limited his inquiry in order to rely solely on eyewitnesses and reach a conclusion as soon as possible after the events. Certainly the intervention of thirty years has handicapped Saville, but the suggestion that proximity is in a directly proportional relationship with truth is a false one, and one implicitly addressed by the film. The cameras in *Bloody Sunday* do not catch everything, partly for practical reasons – it would be impossible to show everything that took place on that day in a length of time acceptable to most audiences – but partly for a more subtle reason. This paragraph from *Sight and Sound* is worth quoting in full:

> Still, once the thud of rubber bullets becomes the crack of live rounds, Greengrass contrives to have his camera elsewhere. We hear the first shots, but know not their provenance. Later, once the Paras

are firing freely, we see angry marchers restraining gunmen among their own numbers (seemingly of the Official – rather than Provisional – IRA). But the Paras' final assault on Glenfada Park is plainly presented as a rampage, and Greengrass foregrounds the worst iniquities: Jim Wray, lying paralysed by one bullet, duly executed by a second at close range; and Barney McGuigan, shot in the head while waving a white hankie. (Kelly)

Greengrass' intention, which seems justified by Richard Kelly's response here, is to provide the essentials of the narrative; in his words "a credible account of the events of that day", what he has also referred to as a "shared story". This would provide an acceptable middle ground for a compromise, an artistic version of what Saville is attempting legally. The aim is to provide the most important and least controversial landmarks that allow the viewer to fill in the gaps with that version of truth that least challenges their preconceptions. To do this, he needs to show certain largely accepted facts, such as the presence of gunmen in the Bogside and the execution of James Wray, but the way he chooses to do so is crucial. As Richard Kelly notes in the quotation above, the camera does not catch those first live rounds being fired, or even hitting home – we see only the wounded Damien Donaghy and Jack Johnston. A similar technique is applied to the other killings, as the camera reacts to the shootings rather than witnessing them. The combined effect of this is to enforce the conception of the camera as a semi-omniscient observer. It doesn't see everything, which reinforces its credibility as an authentic, present, subjective eyewitness, but it does see everything important that we need to construct our authoritative, credible account of events, thus making sure its claim to truth is backed up by all the factual evidence that thirty years of distance has produced. For example, in one scene the marchers pass by a Para wire-cutting party on top of a wall. From the Paras' point of view, their riflemen are protecting the wire-cutters from potential sniper attacks. From the marchers', they are deliberately trying to provoke the crowd by scanning them with high-powered rifles. Greengrass' careful juxtaposition of observer positions shows us how two seemingly opposed versions of events can be reconciled, and a space for a consensual version of reality created.

The strength of *Bloody Sunday's* claim to truth is thus predicated on its negotiation of the space between these two poles, which can be called authenticity and authority. One is based on immediacy and the privileged position of a present eyewitness; the other on historical distance and disinterested objectivity. As the *Los Angeles Times* review stated:

Cinematographer Strasburg deserves special mention for the way his expressive, jittery hand-held *cinéma vérité* camerawork, lurking around corners and eavesdropping on conversations, creates the immediacy of newsreel footage. "Bloody Sunday" plays like it's the work of a documentary crew with great instincts and total access. It manages the difficult trick of conveying chaos while allowing us to recognize the patterns in the madness. It's both spontaneous enough to resemble reality captured on the fly and focused enough to be intensely dramatic. (Turran)

Both authenticity and authority stake a claim to a different kind of truth, and *Bloody Sunday* utilises both of them, which is by no means a simple task. Its use of 'real' people, 'real' locations and of documentary techniques all lay claim to a discourse of unmediated authenticity. However, its meticulous research, careful reconstruction of events from multiple sources and its appeal to an idea of a unitary objective historical truth all depend on the discourse of authority. This tension can be seen in a comment by Mark Redhead, who wrote much of the initial script:

> These are not documentaries. They are dramas based on true stories. Drama-docs have the image of something to do with the job of journalism. The skills of journalism are necessary to do it properly, but it's not a journalistic exercise. Journalism's primary aim is the presentation of facts. We're searching for the underlying meaning of the event. (Redhead)

That meaning, however, is still sought through the methods of journalism, and displayed up on screen through its conventions. *Bloody Sunday* deliberately recreates several of the iconic images of the historical Bloody Sunday, seamlessly transferring still, sometimes black & white photographs into moving colour footage. One example of this is in the sight of Barney McGuigan's body, lying under a bloodstained civil rights banner. Listen carefully to the radio traffic – according to Greengrass meticulously reconstructed from the actual army transcripts – and it is possible to hear someone, presumably a soldier, telling headquarters that the press are taking photographs of this scene. While the army, at one step removed both physically and emotionally from this event, are able to recognise the value of the image as propaganda, those closest to it are shown reacting to the tragedy on a human scale, James Nesbitt as Ivan Cooper in particular overwhelmed by the enormity of the death he has witnessed at first hand. We are, in this scene, privy to both versions of truth. Emotionally invested in the characters and the unfolding tragedy, an audience that is aware of these pre-existing images of Bloody Sunday also recognises this particular scene from an historical distance. By presenting us with the circumstances that resulted in the production of such iconic images, *Bloody Sunday* is able to appropriate their visceral verisimilitude while at the same time laying claim to the status of History with a capital 'H'.

Crucially, this technique poses the least challenge to the willing suspension of disbelief. While, in theory, we as the audience 'know' that what we are watching is a reconstruction (after all, that's Adam from *Cold Feet* up there), Greengrass' successful balancing act pre-empts our concerns about the representation of historical, violent events. It is objective enough to satisfy those who insist on a context, and dramatic enough for those who insist on the emotional, personal impact of this violence. McGovern's *Sunday,* by contrast, approaches its subject in a much more straightforward way, as a linear narrative placed in direct conflict with the official version of truth epitomised by Widgery. By doing so, *Sunday* leaves itself more open to hostile critical analysis than Greengrass' film, since it allows no ground for negotiation. If one disagrees with the presentation of some or all of the events in *Sunday,* the narrative is derailed and there is an inevitable tendency to question the factual basis of the entire film. Because *Sunday* is so overtly didactic, it skews even the presentation of the same accepted facts used in *Bloody Sunday*, until every piece of dialogue sounds like a means of advancing an argument, however impeccable its documentary credentials.

But *Bloody Sunday*'s approach is not without its own risks. Even the most media-literate of us can find the blurring of boundaries between accepted genres disturbing. Kathryn Flett, reviewing *Bloody Sunday* for the Observer, states:

> Even if this was as close to the truth of the events as we shall ever see in the context of a drama (and one strongly suspects that it is), these grainy faux-news images also have the power to superimpose themselves over reality to create a powerful cinematic version of False Memory Syndrome.

The fear of False Memory Syndrome here can be read as patronising – "what if ordinary people believe this is reality?" – but I think the anxiety is well-grounded, at least with regard to Northern Ireland. The debate over revisionism is just one manifestation of the concern that has grown up around the battle between competing discourses that attempt to sideline one version of reality and establish their own as the dominant one. There is, therefore, a corresponding anxiety about the nature of authenticity and the need to preserve its habitat. Post-modern defences that question the bases of these assumptions are often accused of denying the value or even the existence of reality, yet the level of concern over the need to protect the truth suggests that reality is not so robust and self-evident as is often claimed.

Flett also comments that: "*Bloody Sunday* opted for widescreen scratch'n'sniff HyperRealDocuDramaVision. Shot like newsreel footage, replete with camera-wobble, *Bloody Sunday* looked and sounded uncannily like 1972". Although not alone in noticing this technique, none of these first reviewers draw attention to the fact that *Bloody Sunday* is not merely "like newsreel footage". Even the most cursory glance at the BBC's coverage of that day reveals that something far more interesting than simulated *cinema verité* is going on in the scenes of the march itself. Greengrass and Ivan Strasburg, the film's cinematographer, have obviously gone to great lengths to match their production with the news footage shot on the day, in matters such as composition, length of shots and even editing (the cuts to a circling helicopter that act as a signifier of the British military presence in the film perform much the same function in the thirty-year-old news footage). Certain scenes in *Bloody Sunday* are not, therefore, a reconstruction of events, but a reconstruction of the reporting of those events, right down to the interview with General Ford which is reproduced almost word-for-word with Tim Pigott-Smith.[4]

JohnMcGovern's *Sunday* also utilises this interview, but while it seems likely that Piggott-Smith has based his performance on the recorded interview, even down to copying hesitations, Christopher Ecclestone gives a more polished performance, as if his general Ford is giving a speech he prepared earlier. Though on paper these are substantially the same scene, the differing presentations highlight the filmmakers' respective concerns: Greengrass' to produce a 'credible account', McGovern's to show the prejudices of the British and argue the case for the, as he sees it, pre-planned nature of the events of Bloody Sunday. *Sunday* also reproduces the interview with Father Daly, carried out by the same BBC team. In fact, this interview is shown a total of three times in the film – once 'as it happens', and then on TV in a Catholic home and a British army pub. This has the effect of drawing attention to the importance laid on eyewitness accounts as opposed to the official military lies carried by the BBC 'half-way around the world before the truth has done its boots up'. The actor playing Daly in *Sunday* does seem to have based his performance on the actual interview, save for one crucial omission – he does not say "there weren't even stones thrown", which the real Father Daly did say. Now, while this can be interpreted as "there weren't even stones [being] thrown [at that moment]", this would have seriously undermined Daly's credibility as a reliable witness, since we have seen stoning going almost constantly prior to the Paras' attack.

This delicate negotiation of authenticity and authority, so painstakingly constructed, is threatened in several ways by *Bloody Sunday*'s release on DVD. Firstly, the format allows a detailed examination of the film, and makes analysis of its techniques far easier, as well as permitting high-quality freeze-frames, forward and reverse scans and instant jumps to different portions of the disc. Far more threatening than these aspects, however (which are, after all, merely extensions of what is already possible with video), is the addition of so-called special features, extensions to the central text, and the insertion of commentaries – audio tracks superimposed on the film itself. It is these that are most devastating, since they are in not external commentaries like reviews or interviews, but have been reintegrated into the text of the film and alter it significantly (and, I would argue, irrevocably). By explaining the process of construction, and the motivations behind it, the commentaries demolish at least on of the bases of the film's claims to truth. When Don Mullan describes how authentic Derry residents were rounded up by 70s-style loudhailer vans and posters, he draws attention to the artificiality of the exercise. When Greengrass draws attention to the effort involved in reproducing authenticity, he strips that authenticity of the illusion of effortless presentation, of the supposed self-evidential nature of truth. When he also describes the piles of documents, eyewitness accounts, radio transcripts and newspaper reports that were trawled through to produce the initial script, we are made aware of the selective nature of the evidence used, and the subjective basis for what was apparently objective authority. None of this is crippling, or particularly novel; what is, though, is the way in which this supplementary material, designed to reinforce the film's claim to truth, has been absorbed into the complex dynamic of a film that relies on a skilful appeal to the twin poles of authenticity and authority. This supplement was always already latent in the film, but prior to the director's commentary, it was covert and needed to be excavated. Afterwards it is overt and on the surface. However, once we move past this initial recognition and destruction wreaked by the supplementary material, it is possible to regard both the film and its supplement as elements in a wider system, and to see that the damage, while it may be fatal, is not serious. As Derrida himself

---

[4] In the film, this interview is curtailed as Pigott-Smith turns to deal with his troops. Had he gone on to make the claims that the real General Ford did about acid bombs thrown from the Rossville flats, his credibility would have been seriously undermined, since nothing of the missile throwing from the flats was shown in the film.

says: "When the supplement accomplishes its office and fills the lack, there is no harm done" (298). It is only when the supplement goes unrecognised, or is denied, that a dangerous abyss opens and we take the representation of events for the unmediated, revelatory truth.

The relationship between the film *Bloody Sunday* 'proper' and its director's commentary is in this regard, like the relationship between a system and its supplement. The film presents itself as reconstructed actuality, as close to the truth as it is possible to get. It does not, crucially, claim to be unmediated reality, but is much more subtle. It forms its narrative unity around the concept of the 'credible account', the version of events that puts least strain on the suspension of disbelief, and it does this by appealing to the twin poles of authenticity and authority. For every scene of bloody reality, there is a corresponding formal insistence on historical distance, assuring us that this authenticity has been ratified by strict evidentiary standards. I have drawn a great deal of attention to the work and skill that has gone into this operation, partly to highlight that its apparently effortless appearance is nothing of the sort, but also to reveal that its claims to truth are by no means simple. This is also, in an unintentional way, exactly what the director's commentary does. Every time Greengrass or Nesbitt stress the difficulty involved in achieving authenticity, they undermine one of the crucial ideological bases of that authenticity. Every time they imply that this is what really happened, they remind us that this is not what really happened, even if it may well be as close as we are going to get in a film. This is not to suggest that *Bloody Sunday* should be dismissed as false. Rather that we should recognise the nature of the foundations on which its claim to be true are based, foundations that include two very different ideals of truth.

References

Carson, Ciaran. 1990. *Belfast Confetti*. Newcastle: Bloodaxe

Derrida, Jacques. 1997. *Of Grammatology*. Trans. Gayatri Chakravorty Spivak. Baltimore: Johns Hopkins

Pringle, Peter and Philip Jacobson. 2000. *'Those are Real Bullets, Aren't They?' Bloody Sunday, Derry, 30 January 1972*. London: Fourth Estate

Kelly, Richard. 2002. "Bloody Sunday". *Sight and Sound*, March. http://www.bfi.org.uk/sightandsound/2002_03/bloody.html

Flett, Katherine. 2002. "The Art of Darkness". *The Observer*. 27 January http://www.observer.co.uk/review/story/0,6903,639962,00.html

Redhead, Mark. *Press Gazette*. http://www.pressgazette.co.uk/

Turran, Kenneth. "A day of madness made real in gripping 'Bloody Sunday'". *Los Angeles Times*. 18 October 2002. http://www.calendarlive.com/movies/reviews/cl-et turan18oct18,0,7473467.story

Nationalism, Gender, and Irish and Scottish Historiography, 1919-1939: A Comparison of Helena Concannon and Agnes Mure Mackenzie[1]

Nadia Clare Smith

"I am not a professional historian; but then, no-one is perfect," Michel Foucault once claimed. Like Foucault, Helena Concannon and Agnes Mure Mackenzie were not professional historians. These two women, one Irish and one Scottish, wrote most of their historical works in the 1920s and 1930s. This essay argues that their careers are important because they shed light on the interplay between gender, politics, and historiography in Ireland and Scotland during the interwar period.

The careers of Concannon and Mackenzie complicate aspects of the paradigm of Western women historians developed by Bonnie Smith in *The Gender of History: Men, Women and Historical Practice* (1998). Smith argues that between 1800 and 1940, female historians tended to write popular women's, social, and cultural history, while men wrote "high" political history that legitimized the state. They simultaneously gained greater access to political power and raised the profile of the historian-citizen (Smith, 3, 7-8, 11). The university and the state were part of the male public sphere, inaccessible to women, who were originally denied access to higher education and the vote.

The two female historians under consideration do not entirely conform to this model. Concannon entered the Irish Free State's political establishment, becoming a Fianna Fail party TD and later a Senator largely *because* she wrote popular, politicized women's and religious history. Mackenzie, a Scottish nationalist and member of the Saltire Society, wrote a six-volume political history of Scotland, though she also addressed religious, cultural, and women's history.

Concannon and Mackenzie do, however, conform to Bonnie Smith's paradigm in that they, like many other women historians, were not always taken seriously by the university-based historical establishment. These women believed that open identification with non-elite, subordinate groups in history and overt political stances could coexist with sound historical scholarship, rather than being inherently opposed. This view was not shared by many professional historians at the time as the ethos of objectivity and scholarly detachment governed historical practice at the university level. Though influential in shaping the official contours of the discipline, the male-dominated historical establishment in Ireland and Scotland did not write history in a vacuum. They had to grapple with "history from below", which included popular nationalist histories, sometimes written by women. Non-academic, popular women historians played an important if indirect role in shaping modern Irish and Scottish historiography, because they raised a discordant voice against which elite, university-based male historians were compelled to write. As Bonnie Smith contends, "professionalism is a relationship dependent on discredited voices and devalued narratives" (10)

[1] I would like to gratefully acknowledge the Irish Research Council for the Humanities and Social Sciences, which awarded me a fellowship.

Helena Concannon (1878-1952)

Helena Walsh was born in Maghera, Co. Derry (now Northern Ireland) on October 28, 1878. Her parents owned Walsh's Hotel in Maghera. The Walshes were middle-class Catholics and nationalists, and thus belonged to Ulster's minority community. Helena attended a Loreto Convent school in Dublin, and later received a B.A. and M.A. in Modern Languages from the Royal University of Ireland.[2] She married Thomas Concannon in 1906; the childless couple lived in Galway for many years (Macken, 91-4, 96). A supporter of Eamon de Valera and the anti-Treaty side during the Irish Civil War, she later joined his Fianna Fail party. De Valera, shrewdly assessing Concannon as a valuable asset to Fianna Fail, urged her to run for office as a National University of Ireland candidate. He believed that having a devoutly Catholic, popular writer of hagiographical historical works in his new party would enhance Fianna Fail's image in the eyes of the Catholic Church, and generate greater support from the clergy.

Concannon was a nonprofessional historian rather that an academic one. She had no formal training in history, but rather in Modern Languages. She wrote over twenty books, which can be grouped into the following categories: textbooks, women's history, and religious history.[3] In some cases, the last two categories are identical. Two historical textbooks Concannon wrote for schoolchildren are *Makers of Irish History* (1918) and *Defence of Our Gaelic Civilisation, 1460-1660: an Irish History for Junior Grade Classes* (1921). Both reflected Concannon's strong Catholic nationalist beliefs. Her textbooks, because of their ideological dimensions and emotionalism, later attracted criticism from scholars researching the teaching of Irish history. Concannon's first textbook was denounced by William Starkie, the Commissioner of National Education in the immediate pre-Independence period. He complained in his diary that it "[gave] colour to Sinn Fein principles…I can't understand how these publishers can think we can sanction such books".[4] Nationalist history textbooks were regarded with suspicion in the tense days of World War I, particularly after the 1916 Rising. Concannon extolled such history-makers as Brian Boru and Daniel O'Connell. In *Makers of Irish History* (1918) she lauded the Irish Volunteers of the late eighteenth century, which would have resonated with Irish readers who could relate them to the Volunteers of their own era.

Concannon's *Defence of Our Gaelic Civilisation, 1460-1660* antagonized the educational authorities during the turbulent days of the Anglo-Irish War, but was approved by their successors in the Free State era. In this textbook, Concannon asserted that the Irish have historically been a "fit race" and the women of Ireland "fit mates of such men, and fit mothers of a numerous progeny of soldier sons" (Concannon, 1921: 11). She justified Irish armed resistance to English "heretical" rule by citing a 1580 statement by Pope Gregory XIII (Concannon, 1921: 268-70). A major lesson from her study of early modern Ireland was that the Flight of the Earls after the Elizabethan Wars had been a mistake; Ireland should always keep its soldiers at home (Concannon, 1921: 226). Overall, Concannon's textbooks illustrate Gabriel Doherty's assessment that "the dominant theme of history

---

[2] Obituary, *Irish Times*, 28 February 1952; Macken, 91-4.

[3] A volume of her poetry was published posthumously.

[4] Starkie's diary, 31 May 1918, Starkie Papers, TCD MS 9211, 228-9. See Fitzpatrick, 178.

teaching in Ireland was the belief in an inner spirituality of the Irish people, demonstrated by their abiding fidelity to the twin ideals of Catholicism and political freedom" (Doherty, 342). She believed that she would enhance the national pride and self-worth of Irish children by highlighting their nation's spiritual tradition and history of armed resistance.

Books on women's history written by Concannon include *Women of '98* (1919), *Daughters of Banba* (1922), *The Poor Clares in Ireland* (1929), and *Irish Nuns in Penal Days* (1931). *Women of '98* was written to inspire and sustain nationalist women during the Anglo-Irish War, and to urge them to emulate Irish women who had sacrificed their men in a previous struggle for Irish independence (Macken, 96; Bartlett, 64-5). The book consists of biographical sketches of the mothers, wives, sisters, and lovers of famous men in the 1798 Rebellion. The women tend to be idealized as beautiful, sweet, saintly, and self-sacrificing. Overall, *Women of '98* was heavily prescriptive. For example, Concannon stated that "a nation is what its women make its men" and proceeded to describe Mrs. Teeling as an ideal "mother of '98" for "exercising the sweet and lovely rule of the mistress of a Catholic home, training her children to the noblest ideals of life and conduct, [and] directing her servants with gentle authority" (Concannon, 1919: 71). Descriptions such as these underscored the centrality of the ideal of the republican mother for Concannon. She felt that the future of her ideal Irish republic depended on at-home, Catholic nationalist mothers raising virtuous future citizens. She attributed "success for the long fight we have had for our faith and nationality…to Irish mothers and Irish homes",[5] although some women had boldly ventured outside their homes in the struggle for Irish independence.

Daughters of Banba was also heavily prescriptive and sentimental. It described various groups of women throughout Irish history. The non-feminist Concannon declared that she wanted to write a women-centered history of Ireland, maintaining that national histories tended to leave out the female population, and were therefore incomplete (Concannon, 1922: ix). Concannon, in her didactic and presentist book, asked the reader to reflect upon what Irish women suffered during "the tremendous struggle, and then let us resolve to make them the only return they desire—to be faithful, even as they were faithful" (Concannon, 1922: 260-1). In other words, if contemporary Irish women were to reject ideals such as piety, nationalism, and self-sacrifice, they would blaspheme the memory of their foremothers, who would have wanted an Ireland devoted to "Faith and Fatherland."

Helena Concannon's books on nuns, such as *The Poor Clares in Ireland* (1929) and *Irish Nuns in Penal Days* (1931), were also unique for the time in recovering women's history. Although based on scholarly research, they were hagiographical and sought to glorify the Catholic Church, which grew in institutional strength during the Free State years. Concannon's books highlighted the spiritual resistance, tenacity, and courage of the Irish nuns in the face of religious persecution. Her works on nuns differed greatly from her British contemporary Eileen Power's *Medieval English Nunneries* (1921), which critically analyzed convents from the perspective of social and institutional history (Berg, 116-23).

---

[5] Dail Debates, Vol. 67, 12 May 1937, cols. 241-2. Some contemporary historians agree that mothers frequently influenced their sons' decisions to join the IRA in the War of Independence. See Hart, 175. For a sociological perspective on Irish Catholic mothers, see Inglis, 72-3, 187-200.

Why would a historian choose to write in such an emotive, if not melodramatic, way? Literary scholars, examining the device of sentimentality in relation to women poets and novelists, have offered insights that could be applied to Concannon. Jane Tompkins proposes that sentimental literary works could be viewed as "political enterprise[s], halfway between sermon and social theory, that both codif[y] and attempt to mold the values of their time" (126). Sentimental literature may serve to humanize, speak for, and affirm the lived experience of those who have been oppressed and marginalized. One of Concannon's major concerns in her books was to portray the Irish Catholic women as righteous, worthy, completely innocent victims of oppression who in no way deserved their fate. This stood in contrast to Unionist historians of her generation, who identified more with the ruling elites than with their historic subordinates. Her books on Irish women's history received glowing reviews in scholarly and popular Catholic journals (Pierse, 380), but were generally not reviewed in mainstream historical journals.

Helena Concannon served in the Dail from 1933 to 1937, and in the Senate from 1938 until her death in 1952. Her career as a politician in the reigning party (Fianna Fail was in power until 1948) signaled her move away from her earlier status of dissident writer to a position in which she defended power arrangements in the political and intellectual realms. She did, however, advocate for less powerful members of Irish society in her promotion of social welfare legislation. Concannon addressed women's issues in Dail debates on agriculture, social welfare, and the 1937 Constitution, which, unlike feminists, she supported, maintaining that its controversial clauses associating women with the domestic sphere could be used to promote social legislation, such as family allowances. In addition, she favored the Constitution's republican orientation. Concannon set herself up as a spokesperson for women by initiating numerous speeches with "I speak as a woman".[6] In this respect, she was very much like the politically active Irish feminists. She was middle-class, educated, and had a housekeeper, which enabled her to pursue a career outside the home. Irish feminists, however, were frequently vilified as self-appointed and unrepresentative by political and clerical power brokers when they spoke on behalf of women, and she was not.[7]

Concannon's intervention in a Senate debate on censorship, which she herself had had brushes with prior to 1922, highlighted her interest in policing the boundaries of Irish intellectual life in the decades after Independence. Concannon differed with other Irish intellectuals by supporting draconian censorship legislation in the 1945 Senate debate. She believed that "racy" books led to sexual chaos, which could overwhelm and destroy a well-regulated State. Concannon extravagantly praised the men on the Censorship Board who read and banned questionable books, adding, "of course no woman would undertake that revolting task".[8] She denounced another senator for criticizing censorship when the Board "performed the thankless task, the revolting task, of reading the sordid stuff that

---

[6] See, for instance, Dail Debates, vol. 53, col. 1499; vol. 61, col. 1676.

[7] Clear, 179-86. Concannon was at least as unrepresentative of the majority of Irish women as middle-class feminists were. Not only was she an educated, childless married woman with a career, she also represented an elite minority group, Irish university graduates, in the Dail and the Senate.

[8] Seanad Debates, vol. 30, 28 November 1945, cols. 1057-8.

some people tell us is classical".[9] Her performance in this debate revealed that she was now an anti-libertarian republican who believed that individual rights could be sharply curtailed if they appeared to threaten the community.[10]

Helena Concannon died on February 27, 1952, leaving a mixed legacy. As a nationalist prior to Independence in 1922, she was initially a cultural and political dissident, but later gained access to power and became a pillar of the Irish establishment. Concannon was unusual and innovative in writing women's history, but the subversive potential of such a strategy was contained within a conservative intellectual framework. She sometimes played an "enforcer" role, supporting anti-libertarian measures, such as censorship. Concannon had a mixed record on women; while she helped the material condition of some by promoting social legislation, she alienated others by idealizing traditionalist models of womanhood that many could not live up to.

Agnes Mure Mackenzie (1891-1955)

Agnes Mure Mackenzie's major work, a six-volume history of Scotland written between 1934 and 1941, conforms more to the conventions of academic history than does the work of Concannon. However, Mackenzie, like Concannon, was not an academic historian, and had not been trained in historical research.

Agnes Mure Mackenzie was born on the Isle of Lewis in 1891. Her Scottish father was a doctor. Her mother, an Englishwoman from Yorkshire, encouraged Agnes, who had vision and hearing problems, in her academic pursuits. Mackenzie entered the University of Aberdeen in 1908 and graduated with a first-class honors degree in English. Before embarking on her historical project, Mackenzie held various academic posts, such as an assistantship in English at Aberdeen and a lectureship in English at Birkbeck College, London. She also wrote historical novels, reviews for the *Times Literary Supplement* and the *New Statesman*, and literary criticism. She was awarded a DLitt in 1929. By the early 1930s, she was conducting archival research on Scottish history in the British Museum and elsewhere.[11] Her first historical volume, *Robert Bruce, King of Scots* was published in 1934, and was followed by *The Rise of the Stewarts* (1935), *The Scotland of Queen Mary and the Religious Wars* (1936), *The Passing of the Stewarts* (1937), *The Foundations of Scotland* (1938; chronologically it precedes *Robert Bruce*), and *Scotland in Modern Times, 1720-1939* (1941). Thus, her books provide a survey of Scotland from prehistory to 1939, an impressive achievement.

Critics noted that Mackenzie's historical judgments were conditioned by her Tory, Episcopalian, Scottish nationalist outlook. She favored the Stuarts and the Jacobite cause, and was hostile to Presbyterians and Whigs who favored the Union. She tended to use modern political terms to describe historical actors, which sometimes appeared anachronistic. For instance, the Calvinists were consistently described as religious totalitarians or left-wingers. Presbyterian leader John Knox, enemy of Mary Queen of Scots, was compared to Hitler, and Calvin's Geneva was described as "a totalitarian hierocracy that has many affinities in both form and temper with early Bolshevism, Fascism, and Nazism, especially the last" (Mackenzie, 1936: 87).

---

[9] Seanad Debates, vol. 30, 14 November 1945, cols. 989-91.

[10] For a recent discussion and assessment of the Irish censorship policy, see Fallon, 201-11.

[11] Obituary, *Times*, 1 March 1955; Shepherd, 132-40.

Mackenzie believed herself to be a dissident popular historian, rehabilitating Scottish nationalist and Jacobite historiography. This tradition, she believed, had been dismissed by the Whig and Unionist historiography that dominated Scottish academic history. She sounded a subversive note in her foreword to *Robert Bruce*. Writing that academic and popular assessment of Bruce were at odds – the former held that Bruce was initially a "treacherous and rather contemptible figure" who later transformed into an important leader, while the latter rated him an outstanding national hero – she maintained that her research in the primary sources vindicated the popular view of Bruce. Mackenzie announced, "I found to my pleasure that the academic convention as to Bruce ripped into shreds when one tested it by examination of its own data...the popular tradition of history is very often badly wrong, but at times it is truer than the academic...in short, I found the old folk-tradition was right, and that the old popular hero was a hero" (Mackenzie, 1934: vii-viii). This affirmation of popular history over "scientific" academic history would not have endeared Mackenzie to many professionally trained historians at the time.

Unlike Concannon's works, Mackenzie's volumes were reviewed in professional historical journals, such as *History* and *Irish Historical Studies* (I.H.S.). She received mixed reviews, with most reviewers commenting on how her religious and political views shaped her interpretation of historical actors and events. R.L. Mackie, a history lecturer at the Training College in Dundee, reviewed *Robert Bruce* in *History*. He maintained that Mackenzie had been partially successful in rehabilitating Bruce, but that the evidence did not support all of her contentions. Mackie concluded that Mackenzie had written the best biography of Bruce to date: it was "sane and accurate in spite of its enlivening touches of prejudice" (369-70). W.C. Dickinson, a librarian at the LSE, commented on Mackenzie's inaccuracies and bias when reviewing *The Rise of the Stewarts*. However, he added that while Mackenzie's "Stewarts are apt to be kings who can do no wrong," she openly acknowledged that she was responding to "the strong anti-national and anti-Stewart bias of the dominant school." He praised her readable style and her grasp of how European politics affected Scotland (55-6). Historian James Eadie Todd of Queen's University, Belfast wrote one of the harshest reviews of Mackenzie's work in the new *I.H.S.* He worried that the popular readership at whom Mackenzie's *The Passing of the Stewarts* (and other books) were aimed "will fail to realize how far it falls short of dispassionate history, for the work of selection and omission have been skillfully done." He perceived Mackenzie's books as Scottish nationalist propaganda, and argued that she was unfair in judging Presbyterians and Whigs as opposed to Tory nationalists. Todd concluded that Mackenzie's hostile descriptions of Calvinists indicated "her temperamental unsuitability for the task of interpreting the history of a century which, above all others, calls for some sympathetic understanding of religious enthusiasm" (205-6).

Like Concannon, Mackenzie was religious, conservative, and a nationalist, which affected her interpretation of history. A committed Episcopalian, she was relatively tolerant of Catholics, and less tolerant of Presbyterians. Mackenzie was a conservative Scottish nationalist in that she supported the British Empire and British involvement in both world wars. She was also hostile to socialism and communism. Scottish nationalists in the 1920s and 1930s, while united in their advocacy of greater autonomy for Scotland, differed on social and political issues. While Mackenzie was squarely placed in the conservative camp, other Scottish nationalists were anti-Imperialists, pacifists, and socialists (Shepherd, 133-4; Finlay 184-206; Bruce, 14-30). Like Concannon, Mackenzie believed in a wider public role for the historian. She served on a Scottish Education Department committee, presided over the cultural nationalist Saltire Society, and wrote political tracts for the Saltire Society and the National Party (Shepherd, 139).

Mackenzie differed from Concannon in that she was a feminist. She had been involved in the suffrage movement during the prewar years. For Mackenzie, this had involved "[tying] suffrage slogans on the bridge in the middle of the Deeside Golf Course, and [throwing] a hammer wrapped in a huge cabbage of red, white, and blue ribbons on to the lawn of a suburban opponent" (Shepherd, 133). Mackenzie was an unusual historian in that she wrote a sympathetic account of the British suffrage movement in her last book on modern Scotland; few historians of her era discussed feminism in national history surveys. She gave voice to the injustices women faced in nineteenth and early twentieth-century Britain, and wrote of the violence sometimes experienced by feminist activists at the hands of their opponents (Mackenzie, 1942: 222-9). Mackenzie stated that she was reminded of these scenes of brutality when she was researching the persecution of women accused of witchcraft in the early modern period (Mackenzie, 1942: 229). She concluded that "even today a woman of any sort of outstanding achievement may run at times against a surprising rancour, even in men of a normally generous outlook" (Mackenzie, 1942: 338).

Agnes Mure Mackenzie died in Edinburgh on February 26, 1955. Like Helena Concannon, she had been both a conservative and a dissident. She was a traditionalist in that she was formally religious, a supporter of the British Empire, and an opponent of socialism. She dissented from mainstream politics by advocating Scottish nationalism, as well as by openly sympathizing with feminism. Mackenzie's books, while reflecting the author's biases, were significant in the 1930s because they represented an alternative to academic Scottish history, and because they sought to engage with popular historical traditions that Mackenzie believed had been dismissed by professional historians.

In conclusion, the works of Concannon and Mackenzie shed light on several debates in Irish and Scottish historical practice, such as the tensions between political engagement and detachment, popular history and elite history, and the ways in which a historian's gender can shape her or his historical work. Their contributions are significant in the social history of the Irish and Scottish historical professions, because they raised discordant voices with which professional historians were compelled to engage.

References

Bartlett, Thomas. 1998. "Bearing Witness: Female Evidences in Courts Martial Convened to Suppress the 1798 Rebellion". *The Women of 1798*. Ed. Daire Keogh and Nicholas Furlong. Dublin: Four Courts Press

Berg, Maxine. 1996. *A Woman in History: Eileen Power, 1889-1940*. Cambridge: Cambridge University Press

Bruce, George. 1984. *The Saltire Society*. Glasgow

Clear, Caitriona. 1995. "'The Women Can Not be Blamed': The Commission on Vocational Organisation, Feminism, and 'Home-makers' in Independent Ireland in the 1930s and '40s". *Chattel, Servant or Citizen: Women's Status in Church, State, and Society*. Ed. Mary O'Dowd and Sabine Wichert. Belfast 179-86

Concannon, Helena. 1918. *Makers of Irish History*. Dublin: Talbot Press

Concannon, Helena. 1919. *Women of '98*. Dublin: M.H. Gill

Concannon, Helena. 1921. *Defence of Our Gaelic Civilisation, 1460-1660: An Irish History for Junior Grade Classes*. Dublin: Fallon's

Concannon, Helena, 1922. *Daughters of Banba*. Dublin: M.H. Gill

Concannon, Helena. 1929. *The Poor Clares in Ireland*. Dublin: M.H. Gill

Concannon, Helena. 1931. *Irish Nuns in Penal Days*. London: Sands and Co.

Dickinson, W. C. 1936. Review. *History*. 21 (June): 55-6

Doherty, Gabriel. 1996. "National Identity and the Study of Irish History". *English Historical Review*. (April): 342

Fallon, Brian. 1998. *An Age of Innocence: Irish Culture 1930-1960*. Dublin: Gill and Macmillan

Finlay, Richard J. 1992. "'For or Against'? Scottish Nationalists and the British Empire". *Scottish Historical Review*. 71: 184-206

Fitzpatrick, David. 1991. "The Futility of History: A Failed Experiment in Irish Education". *Ideology and the Historians*. Ed. Ciaran Brady. Dublin: Lilliput Press, 1991

Hart, Peter. 1998. *The I.R.A. and its Enemies: Violence and Community in Cork, 1916-1923*. Oxford: Clarendon Press

Inglis, Tom. 1998. *Moral Monopoly: the Rise and Fall of the Catholic Church in Ireland*. 2nd ed. Dublin: UCD Press

Macken, Mary. 1953. "Musings and Memories: Helena Concannon, M.A., D.Litt". *Studies*. 42 (1953): 91-6

Mackenzie, Agnes Mure. 1934. *Robert Bruce, King of Scots*. Edinburgh: Oliver & Boyd Ltd

Mackenzie, Agnes Mure. 1936. *The Scotland of Queen Mary and the Religious Wars, 1513-1638*. London: Alexander MacLehose

Mackenzie, Agnes Mure. 1942. *Scotland in Modern Times, 1720-1939*. London: W. & R. Chambers

Mackie, R. L. 1935. Review. *History*. 19: 369-70

Pierse, G. Review of *Women of '98*. *Irish Theological Quarterly*. 14 (1919): 380

Potts, Donna L. 2000. "Irish Poetry and the Modernist Canon: a Reappraisal of Katherine Tynan". *Border Crossings: Irish Women Writers and National Identity*. Ed. Kathryn Kirkpatrick. Dublin: Wolfhound Press

Shepherd, Nan. 1955. "Agnes Mure Mackenzie, C.B.E., M.A., D.Litt., L.L.D., a Portrait". *Aberdeen University Review*. 36.2: 132-40

Smith, Bonnie. 1998. *The Gender of History: Men, Women, and Historical Practice*. Cambridge, Mass.: Harvard University Press

Todd, James Eadie. Review. 1938-9. *I.H.S.* 1: 205-6

Tompkins, Jane. 1985. *Sensational Designs: The Cultural Work of American Fiction 1790-1860*. New York and Oxford: Oxford University Press

The Nightmare of Shapelessness: The Screen Adaptation of Elizabeth Bowen's *The Last September*

Kersti Tarien Powell

The question of Elizabeth Bowen's (1899-1973) Irishness, (and the consequent difficulty of 'placing' her either in the Irish or British literary canon), has been remarked upon by numerous scholars. Despite the writer's vehement statements such as "I regard myself as an Irish novelist" (Glendinning, 165), critics such as Roy Foster have argued that Bowen's ambivalent life between two worlds – the Anglo-Irish gentry and literary London – left her longing for "order, abstraction, classical symmetry", as a consequence of which she never became definitely rooted on either side of the Irish Sea. According to Foster, Bowen wrote "brilliantly at times of dislocation and conveyed in her best writing a sense of chaos" (103). Her ten novels and numerous short stories can indeed be seen as conveying a sense of chaos. Frequently set either in Blitz-time London or the vanishing world of the Anglo-Irish country estates, her fictions depict transient characters whose real or imaginary journeying turns them into an embodiment of impermanence. The "apparition of tranquillity" that Hermione Lee (1999, 19) detected in Bowen's Irish stories remains the only permanent feature in these characters' lives; it is, however, the permanence of an unachievable goal.

Despite the writer's famous warning that her fictional universe is not to be found on any map – "The Bowen terrain cannot be demarcated on any existing map; it is unspecific" (1975, 35) – this celebrated intransitivity is confined within the framework of recognisable geographical co-ordinates. Indeed, Bowen declared that not only was she "bound to be a writer involved closely with place and time", but for her these "are more than elements, they are actors" (1962, 96). In her autobiography she stated: "No story gains absolute hold on me (which is to say, gains the required hold) if its background – the ambience of its happenings – be indefinite, abstract or generalised. Characters operating *in vacuo* are for bodiless" (1962, 34). This statement indicates that the background – "the ambience of its happenings" – is of vital importance in providing the characters with an identity and bringing them into sharper focus. Importantly, the protagonist of *The Last September* (1929), Lois Farquar, experiences a perceptual crisis which originates from her inability to conceptualise both the country in which she lives and the man she is thinking of marrying. Not only does she experience difficulties with bringing into focus her ('bodiless') suitor Gerald but, inhabiting an abstracted Anglo-Irish world, she herself is left 'operating *in vacuo*'.

The world evoked in *The Last September* belongs to a clearly defined historical and geographical context. Set in the 1920s Ireland, Co. Cork, the novel centres around Lois, the orphaned niece of Sir Richard and Lady Naylor, and her pursuit of personal fulfilment during the War of Independence. Lois, courted by an English subaltern Gerald, is longing to define her true self. Constant tennis-parties and visits to the neighbouring big houses cannot supply her with a desired meaningfulness. Her flirtation with Gerald takes a tragic turn when he is killed in an ambush. Lois is sent to France to learn the language, the visitors leave, and when the IRA sets Danielstown on fire, the Naylors are the only witnesses of the burning of their family home.

The novel is divided into three parts, the titles of which evoke the inherent instability of the characters' lives – "The Arrival of Mr and Mrs Montmorency", "The Visit of Miss Norton" and "The Departure of Gerald" convey a sense of transience and movement. The house, Danielstown, is the scene of constant comings and goings in the midst of which its own rather questionable stability is the only agent of permanence. For example, Hugo and Francie Montmorency, the first visitors to arrive, have sold their house, an act which forces them to keep "visiting" their friends in order to keep a constantly changing roof over their heads. The next visitor, too, the cosmopolitan Marda Norton, is a professional "house-guest". For both Marda and the Montmorencies, Danielstown functions as a stabilising link with the past. In Francie's case the house used to provide her with a clear sense of identity and belonging. Recalling her bridal visit, Francie remembers how she "had had…very strongly a sense of return, of having awaited. Rooms, doorways had framed a kind of expectancy of her" (14). While Francie can easily step into this "framed" expectancy, Lois has an ambivalent attitude towards such a ready-made pattern. When she overhears Francie's attempt to describe her, Lois interrupts her for she "didn't want to know what she was, she couldn't bear to: knowledge of this would stop, seal, finish one" (60). Yet, Lois's resistance contains a detectable element of ambivalence, for her desire to frame is greater than her determination to escape a "seal".

In Lois's case, accepting a "kindly monolithic" Anglo-Irish inheritance would provide her with the desired pattern – a static mould within which to locate a past and, more importantly, build a future. The centre of her perceptual crisis lies in the present, for it is the immediacy of events which blurs her vision, and prevents her from achieving a coherent self-image. Thus for instance she can easily perceive Francie's husband Hugo, her mother's one-time admirer whom she has met as a child, for Hugo is "never out of focus", whereas the young men she meets socially block her mental view by their "extreme closeness" which numbs her imagination (13). Lois finds her suitor Gerald and his immediacy disturbing. She indicates her confusion when she begs him not to be "so actual" (88). Although she would like to love him, she senses that her feelings must be preceded by some sort of a perceptual change: "If there could only be some change, some movement – in her, outside of her, somewhere between them – some incalculable shifting of perspectives that would bring him wholly into focus, mind and spirit, as she had been bodily in focus now – she could love him. Something must be transmuted" (52). Furthermore, in addition to Gerald, Lois also cannot conceive of her country emotionally: "it was a way of living, an abstract of several landscapes, or an oblique frayed island, moored at the north but with an air of being detached and washed out west from the British coast" (34).

The abstractedness of her background indicates that Lois as a character is left *in vacuo*. Her inability to perceive the country she inhabits causes a dislocation in the "ambience of its happenings". Bowen's novel repeatedly draws attention to this double perceptual crisis. During her nocturnal wanderings at Danielstown's outskirts, Lois overcomes her growing fear, and bravely "forces a pass" into the darkness. Hearing footsteps, she notices a nameless, trench-coated passer-by, "a resolute profile, powerful as a thought". This encounter has a profound effect on Lois. The lingering feeling of disturbance does not so much result from the possible threat of the IRA, as from the fact that she had not been acknowledged by the mysterious stranger. Having wilfully resisted Francie's definitive portrait, Lois is suddenly overcome by a desire to be noticed, for "not to be known seemed like a doom, extinction" (34). Importantly, during the course of the novel Lois indicates twice this desire to be known, to be encircled by someone else's vision. The alternative, the visual "extinction" she fears, is to remain a bodiless character, indistinguishable from the background. Her nightmare of shapelessness consists both in an inability to bring the objects of perception into focus, and in the failure to act as the subject of perception – to be a witness and to be witnessed. Marda's advice – "…be interested in what happens to you for its own sake; don't expect to be touched or changed – or to be in anything that you do. One just watches" (100) – ultimately proves to be an unsatisfactory solution for Lois. In her case, both witnessing and being witnessed involve active participation.

The film version of *The Last September* presents Lois's perceptual crisis as originating in the historical and political situation of the Anglo-Irish gentry during the War of Independence.[1] This is evident from the prologue with which the film begins: "For many hundreds of years a tribe ruled Ireland on behalf of the English. They were known as the Anglo-Irish. After the uprising of the 1916 they were caught in the bloody conflict between the Irish Republicans and the British army. This is the story of the end of a world." The prologue indicates that the film version is determined to transform a perceptual problem into a national one while taking advantage of the potential violence inherent in "the end of a   ".

Despite the ambiguous situation of the Anglo-Irish in 1920s Ireland, Sir Richard and Lady Naylor continue hosting tennis parties and entertaining their guests, while ignoring the unrest which has taken over the rest of the country. Although threatened by the IRA, the Anglo-Irish gentry found it difficult to open-heartedly welcome their protectors, the British troops. The Naylors' household is further discomfited when Lois, courted by an English subaltern Gerald, starts secretly seeing her childhood friend Peter Connolly. When Peter's family is insulted by a British soldier, the IRA unit under his command retaliates and executes the soldier. Lois finds her clandestine meetings with Peter in an abandoned mill thrilling, but despite her obvious attraction, she does not become Peter's lover. The love-triangle finds a bloody end when Peter shoots Gerald after he followed Lois to the mill. The film ends with Lois leaving Danielstown with Marda in order to find solace in the excitements of London.

Compared to the colourful portrayal of the conflict, the portrayal of the ambiguous situation of the Anglo-Irish in the film is vague and unfocused. Defining the Anglo-Irish along national lines proves to be a less straightforward demarcation than the one between the IRA and the British army. Sir Richard and Lady Naylor stress their difference from the English on a number of occasions; for instance, when Francie and Hugo indicate that in Danielstown they remain outsiders by dressing for dinner, their sartorial *faux pas* prompts Lady Naylor's shocked comment: "You've dressed?! We're getting so bucolic down here…" More importantly, Sir Richard snubs Francie at the dinner table by declaring: "I am Irish. We all are here. Except you, my dear." These declarative scenes fail to define the Naylors' position – or their reasons for not taking one. While the novel

[1] The screenplay for *The Last September* was written by John Banville and directed by Deborah Warner, and was released in 2000.

evoked the vanished world of the Anglo-Irish big houses, the film is centred around a portrayal of violent events surrounding the detached insular estates. That the main difference between the novel and the film lies in the difference of emphasis is evident from the fact that the novel was also intended to be emphatically "historical". In the preface to the 1952 American edition of *The Last September* Bowen said: "From the start, the reader must look, be conscious of looking, backward – down a backward perspective of eight years. Fear that he might miss that viewpoint, that he might read so much as my first pages under misapprehension, haunted me" (1962, 97). Having declared the ordinary narrative past tense, though "so much in usage", insufficient for her purposes – "the cast of my characters, and their doings were to reflect the mood of a vanished time" – she decided to open the second paragraph with a temporal "pointer": "In those days, girls wore crisp white skirts and transparent blouses clotted with white flowers; ribbons threaded through…." As the preface stated: "Lois's ribbons, already, were part of history" (1962, 97). While the novel uses its heroine's ribbons in order to attest its incontestable historical nature, the film version resorts to "some serious bodice-ripping", provoking the disapproval of a number of film critics.[2]

The film version offers a new and controversial reading of *The Last September*. The novel's complexities appear in the film in a rather simplified form, as the elegiac mood of a vanished time is in the film enriched by sexual passion. In the novel, having entered an abandoned mill, Lois stumbles upon a sleeping IRA man, a nameless figure whose calculating intentness and immobile face suddenly provide her with a desired "pattern". Framed by the stranger's gaze, she feels "rather conscious" as though "confronting a camera". Under this unflinching immobile camera eye, her thoughts turn unaccountably to Gerald, and she feels that she "must marry him". In *The Anglo-Irish novel and the Big House* Vera Kreilkamp noted that this scene "provides a sexual initiation of sorts for Lois" (157). In the novel, the mill scene is governed by an overall sense of mystery; the reader never learns, for instance, why Lois is so reluctant to enter the mill. The film attempts to "flesh out" the sense of mystery by transforming the nameless man into Peter Connolly. This is the more controversial of the two major changes introduced to the film version (the second one being the decision not to show the burning of Danielstown at the end of the film), and it attempts to bring her inner crisis into the open.

By helping Connolly, who is on the run from the British and hiding in the mill, Lois encounters an element of danger which so far has been missing from her cocoon-like existence. Yet it is difficult to see the overpowering attraction of his tough macho stance on Lois. During their few meetings, the film shows Connolly playing with a pistol in front of a girl, taking an evident pride in having executed the British soldier. Convinced of his hold over Lois, Peter tries to rip off her clothes. His exaggerated Celtic masculinity offers a striking contrast to the bland English Gerald. While Connolly's intentions towards Lois remain unambiguous, this demonstration of masculinity turns Gerald – according to Hermione Lee the only truly romantic figure in the story – and his 'honourable intentions', into a farce. Lois's perceptual problems relating to Ireland and Gerald are in the film

---

[2] "Bowen's virginal Lois imagines what a kiss would be like; her film counterpart goes in for some serious bodice-ripping." See McCarthy, 'Settling on A Past Imperfect.' *Times*, 23 April 2000.

version translated into an indecision between an English marriage or an Irish affair. Yet, this attempt to translate Lois's longing for a perceptual change into sexual initiation is not fully convincing, as it offers a radically different reading of Lois who after all in the novel had asked Gerald not to be "so actual". The director, Deborah Warner tried to justify introducing the Peter Connolly figure by claiming that "He's what's out there in the landscape…You've got to make it more tangible if you're making a film; you've got to make passion visible." (Lee, 2000, 6). The film critics remained dissatisfied, saying that the film solution was "crude", and that "even as a metaphor the image is inappropriate".[3]

The film version attempts to contrast the English and the Irish, and the English and the Anglo-Irish. Yet, despite its endeavours to be as explicit and unequivocal as possible the film fails to portray the story's central concern, the complexity of Lois's perceptual crisis, depicting her as a girl "determined to love and love well" – as Marda perceptively observes. A longing for love, though incontestably among her desired objectives, does not constitute the centre of her "crisis". Her ultimate dissatisfaction resides in a "frame of expectancy", being a passive recipient framed by and for others.

Instead of the immobile camera eye of a stranger from the mill, the film version introduces a different visual metaphor, as in several scenes the audience is shown Lois playing with a spyglass. As a means for creating an artificial distance between the object of perception and the perceiving subject, the spyglass represents another way of depicting a perceptual crisis. Yet, in this case it remains as inappropriate a metaphor as sexual passion. Lois's crisis is not caused by distance, but rather by the lack of it. Although the spyglass seemingly offers an opportunity to bring Gerald into focus, it is the immediacy of the present which disturbs Lois's vision.

In addition to the problematic portrayal of her perceptual problems, the film version presents a rather disturbing projection of Lois's future. Showing her leaving Danielstown with Marda, the film implies that she will eventually turn into another Marda. According to the screenwriter, John Banville, "you'll see her in 10 years' time sashaying through a hotel on the Riviera with a cigarette holder, a hard-eyed bitch" (Lee, 2000: 6). Lois's conspicuous absence from both the final scene of the original novel format and the screen version leaves room for speculation. The ending of the novel, the oft-quoted scene of the burning of Danielstown, is unquestionably a powerful metaphor for depicting "the end of a world". While the reader is left with the image of the Naylors witnessing the burning of their family home – "Sir Richard and Lady Naylor, not saying anything, did not look at each other, for in the light from the sky they saw too distinctly" – the novel only offers what seems like a passing note on its heroine's fate. The reader is never given a full description of Lois's departure; instead, we have Lady Naylor's chance remark on Lois having gone to France to study the language. The news of Gerald's death in an ambush brought about the qualitative perceptual change Lois had been looking for; her "focus" is the present – hence her conspicuous absence from the burning of the last remains of the vanishing world. As she finally sees, "there are things which one cannot get past".

---

[3]See for instance Lee 'Love and Death in Old Ireland', McCarthy 'Settling on a Past Imperfect' and A.O. Scott, 'Oblivious to Revolution, The Gentry Loses Ground', *New York Times*, 21 April 2000, 18.

The film shows Lois driving away with Marda on their way to England, leaving the Naylors alone in the house, which does not burn. According to Warner, this ending leaves the audience with the "right level of ambivalence". The inevitability of the slow fading of the Naylors' world is conveyed by the film's last shot where the camera moves from the ground to the trees, "as if giving release to a new world" (Lee, 2000, 6).

According to Bowen, shape is "possibly *the* important thing... Shapelessness, lack of meaning, and being without direction is most people's nightmare, once they begin to think."[4] Attempting to portray Lois's perceptual crisis, the film version of *The Last September* located her nightmare of shapelessness in a definitive mould of (an adolescent) romantic entanglement. Although determined to take advantage of the potential violence inherent in "the end of a world", the film version chose to omit the most spectacular 'eschatological' sign, the burning of Danielstown. This omission is emblematic to the film's indecision between its art-house aspirations and courting of commercial success. Lois might end up sashaying somewhere in Riviera, yet one feels convinced that instead of passivity suggested by Marda, her witnessing will be active.

References

Bowen, Elizabeth. 1962. "The Last September." *Afterthought: Pieces about Writing* London: Longman

Bowen, Elizabeth. 1975. "Pictures and Conversations." *Pictures and Conversations* London: Allen Lane

Bowen, Elizabeth. 1998. *The Last September*. 1929. London: Vintage

Foster, Roy F. 1993. "The Irishness of Elizabeth Bowen." *Paddy and Mr Punch: Connections in Irish and English History*. London: Allen Lane

Glendinning, Victoria. 1993. *Elizabeth Bowen: Portrait of A Writer*. London: Phoenix

Innes, C.L. 1993. *Woman and Nation in Irish Literature and Society, 1880-1935*. Atlanta: University of Georgia Press.

Kreilkamp, Vera. 1998. *The Anglo-Irish Novel and the Big House*. Syracuse: Syracuse University Press

Lee, Hermione. 1999. *Elizabeth Bowen*. London: Vintage

Lee, Hermione. 2000. "Love and Death in Old Ireland." *Guardian*. 28 April

McCarthy, Gerry. 2000. "Settling on A Past Imperfect." *Times*. 23 April

Scott, A. O. 2000. "Oblivious to Revolution, The Gentry Loses Ground." *New York Times*. 21 April

---

[4] From a letter to V.S. Pritchett cited in Innes, 169.

The Maddest of Companies: Joyce and the Occult[1]

Enrico Terrinoni

In a letter from Rome written in 1907, in which Joyce told his brother Stanislaus, then living in Trieste, about the riots at the Abbey Theatre after the staging of Synge's play, *The Playboy of the Western World*, and about the role played by W.B. Yeats in defending the play, he referred to the young Dublin intellectuals belonging to the circle of the mystic poet George Russell, calling them derisively 'Hermetists' (1957, 144). Many biographical sources, as well as the artist's own accounts, indicate that there had been a period in Joyce's life, accordingly the last three or four years before his leaving of Dublin in 1904, in which the Irish writer took a serious interest in occult matters. The nature of that interest, and whether it may have been a sincere commitment or just a mocking curiosity, is still to be established. In this paper I will try to speculate on the often overlooked possibility that Joyce's own position towards the occult requires serious attention from Joyce scholars and readers. Of course, this is not to suggest that Joyce was an occultist, a magician or anything to that effect. In fact, the term "occult" is here used in its literal sense. The adjective occult comes from the latin *occultum* and points to something that is hidden, secret, and has etymologically speaking little to do with the supernatural. Such an outlook will lead us to consider what could be described as the occult side of Joyce's mind.

In the famous autobiographical essay, "A Portrait of the Artist", written in 1904 and rejected by the editors of the Irish periodical, *Dana*, Joyce gives the following account of the extravagant mystical and occultist period of his youth:

> [H]e established himself in the maddest of companies. Joachim the Abbas, Bruno the Nolan, Michael Sendivogius, all the hierarcs of initiation cast their spells upon him. He descended among the hells of Swedenborg and abased himself in the gloom of Saint John of the Cross. His heaven was suddenly illuminated by a horde of stars, the signature of all nature, the soul remembering ancient days. Like an alchemist he bent upon his handiwork, bringing together the mysterious elements, separating the subtle from the gross. (in Beja, 44)

Here Joyce had put together Catholic mystics such as Joachim, John of the Cross, the unorthodox mystic and visionary, Swedenborg, and the heretic, Giordano Bruno. Moreover, anyone equipped with a little knowledge of the occult tradition would have recognised in the text's allusions to the unorthodox mystic, Jacob Boehme ('the signature of all nature'), to the occultist physician, Paracelsus ('separating the subtle from the gross'), who was also alleged to have been a member of the original Rosicrucian society, and finally an explicit reference to

---

[1] The present research is funded by the Government of Ireland, under the IRCHSS postgraduate scheme. The title of this essay recalls a 1995 paper by Franca Ruggieri, "The Maddest of Companies", in *Intorno a Joyce. Cinquant 'anni dopo*. Roma: Cosmopoli.

Alchemy.

Such a cluster of different traditions suggests that Joyce must have considered the occult as a very multifaceted subject during his youth. As a matter of fact the idea of occulta philosophia as an amalgam of different secret traditions is now an accepted notion among scholars, and has been exhaustively discussed, for example, in the works by the historian Frances Yates[2] and in many recent books by occult studies critics. Judging by the volumes shelved in Joyce's personal libraries – especially the one he left behind him in Trieste when he moved to Paris in 1920, and also the Paris Library – we are led to believe that he also had an eclectic knowledge of the subject.[3]

In fact, among the volumes present in Joyce's Trieste library we find a copy of Boehme's *The Signature of all Things*, Swedenborg's *Heaven and Its Wonders and Hell*, two books on theosophy and discipleship by Annie Besant, a book on the occult meaning of blood by Rudolph Steiner, a study in French on Spiritism, a volume by Merlin called *The Book of Charms and Ceremonies Whereby All May Have the Opportunity of Obtaining Any Object They Desire*, a translation of Plutarch's theosophical essays, a study on Yogi philosophy and oriental occultism, a book by Giordano Bruno and a study on him, and finally several works by Blake and Yeats. On the other hand, in his Paris library, among other books on similar matters, we find also a copy of *The Occult Review* (July 1923) in which essays and articles on Practical Qabala, the Akasic Records, and 'the alleged communication with Madame Blavatsky' are published.

This last evidence would alone suffice to show us that Joyce's interest in the occult may not have been an occasional phenomenon which occurred during his youth; but rather, it lasted through the years till his most mature days. Craig Carver outlines the argument as follows:

> His open curiosity for all facets of experience inevitably led him to explore the literature written on a very curious aspect of the human spirit: occultism. Joyce read or was familiar with not only many of the modern works on the occult, but also many of the older traditional works. He read, for example, the writing of Swedenborg and Paracelsus, the works of Blake (in the Ellis-Yeats edition), the prophecies of Joachim Abbas, the Kabbalistic works of Giordano Bruno and perhaps of Pico della Mirandola. He had also perused the works of Hermes Trismegistus, Cornelius Agrippa, and other alchemists, such as Michael Sendivogius. As he says in his early essay "A Portrait of the Artist", "all the hierarchs of initiation cast their spells upon him". (201)

Joyce's first contacts with the occult must have occurred in Dublin, as many references in the Dublin critical writings clearly show. Yet, other writings like, for

---

[2] See Frances Yates. 1972. *The Rosicrucian Enlightenment*. London: Routledge & Kegan Paul, and Frances Yates, 1978, *The Occult Tradition in the Elizabethan Age*. London: Routledge & Kegan Paul.

[3] See Richard Ellmann. 1977. *The Consciousness of Joyce*. London: Faber and Faber, and T. Connolly. 1955. *The Personal Library of James Joyce: A Descriptive Bibliography*. Buffalo: Buffalo University Press.

example, an Italian conference paper given at the University of Trieste in 1912, *Giacomo Joyce*, certain sections of *Stephen Hero*, the fifth chapter of *A Portrait of the Artist as a Young Man*, and many places in *Ulysses* and *Finnegans Wake*, provide the evidence that the occult may have remained a constant in his literary developments. I will not touch on all such occurrences here. Instead, I will try to briefly mention some references to occult authors and themes in Joyce's works. Among the authors, beside the ones already quoted, we find for instance the theosophist Madame Blavatsky, the mystics Miguel de Molinos and Dyonisius the Pseudo-Aeropagite, and many others.

Among the themes which contribute to form what could be described as an occult outlook in Joyce's works, we find the alchemical microcosm/macrocosm correspondence, the Cabalistic theory of the Androgynous Man, the theory of metempsychosis or reincarnation, the 'apophatic theory' of Dyonisius, also known as theology of the negation, many references to secret societies such as the Freemasons and the Rosicrucians, Satanic symbolism and many others. All these themes and authors blended together, in what could be precisely described as an occult amalgam, contribute to give Joyce's works a touch of secrecy and make them almost cryptic texts. Such an arcane quality is clear in the various levels of interpretation to which most of them are open, and the hidden meanings they often refer to. Yet, Joyce's use of occult ideas in his works, suggests that such an obscure territory of knowledge may be in a way a sort of secret 'inscape', a mnemonic mental frame in which the writer may find occasionally a useful methodology, enabling him to conceal from the reader's perception as much as he can in terms of understanding.

This point of view is shared by Joyce's brother, Stanislaus, who in *My Brother's Keeper*, while recounting how Joyce indulged in a night-time conversation on theosophy with George Russell, acknowledges that 'he had been even then as much in earnest as Russell himself' (180). In an article written in Italian in 1941, a few months after Joyce's death, Stanislaus had in fact suggested the idea of 'occult knowledge' as a mental outlook, despite acknowledging his brother's instrumental use of the subject. The following quotation is from the translation into English of Stanislaus' article, which first appeared in the *Hudson Review*, in 1949:

> Theosophy was perhaps the only one of his enthusiasms which he came to regard as a total loss; all that was to remain of it was his interest in dreams. He used to make notes of the dreams that impressed him most, interpreting them and investigating their causes after a method of his own. This habit continued at Trieste. The importance he attached to them may be deduced from the fact that his last book, to which he devoted seventeen years, takes the form of an extremely long dream. (493)

Stanislaus's remarks point rightly to the consideration of the presence, which happens to be particularly relevant, of dreams and visions in the structure of both *Ulysses* and *Finnegans Wake*. In this light, Joyce's brother's biographical recollection would be tremendously important in leading us towards the understanding of some half-oneiric techniques implied in Joyce's art. Yet, such a discussion would take us too far. Instead, I think it may be useful to review the actual process through which Joyce may have come in contact with the occult, and perhaps give a couple of examples of how he would hide secret meanings beneath the surface of his texts.

A certain amount of biographical evidence suggests that, while in Dublin, one of his early mentors must have been the poet W.B. Yeats. Joyce's love for Yeats's hermetic prose works is well known. As early as in *Stephen Hero*, Stephen Dedalus admits to knowing by heart the two esoteric short stories called 'The Table of the Law' and 'The Adoration of the Magi'. In later years, statements of admiration for Yeats are ever-present, especially in the correspondence. In a letter in Italian to his son, Giorgio, written on June, 1935, Joyce mentions what had happened to him during an evening among friends:

> They all begged me to recite something beautiful. I smiled modestly but then began. For a couple of hours there followed a succession of poems by Yeats. Everybody congratulated me on my extraordinary memory, my clear diction and my charming voice. Someone added: What a pity he is such a fool! (1957, 371-2)

The influence of Yeats on Joyce, particularly in the development of his own aesthetics and his approach to the occult, seems unquestionable. It was through Yeats's edition of Blake's works that Joyce came to know and admire intensely the English poet. Both Blake and Yeats constantly refer to mystics and visionaries such as Boehme and Swedenborg. They were also very important to Joyce and continued to be so since the early years till the later phase of his career, when he worked on *Ulysses*.[4]

Joyce derived directly from Swedenborg the idea of writing *Ulysses* according to a correspondence between the episodes of his book and the various organs of the human body, a correspondence described in the Linati and Gorman schemas. In *Heaven and Hell*, one of the books Joyce had in his Trieste Library, Swedenborg had in fact proposed an interpretation of the Bible according to a general correspondence between the body of man and the body of heaven. Joyce mentions the idea in the above mentioned Italian conference paper on Blake, long before starting to write *Ulysses*. Moreover, just as happens in *Ulysees*, Swedenborg had invented a more particular correspondence between the various organs of the human body and the organs of heaven, otherwise called 'the divine man'. On the other hand, with regards to Jacob Boehme, his book, *The Signature of All Things*, is in fact literally the author's imaginary 'signature' in Joyce's great work. It is in fact quoted in the very first paragraph of one of the most complex chapters, from an oneiric perspective, of the whole book, namely 'Proteus', and it is hidden behind the whole reinventing of a half-visionary theory of perception partly derived from Bishop Berkeley, while Stephen walks on the strand at Sandymount. When Stephen Dedalus says, in the episode, 'signature of all things I am here to

---

[4] I have discussed Boehme's and Swedenborg's influence elsewhere. See Enrico Terrinoni, "James Joyce and the Hyperborean Dedalus", *PaGes* 9 (2003); "Blakian Ghosts and Shadows in Proteus", in Franca Ruggieri, Ed. 2003. *Romantic Joyce*. Roma: Bulzoni; "L'Ulisse delle Corrispondenze", in Enrico Terrinoni. Ed. 2001. *Voci d'Irlanda: oralita e tradizione nella cultura irlandese*. Roma: Il Bagatto

read' (1992, 45), he is referring to the possibility of decoding the secrets of nature that lie scattered around, in chaotic fashion, in front of his very eyes. Bloom seems to have something similar in mind, when he reflects on the reality that surrounds him along the same beach, towards the end of 'Nausicaa': 'All these rocks with lines and scars and letters' (1992, 498). In feeling the ineluctable fragmentation of the real, they both seem to attempt to make sense of external reality, and try to recompose a lost unity which the reader of Joyce faces in many places in *Ulysses*. Hence, they are also silently expressing a belief in the primordial unity of things, of which superficial signatures of this vegetable world are, in the words of Blake, but a shadow. It is interesting to note that the copy of *The Signature of All Things* Joyce had is dated by Ellmann 1912, but the above quotation from the early essay, 'A Portrait of the Artist', shows us that he must have known the book at least as early as in 1904, while he was still in Dublin.

Apart from those observations, which no doubt help in suggesting a very close connection between Joyce and Yeats in terms of source material for their mutual visionary techniques, I will mention a case in particular, in which Yeats's influence on Joyce is peculiarly evident. It relates to the above-mentioned esoteric short stories by Yeats. Craig Carver explains:

> Two stories by Yeats which were replete with the magical paraphernalia of apparitions and rituals, "The Adoration of the Magi" and "The Tables of the Law", were particularly admired by Joyce, who, like Stephen Dedalus, was fond of reciting the latter, "every word of which he remembered". (202)

"The Tables of the Law" appeared in *The Savoy* in 1896, while "The Adoration of the Magi" was published privately, in a separate volume, along with the other short story. Originally, they were intended to follow another esoteric short story called 'Rosa Alchemica', in the volume known as *The Secret Rose*, a collection published in 1897. In fact, they represent the follow-up to 'Rosa Alchemica'. Joyce's copy of the volume in the Trieste library dates 1904 but he must have read them well before that date. This is suggested by the prefatory note to the 1904 edition where Yeats makes a veiled allusion to the young writer:

> These two stories were privately printed some years ago. I do not think I should have reprinted them had I not met a young man in Ireland, the other day, who liked them very much and nothing else that I have written. (1904, n.p.)

Yeats's first encounter with Joyce occurred in early October 1902. A few days after their meeting, on October 22 and 23, 1902, Joyce went to the Marsh's library, close to Dean Swift's Cathedral, in the Liberties. On that occasion, it is recorded, he read a copy of the prophecies attributed to Joachim of Flora. The library stocks other books by the Italian mystic. The copy of *Vaticinia* Joyce consulted is the only bilingual one (Italian and Latin), while the other books are only in Latin. Joyce will quote the circumstance in the third episode of *Ulysses*:

> Houses of decay, mine, his and all. You told the Clongowes gentry you

had an uncle a judge and an uncle a general in the army. Come out of them, Stephen. Beauty is not there. Nor in the stagnant bay of Marsh's library where you read the fading prophecies of Joachim Abbas. (1992, 49)

A few lines below, Joyce quotes from the text, although trickily changing the actual sentence of Joachim, and, what is more important, he suggests a connection between the Italian mystic and the Dean of Saint Patrick's Cathedral, Jonathan Swift: "Abbas father, furious dean, what offence laid fire to their brains? Paff! Descende, calve, ut ne nimium decalveris" (1992, 49). In order to show how Yeats's occult influence on Joyce, although subliminal, must have been relevant, we may consider that both 'The Tables of the Law' and 'The Adoration of the Magi' are strictly connected with Joachim's ideas on religion and the history of the world, as exposed in his imaginary secret book called *Liber Inducens in Evangelium Aeternum*. Moreover, in 'The Tables of the Law' we find precisely a link between the Italian mystic and Jonathan Swift. After having explained Joachim's theories on the 'Kingdom of the Spirit', one of the characters, Owen Aherne, in answering to the narrator's scepticism about Joachim's revolutionary theology, paraphrases one of Swift's expressions in *A Tale of a Tub*, by saying, "Jonathan Swift made a soul for the gentlemen of this city by hating his neighbour as himself" (1995, 207). Other references in the short story are relevant for they are parallel to some occurrences in the third episode of *Ulysses*. For instance, one of them is Yeats's allusion to "the kabalistic heresies of Pico della Mirandola" (1995, 204). In Joyce's 'Proteus', besides all the references to various heretics, there is also an allusion to Pico della Mirandola (1992, 50) and to the Kabbalistic Primordial Man, Adam Kadmon (1992, 46).

The idea of taking some of Yeats's intuitions concerning occult knowledge and using them in subliminal fashion in the unfolding of his works, suggests precisely the existence of what we may call an occultist method, by which Joyce manages to conceal obscure meanings and references behind half-secret allusions. Biographically speaking, we don't know, for it is not recorded anywhere, whether or not Yeats suggested that Joyce should go to the Marsh's library to find books by the mystic Joachim Abbas. Yet this could very well be the case for, as I have said, they met just a few days before his visit to the library, and in that occasion they very likely talked of the two esoteric short stories Yeats would have reprinted some time later. Morever, in 'The Tables of the Law' there happens to be also a reference to the 1527 edition of Joachim's book *Expositio in Apocalypsin*. As a matter of fact, a copy of the same volume, published in Venice in 1527, is the property of Marsh's library, along with three other works and a biography of the mystic. Therefore, we may assume that Joyce not only must have followed the older artist's advice, but he took his suggestions so seriously that he ended up using them later on, in one of the most cryptic passages of his masterpiece.

In the case just mentioned, Joyce's use of one of Yeats's intuitions is clearly recognisable. In order to reinforce this idea, I wish to quote another passage in *Ulysses* where Joyce's debt to Yeats is displayed, I would say, in an obscure fashion. I'm thinking of the other episode of the book which, just like 'Proteus', may be considered an ultimately oneiric and visionary chapter: 'Circe'. With regards to 'Circe', in the Linati schema of *Ulysses* – which Joyce had written to facilitate the understanding of his book's inner structure – the 'science' category appears to be 'dance'. Towards the ending of the chapter, almost all the characters 'on stage', the imaginary as well as the real ones, take part in a queer fanciful dance, possibly half-macabre, which makes all 'wheel, whirl, waltz, twirl' (1992, 279). This event is described as follows in one of the 'stage directions' : "Twining, receding, with interchanging hands, the night hours link, each with arching arms, in a mosaic of movements" (1992,679). Bearing in mind this image of the mosaic and its connection to dance, we may consider a passage from the final stages of Yeats' 'Rosa Alchemica' – the short story which would have been published along with 'The Tables of the Law' and 'The Adoration of the Magi', had not Yeats's publisher refused to print the latter stories on the ground of their obscenity. In the story we encounter the following account of a dreamy and visionary dance experience, during a ritual of initiation to a secret alchemical society:

> [G]radually I sank into a half-dream, from which I was awakened by seeing the petals of the great rose, which had no longer the look of a mosaic […]. Still faint and cloud-like, they began to dance, and as they danced took a more and more definite shape […]; and soon every mortal foot danced by the white foot of an immortal […]. While I thought these things, a voice cried to me from the crimson figures: 'Into the dance, there is none that can be spared out of the dance […].' (1995, 195-6)

This sense that Yeats and Joyce are closer to each other than one may well imagine, seems to me to be somehow shared by Richard Ellmann, who in his *Ulysses on the Liffey* states: "Joyce was much concerned with the idea of a precursor: in his youthful letter to Ibsen he assigned that role to Ibsen, then, in 'The Day of the Rabblement', to Ibsen and Hauptmann; but his final decision was for Yeats" (148).

However, in spite of this, my conclusions on the relationship between Joyce and the occult, in which Yeats seems to me to play a fundamental role, are by no means definitive, the present paper having focused on an aspect of Joyce studies which is very much open to different perspectives and approaches. In fact, the main aim of a discussion of such an obscure topic is to help in suggesting a point of view which so far has been somehow unjustly overlooked by scholars, despite its great potentialities in interpretative terms. It is an outlook which can certainly open new grounds for the understanding of Joyce's own methodology, as well as for the reassessment of the artistic relationship between two of the most important writers of the twentieth century, and the common ground on which they occasionally move. An analogous perspective is therefore certainly useful not only in order to acknowledge the massive presence of occult contents in *Ulysses*, but also to show that the tension towards the occultum – i.e. the hidden – is a structural factor in Joyce's vision of his own art, and deserves further attention from critics. The occult pertains to the act of telling, but also of representing fictionally and constructing a visionary universe of the mind through the elaboration of empirical perceptions. Often in Joyce's works, those impressions appear filtered in the text by the opaque and sometimes mocking mirror of a secret tradition, hidden or lost along the paths of the developments of culture. Such a tradition, which, in Jungian terms, is intended by Joyce as a mythical projection of the unconscious, besides informing some aspects of his subtle technique, lies also behind some of the most remotely accessible explanations of particular meanings of his great work.

References

Beja, Morris. 1980. *James Joyce – 'Dubliners'* and *'A Portrait of the Artist as a Young Man': A Casebook*. London, Macmillan

Carver, Craig. 1983. "James Joyce and the Theory of Magic". *James Joyce Quarterly*. 20.3: 201-10

Ellmann, Richard. 1972. *Ulysses on the Liffey*. London: Faber and Faber

Joyce, James. 1957. *Letters of James Joyce*. Ed. Stuart Gilbert. London: Faber and Faber

Joyce, James. 1992. *Ulysses*. London: Penguin

Joyce, Stanislaus. 1949. "Memoirs of James Joyce". *Hudson Review*: 486-514

Joyce, Stanislaus. 1959. *My Brother's Keeper*. London: Faber and Faber

Yeats, W.B. 1995. *Short Fiction*. London: Penguin

Yeats, W.B. 1904. *The Tables of the Law & The Adoration of the Magi*. London: Elkin Matthews